STARTING A LIMITED LIABILITY COMPANY

STARTING A LIMITED LIABILITY COMPANY

Second Edition

Martin M. Shenkman
Samuel Weiner
Ivan Taback

WILEY

John Wiley & Sons, Inc.

Published by John Wiley & Sons, Inc., Hoboken, New Jersey.
Published simultaneously in Canada.

Limit of Liability/Disclaimer of Warranty: While the publisher and author have used their best efforts in preparing this book, they make no representations or warranties with respect to the accuracy or completeness of the contents of this book and specifically disclaim any implied warranties of merchantability or fitness for a particular purpose. No warranty may be created or extended by sales representatives or written sales materials. The advice and strategies contained herein may not be suitable for your situation. The publisher is not engaged in rendering professional services, and you should consult a professional where appropriate. Neither the publisher nor author shall be liable for any loss of profit or any other commercial damages, including but not limited to special, incidental, consequential, or other damages.

For general information on our other products and services, please contact our Customer Care Department within the United States at (800) 762-2974, outside the United States at (317) 572-3993 or fax (317) 572-4002.

Wiley also publishes its books in a variety of electronic formats. Some content that appears in print may not be available in electronic books. For more information about Wiley products, visit our Web site at www.wiley.com.

Library of Congress Cataloging-in-Publication Data:

Shenkman, Martin M.
　　Starting a limited liability company / Martin M. Shenkman, Samuel Weiner, Ivan Taback.—2nd ed.
　　　　p.　cm.
　　Includes bibliographical references and index.
　　ISBN 0-471-22664-5 (pbk. : alk. paper)
　　1. Private companies—United States.　I. Weiner, Samuel, 1955–　II. Taback, Ivan.
III. Title.
KF1380 .S53 2003
346.73′0668—dc21

2002190749

Printed in the United States of America.

10　9　8　7　6　5　4　3　2　1

ACKNOWLEDGMENTS

A number of people were of considerable assistance in the preparation of this book, especially Michael Hamilton of John Wiley & Sons, whose support and encouragement were outstanding, as usual. Special thanks to Joshua Klavan for his research and drafting assistance on the first edition. The book could not have been completed without their able assistance.

Any errors or omissions are ours.

MARTIN M. SHENKMAN
SAMUEL WEINER
IVAN TABACK

CONTENTS

Part One

INTRODUCTION TO LIMITED LIABILITY COMPANIES

1 WHAT IS A LIMITED LIABILITY COMPANY?

The **limited liability company** (LLC) has become the most popular form for organizing business and investment activities. It can provide tremendous benefits. For example:

- For a modest cost and no additional annual tax filing requirements, you can make your home-based business sound more professional; and most importantly, you can protect your personal assets from claims relating to your business by setting it up as an LLC.

- An entrepreneur starting a new business will likely have tax losses for the first year or two until sales grow. An LLC provides an approach to dealing with these losses.

- For doctors, lawyers, and other professionals seeking to protect assets from malpractice and other claims, the LLC is a key tool in their **asset protection** arsenal. Owning nonrisk assets (e.g., a doctor's personal investment portfolio) in an LLC with other family members and **trusts** can make it more difficult for claimants to reach those assets.

- A parent wants to minimize **estate tax** costs while retaining considerable control over family business and investment assets. Transferring assets into an LLC with the parent serving as the **manager** or sole voting **member** of the LLC can accomplish these two important goals.

- A real estate investor owns five rental properties. Each can be owned by a separate LLC to insulate each property from claims on the other properties and to protect personal assets. Thus, if there is a suit by a tenant on one property, only the assets of the LLC owning that property can be reached.

- A business owner wants to start a new retail store but wants to keep the liability of that store independent of other retail stores he owns. A separate LLC can own each store.

This book tells you how to use LLCs to deal with these situations, and more. This book guides you step by step through understanding, forming, operating, and eventually winding down and dissolving an LLC. This book also describes the many benefits that make the LLC form of business organization a practical way of doing business, managing investments, and handling personal issues.

WHAT IS A LIMITED LIABILITY COMPANY?

An LLC is an entity formed under state law with both tax and legal advantages. It separates business assets from personal assets and thus can generally limit business-related claims on the business assets. It has relatively simple and favorable income tax attributes because it is generally taxed as a **partnership** if there is more than one member. This means income is taxed to the members, not the entity. If there is only one member of the LLC, the income tax situation is even simpler; it is ignored. Most importantly, you can choose the intended income tax result. Tax regulations, called *Check the Box Regulations*, let you check the appropriate box on a federal tax filing to obtain the desired tax status. This law provides certainty and simplification, and assured income tax results.

An LLC is a hybrid between a **corporation** and a partnership. The tax and legal advantages that the LLC form offers may make it the preferred choice for new transactions.

LLCs ARE STILL NEW

Although LLCs have been in use for a number of years, they are still quite new compared with other forms of ownership for businesses and investments. Thus, some caution must be exercised. There are likely to be changes in state laws. Court cases interpreting both the tax and legal rules will take years to develop a thorough and consistent resource. The concepts explored throughout this book are unlikely to change, but the nuances—in particular, the rules applicable in your state or for your specific legal or tax situation—could change. Therefore, it is essential to consult competent legal, tax, and accounting advisers before making any decision about using the LLC structure.

THE NATURE OF YOUR LLC DEPENDS ON STATE LAW

LLCs are formed and exist solely in accordance with the specific state law under which they were formed. Hence, to properly understand any LLC that is in existence, you must examine the state statute under which that particular LLC was organized. There can be important differences from state to state.

CAUTION: Make certain that the lawyer who assists you in the organization of an LLC has knowledge and experience with your particular state's LLC laws. If the business your LLC will operate extends beyond your state's boundaries, your lawyer must be familiar with the other states' LLC laws, or must hire counsel in those states who have this specialized knowledge.

Most statutes, known as *flexible* statutes, permit members (who are the owners) of an LLC to enter into any agreement they desire to govern internal relationships within the LLC; they are only limited by broad public policy restrictions. Most statutes are written in this manner "unless the **operating agreement** provides to the contrary. . . ." In other words, you can agree in the contract between the members (the operating agreement, which is analogous to a shareholders agreement for corporate shareholders or a partnership agreement in the partnership context) to almost anything you wish. If, however, you don't agree as to a specific matter (your LLC's operating agreement may not address that particular matter) then the rules of the state law where the LLC is formed will apply. These rules are thus called **default rules** (they apply in default of your providing otherwise). Because these rules can differ in important ways from state to state, it is important that you have some familiarity with them. They really are not that complex to read; and you can find them in your public library, or on the Internet. These differences make it imperative that the attorney you hire be familiar with the LLC law in the state where your LLC is formed and operates.

NOTE: Prior to the IRS permitting LLCs to simply check off a box on a tax filing indicating whether they should be taxed as a partnership or corporation, the state laws were critical to determining the income tax status of the LLC. Even following these rules, important nuances in state law can still have significant tax impacts. The different default rules under state law can be critical when valuing LLC interests for estate and **gift tax** purposes and determining **discounts,** in particular (see Chapter 12).

The contract between the parties, known as an *operating agreement,* must also be reviewed when analyzing an LLC. Many states provide substantial latitude in the provisions that can be included in such an agreement. Other states mandate certain provisions that cannot be modified by an operating agreement.

LLC RULES DIFFER BY STATE

Despite the tremendous benefits derived from using limited liability companies, LLC statutes throughout the United States are very diverse. Many businesses engage in multistate activities. States vary in their recognition of out-of-state LLCs. As a result of the lack of uniformity among the states, there are a multitude of basic questions, such as:

- May an LLC be engaged in not-for-profit activities?
- Can a member withdraw from an LLC and mandate the payment of fair **value** for the member's **interest**?
- Are one-member LLCs permissible?
- Who can bind an LLC and are there any limits on this authority?
- What fiduciary obligations to the entity and its members are imposed on LLC owners and managers?
- Do the LLC members have the authority to sue the LLC on their own as well as on behalf of the LLC?
- Can general and **limited partnerships** be converted to LLCs and how is this accomplished?
- Which law governs out-of-state LLCs?
- How is the LLC managed?

The differences in state laws may create some uncertainty when you utilize a limited liability company beyond the state of formation.

UNIFORM LIMITED LIABILITY COMPANY ACT

The National Conference of Commissioners on Uniform State Laws prepared a uniform model LLC Act, known as the **Uniform Limited Liability Company Act** (Model Act). Many states model their laws on this act. Therefore, a brief overview of the Model Act provides a good introduction to the laws likely to affect your LLC. Even with a uniform act, many state legislatures have and will continue to put their own interpretation on the uniform act in their laws.

As presently drafted, the Model Act is a flexible statute containing numerous *default provisions*. These default provisions apply unless you affirmatively take steps to have a different result (i.e., unless you provide otherwise in your LLC's operating agreement or organizational documents).

General Provisions of the Model Act

Some of the general provisions of the Model Act include the following:

- An LLC is a legal entity separate from its members. This is important for many reasons. Its separate nature means that formalities relating to this separate identity (e.g., separate bank accounts) should be maintained. This is also the basis for limiting your exposure to lawsuits by using an LLC.
- An LLC may be for-profit or nonprofit.
- An LLC may have one member. One-member LLCs can offer a simple, flexible, and cost-effective method of owning and operating many types of investment and business transactions.
- No **distributions** to members may be made if the LLC cannot pay its debts, or if the LLC's assets are less than its liabilities plus amounts necessary to satisfy preferential rights on dissolution.
- A member has no transferable interest in an LLC's property, but does have a transferable interest in distributions from the LLC and return of capital. The right to transfer LLC equity (membership) interests is a major focus of most LLC operating agreements, which generally try to restrict such transfers.

Key Rules from the Model Act

The Model Act establishes mandatory provisions that cannot be overridden by your LLC's operating agreement. Under these provisions, which your state's statutes may reflect, you cannot:

- Unreasonably restrict a member's right to access the LLC's books and records. Often operating agreements include express provisions requiring that members be sent certain reports within specified time periods. If not, a state law providing the right to access the records often is available.
- Eliminate a member's or manager's statutory duty of loyalty to the LLC and other members.
- Unreasonably reduce a member's or manager's statutory duty of care. For example, a manager operating the LLC will have to conduct LLC affairs in a manner that reasonably protects the member's economic interests in the LLC.

- Eliminate a member's or manager's obligation of good faith and fair dealing. For example, a manager or member cannot sell real estate to their LLC at an inflated price, to the detriment of the other members.
- Restrict the rights of third parties (i.e., non-members).
- Vary the statutory requirement to end an LLC in certain limited circumstances.
- Vary the statutory right to expel a member in the case of a judicial determination that the member engaged in wrongful acts adversely affecting the LLC's business, committed a material breach of the operating agreement, or engaged in conduct that makes it impractical for the LLC to carry on any business with the member.

Flexibilty Provided by Modifiable Provisions

The Model Act is a lengthy document containing over 80 pages of default provisions. These provisions, however, may be modified in a particular LLC's operating agreement or articles of organization to meet the requirements of a particular business. Some examples of the default provisions that you might modify are:

- *Limited Liability:* Debts of an LLC are solely those of the LLC unless the **articles of organization** provide otherwise. A limited liability company is legally distinct from its members, who are not normally liable for the debts, obligations, and liabilities of the LLC. Accordingly, members are not proper parties to suits against the LLC.
- *Agency of Members and Managers:* Members of a member-managed and managers of a manager-managed company serve as agents of the company and can therefore bind the company to third parties. Members in a manager-ruled LLC are not such agents and do not have the power to bind the LLC. Acts beyond the scope of the Model Act can only bind the LLC if they are ratified after the act. A member or manager, as agent of the LLC, is not liable for the debts, liabilities, and obligations of the LLC simply because of the agency.
- *Existence:* LLCs may have a specific term or be *at will.* Members of an LLC must agree to remain as members until the expiration of the term. A term company will generally dissolve at the expiration of its specified term unless the articles of organization are amended before the term expires providing for an additional specified term, or the members or managers simply continue the LLC as an at-will entity. Preexisting operating agreement provisions will govern the relationship of the members except to the extent inconsistent with rights and

duties of members of an at-will company with an operating agreement containing the same provisions.

- *Transferees and Creditors of a Member:* Generally, members have no property interest in property owned by an LLC. This interest may be evidenced by a certificate of the interest issued by the LLC and may also provide for the transfer of any interest that the certificate represents. The only interest a member may freely transfer is the member's rights to distributions from the LLC. A transferee may only acquire the remaining rights by being admitted as a member of the LLC by all of the remaining members. A transferee who is not admitted as a member is not entitled to participate in management, require acts to obtain information, or inspect a copy of the LLC records. The only rights of a transferee are to receive the distribution to which the transferor would otherwise be entitled, receive a limited statement of accounting, and seek a judicial dissolution under the Model Act. A judgment creditor may only receive the member's right to receive distributions from the LLC and seek judicial **liquidation** of the LLC. This is accomplished by obtaining a charging order.

- *Dissolution:* An LLC is dissolved on: (1) the occurrence of a specific event described in the operating agreement, (2) the consent of the number of members specified in the operating agreement, or (3) the dissociation of a member-manager, or if none, a member of an at-will LLC, for any reason. The term *dissociation* relates to the change in relationships among the dissociated member, the remaining members, and the LLC. If the member files a bankruptcy or the equivalent thereof, dies, or is deemed mentally incompetent, the LLC will dissolve unless continued by a vote of a majority of the remaining members.

HOW CAN AN LLC BENEFIT YOU?

An LLC is a flexible and relatively easy-to-use form of owning a business or investment. It can provide you with favorable income tax results (flow through—see Chapter 3), liability protection (see Chapter 3), avoidance of ancillary probate (see Chapter 12), control (see Chapter 16), estate tax benefits (see Chapter 12), and other benefits as well.

LLCs Combine the Best of Corporate and Partnership Attributes

An LLC can be viewed as a hybrid entity combining the characteristics and, importantly, the benefits of a corporation and a partnership. If an LLC is properly structured, it will be taxed as a partnership (unless there are specific reasons why corporate taxation is preferred). This means that only one level of taxation will occur, not two layers as with a corporation (C or regular corporation). (**Note:** Proposals have been made to eliminate this double taxation by making shareholder receipts of dividends tax free. As of the date this book went to press, these proposals had not been acted upon.) This benefit can be obtained without the complexity required for an **S corporation,** which also has one level of tax. Prior to LLCs, the S corporation had been the most popular way to organize businesses because it afforded owners **limited liability** (like a corporation) and flow-through tax treatment (like a partnership). However, qualifying as an S corporation involves complex requirements and limitations as to type of stock, shareholders, deductibility of losses, and so on, which an LLC does not.

With limited liability for its members, an LLC resembles a corporation. The members of an LLC, like shareholders of a corporation, are generally not responsible for the debts and obligations of the LLC beyond their **contributions** to it. This is a tremendous benefit for anyone owning real estate or a business that could trigger a suit or claim. An LLC, if properly structured, is not taxed at the entity level like a regular corporation. Instead, LLC profits are taxed on its owners' individual tax returns, like partners in a partnership.

ABILITY TO CONTROL BENEFITS

A third and equally important benefit of an LLC is the ability of all of its members to manage and control the business without causing the LLC to be taxed as a corporation. For businesses, but especially for family investment companies, this is an important attribute. Many parents would not make **gifts** of equity in a family business if they could not continue to control operations. For family or other **closely held businesses,** it can be desirable to give management participation to a child or other key person. An LLC can permit this. Members of an LLC can directly participate in the company's management or can elect business managers. The members' ability to participate in the LLC's management distinguishes LLCs from limited partnerships in which only the **general partner** can be involved in management. If **limited partners** engage in management, they risk losing their limited liability. Many benefits of an LLC are available without the restrictions faced by corporations and partnerships.

NOTE: The ability of all members to manage is something that should be addressed very carefully in the operating agreement. What decisions can various members make? What percentage of members should approve a major decision, for example, selling the business?

An LLC is governed by a contract between its owners (members) called an *operating agreement*. This is analogous to a shareholders' agreement for the owners (shareholders) of a corporation, or a partnership agreement among partners. The operating agreement can address an almost endless array of control and management provisions. This flexibility is a major benefit of the LLC format.

An LLC Provides Limited Liability

For any business or real estate owner, protecting the nonbusiness or non-real estate assets from lawsuits emanating from the business or real estate is a key planning goal. If an LLC owns your widget factory or rental house, a lawsuit should not be able to reach your personal assets.

Although the LLC can solve many of the problems associated with the previously mentioned business entities, it does not eliminate all problems of business owners. For most closely held small businesses, the principal owners likely will be required to personally sign leases, bank loans, and other legal documents, and provide personal guarantees, whether the business is a corporation, partnership, or LLC. Thus, an important practical limitation on achieving limited personal liability of a business' owners will remain despite using the LLC format. In addition, the members could still be liable for certain liabilities such as the nonpayment of payroll taxes that have been withheld from employees and not turned over to the IRS or the state taxing authorities. The same holds true for sales taxes and for infractions of certain environmental regulations.

This practical limitation, however, does not negate the importance of achieving limited liability to a business' owners. This is because an LLC, like a **C corporation,** S corporation and limited partnership with a corporate general partner, provides limitations on nonmonetary liabilities (e.g., a customer slipping and injuring himself on the business premises). While a principal owner in any of these entities may have to personally guarantee a bank loan, the proper use of an entity to own and operate the business will provide limitations on an owner's liability from lawsuits and other claims (e.g., environmental and tort liabilities). To the extent that an LLC can provide a simpler method of achieving limited liability it will be more effective and practical. The simplicity of an LLC is attractive to business owners and investors and is increasingly used by them.

Estate Planning Benefits

With or without an estate tax, LLCs can be useful in avoiding ancillary probate (i.e., the process of proving and admitting your will in a state other than the state in which you live) and taxes. If you have real estate in another state, having an LLC own it can avoid the costs, taxes, and difficulties of ancillary probate. For parents or others looking to transfer assets or business interests to children in a controlled manner, using an LLC is an excellent technique. If you have an expensive asset that you want to give to your children using the annual gift tax exclusion (currently $11,000, but inflation indexed), you can give it to an LLC and then give ownership (membership) interests in the LLC to your children or a trust for their benefit. Thus, an LLC provides a way to divide ownership into small pieces to facilitate gift giving.

USAGE AND TERMINOLOGY

Since almost every LLC with more than one member will be treated as a partnership for income tax purposes, the terms *partnership* and *LLC* are interchangeable in the tax aspects of the discussions. Since partnerships have been around for decades longer than LLCs, most of the tax laws, cases, and regulations and rulings issued by the IRS refer to partnerships. For most of these, however (except to the extent that the decision is based on underlying state laws that can differ in important ways for partnerships and LLCs), the analysis is interchangeable. Thus, although this book is about LLCs, many of the income tax comments may mention, or be based on, partnership terminology.

Explaining complex LLC tax, legal, securities, and other concepts to those without legal training is quite a challenge. Because our focus is on these matters, we have opted not to complicate sentence structure or examples to make them gender neutral or equal. Throughout, the discussions pertain to both male and female readers.

SUMMARY

The LLC is a relatively new form of business entity that has come into existence in the United States largely in the past 10 years. The LLC combines the best tax and legal features of a partnership and a corporation. The LLC can provide its owners with the tax benefits traditionally associated with the partnership business entity and the limited liability protection traditionally associated with the corporate form of doing business. The result is that LLCs have become the favored form for new business and investment undertakings.

2 UNDERSTANDING THE TERMINOLOGY OF LIMITED LIABILITY COMPANIES

To work with limited liability companies (LLCs) requires learning new legal jargon. Although the terms are similar to those used in discussing other entities such as partnerships or corporations, there are differences.

MEMBERS

The owners of an LLC are called *members*. A member is analogous to a shareholder in a corporation, or a partner in a partnership. An LLC must have at least one member. A one-member LLC is similar to a **sole proprietorship.** If there are two or more members, the LLC resembles a partnership. There is no limit on the maximum number of the members and no restrictions on their identity or type. Thus, an LLC may have more than 75 members, which is the current limit for an S corporation.

Some state statutes specifically define "member," and other state statutes do not. Some states that define the term provide that a member is a person with a membership interest; some states provide that a member is a "person who has been admitted to membership . . . and has not ceased to be a member"; and one state defines a member as a "person reflected in the required records of an LLC as the owner of some governance rights of a membership interest."

A member may or may not participate in the management of the LLC. If not, then another category of person, called a *manager* will be responsible for operating the LLC, as discussed later in this chapter.

MEMBERSHIP INTERESTS

The states that have enacted LLC statutes have given varied names to the ownership interest in an LLC. In some states, the ownership interest is referred to as a *membership interest.* Other states merely refer to it as an *interest.* There are also states that use the term *limited liability company interest.* In all cases, the ownership is the same—the interest you own in the LLC as a member is analogous to the stock a shareholder owns in a corporation.

Personal liability aside, members of an LLC are similar to partners in a partnership. Members have *interests* or *membership interests,* not shares or stock in the LLC. However, the LLC can issue a share (not stock) certificate to evidence your membership interest. Many LLCs issue such certificates; some do not. If there is no membership share certificate, your ownership interest should be set forth in a contract between members called an *operating agreement* (even with certificates, your LLC should still have an operating agreement).

Some states expressly provide that a member's interest in an LLC is **personal property,** and other states do not address this issue. In the states that are silent in this regard, it is improbable that an interest in an LLC is anything but personal property.

TIP: The issue of whether your interest in an LLC is personal property can have important ramifications. If you live in First State, but own real estate in Second State, at your death your estate would have to go through probate (the process of proving a will and marshaling assets) in Second State (for the property located there) and may even owe Second State estate and/or inheritance taxes. If you transfer your real estate in Second State to an LLC and if the LLC member's interest may be considered personal property under Second State law, you would not be subject to probate or taxation on death as a result of owning the real estate there.

A membership interest, as a property interest, may be held in many forms. The simplest and most common ownership form is a *sole owner.* A second form of ownership is as *tenants-in-common,* where the parties hold their interest together, but it is subject to division by each owner. With the tenants-in-common property interest, the share of each tenant is distinct from that of other owners, and if a co-owner dies, that person's interest does not automatically pass to the surviving co-owners. Until the interest is divided, no member can claim a specific portion of the membership interest. A tenant-in-common is allowed to transfer his interest in the membership interest without affecting the interest rights of other co-owners.

A third form of ownership that can be used for an LLC membership interest is the *joint tenancy with rights of survivorship.* Typically used by husbands and wives (also known as a tenancy-by-the-entirety), the parties own an undivided interest in the LLC that was acquired at the same time. Neither the husband nor the wife can transfer his or her interest without the consent of the other. A joint tenancy is terminated by divorce, death, or voluntary separation.

LLC statutes allow the creation of different classes of membership interests in an LLC. There may be members who participate in management and other members who have an economic interest but have no right to participate in the LLC's management. Additional classes of members may be created, if not restricted by state law. For example, some classes of membership interests may be entitled to distributions before other classes of membership interests.

CONTRIBUTIONS

Contributions (investments) are assets that members contribute to the LLC to obtain their membership interests. Unless state law or the operating agreement (the contract governing the relationship of the members) imposes restrictions, contributions may include almost any type of asset (cash, property, services rendered, or a promissory note or other obligation). Members generally contribute assets to the LLC in their capacity as members.

> **EXAMPLE:** Fred and Joe organize an LLC to operate a store. Joe contributes land and a building worth $200,000 to the LLC in exchange for two-thirds of the membership interests. Fred contributes fixtures and inventory worth $100,000 for one-third of the membership interests.

For services to be treated as a contribution, however, they must be designated as a contribution in the LLC's operating agreement. In some instances, services may include furnishing guarantees of LLC debt, which may be valuable to a thinly capitalized LLC (i.e., not enough equity to reasonably support operations).

DISTRIBUTIONS

What Are Distributions and What Is Distributed?

Distributions are what you receive from your LLC. Distributions will generally be in the form of cash, like a dividend from a corporation (but the tax results, as explained later, are different), but the law for corporate dividends may change. Distributions may also be made in property.

Distribution from LLC Operations

Distributions can occur during the operation of your LLC and will typically be distributions of earnings of the LLC.

Distributions to members other than on the LLC's liquidation, otherwise known as *interim distributions,* can be made on the basis of the following factors (these may vary from state to state):

- On the same basis as profits and losses are allocated.
- In accordance with adjusted contributions of the members.
- On a per capita basis (each member receives an equal share).
- Based on the book value of the contributions made by members.
- Based on the capital value of each member (the value of what you contributed, adjusted for distributions and earnings, compared with similar calculations for other members).

The preceding methods are various default rules in the statutes of the states that have enacted LLC legislation. These rules can generally be modified for specific situations in the LLC's operating agreement.

EXAMPLE: Don't let your state's LLC laws tell you when money can be distributed from your LLC. All the members should come to some basic agreement. This may include a formula (e.g., a percentage of profits or sales) or a fixed amount for salary. You may also consider a point system for distributing profits above salaries (e.g., each member active in the LLC is assigned points by agreement of the members for generating business, hours worked, etc.; and then profits are distributed based on the number of points each member has). As circumstances change in the future, you can revise these arrangements by simply amending your LLC's operating agreement.

Distributions on Significant Events

Distributions can also occur when a significant event occurs. Such events might include:

- Distributions when the LLC ends or is terminated. These are called *liquidating distributions* and will include a distribution of your original capital contributions (or what remains of them). LLC members are generally not entitled to distributions from the LLC, other than on the LLC's liquidation, unless provided otherwise in the articles of organization (the legal document used to form the LLC) or operating agreement.
- Distributions to liquidate your interest when, for example, the LLC buys you out. This could occur for a host of reasons that may be listed in the operating agreement.

- Distributions of bonus payments following year-end or a significant event. Many LLCs will make periodic payments (e.g., monthly) and will make a larger or bonus distribution when the LLC accountant finishes the books at year-end.
- Distributions if real estate owned by the LLC is refinanced.

Once entitled to a distribution, a member becomes a creditor of the LLC with respect to the distribution. This gives the member the same rights as a creditor to sue for the money, put a lien on the LLC or its assets, or take any other steps the law permits.

Income Tax Consequences of Distributions

The tax implications to members for the distributions they receive may depend on the type of distribution. Partnership tax law distribution rules govern distributions from an LLC to its members, assuming you elect that your LLC be taxed as a partnership (which is what most should be). When an LLC is taxed as a partnership, members generally may receive distributions of appreciated property without recognizing gain.

CERTIFICATE/ARTICLES

Your LLC can only exist because your state law provides a method for setting up an LLC. If you don't comply with the state law requirements, you may not have created an LLC. One of the first and key steps in creating an LLC is to complete a simple legal document, which might be called a **Certificate of Formation,** *Articles of Organization, LLC Formation Certificate,* or some similar name. This document has to be signed in a specified manner and filed with (sent with the appropriate fees) the appropriate state authority. Although additional steps may be necessary for the formation of your LLC (and those steps will differ by state), filing this initial document is key. This is analogous to forming a corporation by filing a Certificate of Incorporation, or forming a limited partnership by filing a Certificate of Limited Partnership.

OPERATING AGREEMENT

Most entities have a contractual document that governs the relationship between their owners. The owners of a corporation should have a contract between them called a shareholders' agreement. Partners in a partnership should have a contract between them called a partnership agreement. The owners of an LLC, called members, should similarly have a contract between them called an operating agreement. In some ways, it can be more important for an LLC to have an operating agreement than it is for a corporation to have a shareholders' agreement. This is because corporations also have bylaws, which are formal rules adopted to address many of its operating and business decisions. LLCs do not have bylaws so if the state laws governing your LLC are silent, vague, or contrary to your intent, an operating agreement is the only way to address these points.

Operating agreements should not be viewed as legal boilerplate (the same document used for everyone by inserting the appropriate names). They must be carefully tailored to your business or investment, member goals, and other unique circumstances. To be certain that the operating agreement reflects everyone's collective agreement, each member should read a draft and understand it before signing the document. Chapter 4 describes in detail what should be in your operating agreement and includes a sample agreement.

MANAGERS

In the simplest LLCs, the members owning it are also responsible for operating or managing the LLC's business and other activities. In many LLCs, however, it is advisable or desirable to have specified persons run the company. These people are called managers and are analogous to the directors or officers of a corporation or the general partner of a partnership (although there are differences). If one or more managers are going to run the LLC, the certificate filed to form it and/or the operating agreement should indicate this fact. In every situation when a manager will run your LLC, you should have detailed rules in the operating agreement stating the manager's rights, authority, and responsibilities.

COMPARING LLC JARGON TO PARTNERSHIP AND CORPORATE JARGON

LLCs use disparate terminology for concepts that are similar to those used in corporations and partnerships. Although there may be important differences, a simplistic comparison will help you better understand the LLC jargon, the legalities of your LLC, and the detailed discussions in Chapter 3.

	C Corporation	S Corporation	Limited Partnership	General Partnership	LLC
Owner	Shareholder	Shareholder	General or Limited Partner	General Partner	Member
Distribution	Dividend	Dividend or S corporation distribution	Partnership distribution or guaranteed payment	Partnership distribution or guaranteed payment	LLC distribution or guaranteed payment
Agreement between owners	Shareholders' agreement	Shareholders' agreement	Partnership agreement	Partnership agreement	Operating agreement
Person managing	Director or officer	Director or officer	General partner	General partner	Member or manager
Document used to form	Certificate of Incorporation	Certificate of Incorporation	Certificate of Limited Partnership	Business or Partners Certificate	Formation Certificate or Articles of Organization

SUMMARY

This chapter has provided an overview of some of the key terms and concepts that you must understand to evaluate the decision to form an LLC, or to run an existing LLC. In the following chapters, these definitions will be analyzed in great detail and from several perspectives. If you can keep the big picture and key definitions of this chapter in mind, the later discussions will flow much easier.

3 COMPARING LIMITED LIABILITY COMPANIES WITH OTHER BUSINESS ORGANIZATIONS

Perhaps the best way to define a limited liability company (LLC) and assess its advantages is to compare it with the other common forms of business and investment organizations. These include C corporations, S corporations, limited partnerships (LPs) or **family limited partnerships (FLPs),** and **general partnerships (GPs).** These comparisons highlight many of the tax and legal characteristics of an LLC. Even if you are convinced that a limited liability company is the best way to go (and it usually is!), reviewing this chapter will help you get the most out of your LLC.

TIP: An LLC offers tremendous benefits. It has become the favored form of operating most closely held businesses and investments. Whether you run a retail store, own a small rental property, operate a home-based business, or have a family manufacturing enterprise with $10 million in sales, it pays to consider the LLC. When you are starting a new business or investment endeavor, the question to ask is not "Should I organize an LLC?" but instead, "Is there any reason to consider any approach other than an LLC?"

COMPARING THE DIFFERENT ENTITIES

Factors to Consider

When comparing the types of entities that you can use, consider the following key factors:

- *Federal income taxes:* What are the income tax consequences of using the entity? Some entities pay their own tax, other entities pass the income through to its owners, but few are perfect conduits. The differing imperfections in how entities pass income to their owners are potentially important.

- *State income taxes:* Tax rules differ markedly from state to state. Depending on the state where you will conduct your business or investment activities and the entity that you use, you may realize different tax results. This book addresses LLCs generally and does not provide detailed state tax advice. Your best approach is to understand the general concepts herein and then review the unique details of your situation (i.e., the state, legal, tax, and other ramifications) with your attorney and accountant.

- *Liability protection:* Business owners uniformly want to have limited personal liability. With limited liability, you should not be liable personally (your house and bank account should not be at risk) for a business claim. You can only achieve this protection by separating business and personal risks.

EXAMPLE: Larry Lawn started a lawn mowing business. He purchased equipment and hired college kids part time to help. The first day of work, a worker lost control over a mower and it ran over a coworker and young child, both of whom sustained serious injuries. The lawsuits that follow will likely be expensive and must be satisfied out of Larry's personal assets. Had Larry taken the precaution to organize an entity such as an LLC to own and operate his lawn mowing business, he might have safeguarded his personal assets.

Malpractice is generally an exception to these rules, and a malpractice claimant can generally reach a professional's personal assets to satisfy a claim (unless it is covered by insurance).

- *Legal distinctions:* The legal implications of different entities determine the rights of owners, create other types of persons distinct from owners who may manage or operate the entity (trustees, managers, general partners), and affect other important attributes. Depending on your goals and the state law where your entity will be formed, one entity may have advantages over another.

Summary of Key Considerations for Each Entity

Although each common entity is discussed in detail later in this chapter, the following salient distinctions carry the most weight in deciding which form of entity to use:

- C corporations provide limited liability for owners and have a flexible ownership structure (you can have many classes of stock), but they face double taxation, unless current tax proposals make dividends tax free.

- S corporations provide limited liability for owners, but face severe restrictions on the structure of equity interests and shareholder number and characteristics. There is generally no corporate taxation, but it is not a perfect conduit. At the state tax level, many states impose a corporate-level tax on the income of an S corporation, which reduces its attractiveness.

- Limited partnerships have a separate entity as a general partner (e.g., an S corporation) or face unlimited liability if an individual serves in that position. There is no entity-level taxation. In any limited partnership, at least one partner must be liable for the business's debts. A solution is to use a limited partnership with a corporate general partner (or sometimes now an LLC as a general partner). This requires forming two entities (i.e., a corporation as a general partner and the limited partnership itself) with the resulting complications, multiple tax returns, and costs.

- General partnerships do not have entity level taxation, but owners all risk unlimited personal liability.

- LLCs provide limited liability to all owners and do not face entity level taxation. A few states impose a tax on the income of an LLC.

- Trusts face a hybrid of entity versus beneficiary taxation but do not provide limited liability. Trusts are often used in conjunction with the preceding entities when business or investment activities are being structured, instead of being used alone.

NOTE: William Wealthy wants to buy rental real estate and give it to his child, Sally Spendthrift. He forms an LLC that purchases the property; then he gifts equity in the LLC (membership interests) to a trust he forms for Sally's benefit. This gives William two levels of control over the underlying economic benefits.

PARTNERSHIPS COMPARED WITH LLCs

Partnerships, especially family limited partnerships (FLPs) continue to be a commonly used entity for investment holdings, and to a lesser extent for business endeavors. Most LLCs, other than those with just one owner (member), are taxed as partnerships. Thus, limited partnerships are the most important entities to compare with LLCs.

What Is a Partnership?

For federal income tax purposes, a partnership is a syndicate or group for conducting any business, financial operation, or venture. A partnership is an association of two or more people to co-own a business for profit. This can be contrasted with the mere co-ownership of property, which may not constitute a partnership. Similarly, a joint undertaking merely to share expenses may not be a partnership.

General Partnerships

The simplest and most common type of partnership is a general partnership. It is formed where you, and at least one other person, conduct a business with the intent to make a profit. Legally, you should file a certificate (form of legal statement) with the appropriate government agency, usually the clerk of the county where you reside. This certificate states that you and your partners are going to conduct business as partners, gives the name and address of the partnership, and notes other pertinent facts. This filing is usually simple and inexpensive (fees can be $50 or less, but check with your county clerk). In addition, partners should, and often do, hire an attorney to prepare a partnership agreement. This is a legal contract between the partners that sets forth the details of their relationship.

A general partner can be held personally liable on all partnership debts (even beyond his capital contributions). A general partner may actively participate in the management of the partnership's affairs. Thus, if the partnership constitutes an active business, instead of a passive investment, and the partner materially participates in those activities, then the general partner will receive active income or loss for purposes of the passive loss rules.

Limited Partnerships

A limited partnership is more complex and costly to establish and maintain. It offers, however, some valuable advantages over the general partnership form. A limited partnership has two types of partner. There must be at least one general partner who is personally liable for all partnership debts and is authorized to participate in the partnership's management. There must also be at least one limited partner who is not personally liable for partnership debts; and to maintain that status, he cannot participate in the active management of partnership activities. The limitation on the personal liability of a limited partner is a major factor encouraging the use of limited partnerships over general partnerships.

A limited partnership is formed by filing a certificate that states the names of the partners, which are limited and which are general, the name and business of the partnership, and other information required by the laws of your state. The certificate is more complex and expensive. Also, it is more common to have a detailed and often complex partnership agreement. Some states may even require the formal publication of a summary of the limited partnership certificate in specified papers. This could cost $1,000 or more.

Limited Liability Partnerships

Limited Liability Partnerships (LLPs), also called registered limited liability partnerships, are recognized in many but not all states. LLPs are commonly used for professional practices (lawyers, accountants, doctors, etc.). An LLP is a general partnership that files a registration form with the appropriate state filing authority. The registration provides information relating to the partnership and its partners, with such information requirements varying from state to state. LLPs will generally be treated as a partnership for federal tax purposes, just as will most LLCs. An LLP retains the entity's original general partnership form, but provides a partial liability shield to the partners. Most state statutes provide that a partner in an LLP is not personally liable for debts, obligations, and liabilities chargeable to the partnership arising from negligence, malpractice, wrongful acts, or misconduct of employees not under the direct supervision of that partner. The partners in an LLP formed in those states, however, are generally liable for the commercial obligations (i.e., contract liability) and tort liability of the LLP. With the recent development of the LLP, the advantage of the LLC over a partnership has slightly diminished.

EXAMPLE: Able, Baker, and Charles form a law firm. They set up the firm as an LLP. They sign a **lease** for an office. Baker commits malpractice, and the firm is sued and eventually dissolves. Able and Charles cannot be sued for the malpractice Baker committed (if they were not involved in the case), but all three remain liable for the LLP's lease obligations.

In contrast to LLPs, LLCs provide limited liability to its owners with respect to contractual and tort liabilities of the entity. In certain states where professional LLCs are permitted, however, a member in a professional LLC will generally not be protected from liability resulting from his own malpractice or the malpractice of someone directly under his supervision.

EXAMPLE: Able, Baker, and Charles form a law firm. They set up the firm as an LLC. They sign a lease for an office. Baker commits malpractice and the firm is sued and eventually dissolves. Able and Charles cannot be sued for the malpractice Baker committed (if they were not involved in the case and did not supervise anyone involved in the case); further, none of the members in the LLC are liable on the LLC's lease obligations.

Whereas the LLC thus provides better personal liability protection to its owners than the LLP, legal impediments may prevent its use in some situations. Further, if the landlord were to insist on a personal guarantee of the partners, which is often the case, there would be little practical difference between using an LLP or an LLC.

There are a few states where partners in an LLP are protected from all of the LLP's debts and obligation. In such states, there might be little practical difference between LLCs and LLPs.

LLPs have been enacted primarily for use by national accounting and law firms. Large accounting firms have opted to be LLPs rather than LLCs because LLPs are taxed as partnerships at all state levels, whereas LLCs are taxed by some states at the entity level.

Converting to an LLP is a much more streamlined procedure than converting to an LLC, which necessitates the creation of a new entity. An LLP is the existing partnership, which files a registration statement. Some people may prefer the LLP because of the convenience of conversion.

Income Tax Advantages and Disadvantages of Partnerships

Flow-Through to Partners of Tax Consequences

The most important aspect of a partnership structure, from a tax perspective, is that the partnership itself is not subject to taxation. All of the income, deductions, credits, and so on flow-through to the individual partners to be reported on their individual tax returns. This is advantageous for two reasons. First, there is no tax at the entity level. As a general rule, this compares favorably to a C corporation, whose income is taxed at the corporate level (S corporations generally have pass-through tax treatment similar to that of a partnership, but are subject to more complex rules and tax traps). Distributions from a C corporation are also taxed to the recipient shareholders, resulting in two layers of taxation. Partners and partnerships avoid double taxation. This conduit character of a partnership has caused this form of organization to be a preferred vehicle for structuring many business and real estate transactions.

NOTE: At some points in time, corporate income tax rates are lower than individual rates. At those times in "tax history," to the extent income is not going to be distributed to the individual owners, overall taxes could be lower with a C corporation. However, this comes with substantial tax problems of two layers of tax on liquidation, the vagaries of congressional changes in marginal tax rates, and so on.

Second, the flow-through feature of partnership taxation may enable individual owners/partners to use the losses generated by the partnership to offset other income they may have. However, this ability to offset other income with partnership losses may be subject to the so-called passive loss rules and other restrictions.

Passive Loss Limitations

The **passive loss** rules generally treat any income or loss received by a limited partner in a limited partnership as **passive income** or loss (subject to restrictions that may prevent you from deducting those losses currently, e.g., loss on a real estate rental property). Thus, if an investor has passive losses and cannot use them to offset active income, and is contemplating another income-producing investment, a limited **partnership interest** that will produce passive income to offset the investor's otherwise unusable passive losses may be preferable over a general partnership. Obviously, the investor's involvement in each situation must conform to the active or passive result desired.

Limitations Affect a Partner's Ability to Deduct His Share of Partnership Losses

There are several restrictions on a partner's ability to deduct his share of partnership losses. A partner, for example, cannot deduct a loss that exceeds his **tax basis** (roughly equal to investment, increased by income plus his **pro rata share** of the partnership's debt, reduced by distributions and losses) in his partnership interest.

Passive Loss Rules

The passive loss rules can limit a partner's ability to deduct certain partnership losses. The passive loss rules generally divide all activities (and the income or loss they generate) into three categories:

1. *Passive:* Activities in which the family business owner does not materially participate, such as a passive tax shelter investment. Income and loss allocated to a limited partner of a limited partnership are per se passive.
2. *Active:* Activities in which the family business owner does materially participate, such as a full-time profession.
3. *Portfolio:* Interest, dividends, and so on.

Passive losses generally cannot offset income in the other two categories. Unused passive losses are carried over to future years until they offset other passive income or the family business owner's entire interest in the activity is sold. The passive loss rules may be important in choosing between types of partnerships because general partners can earn active income; whereas limited partners cannot participate in the management of the partnership without losing their limited liability. Thus they can only earn passive income. The IRS has not stated how the passive loss rules apply to managers and members of LLCs.

At-Risk Limitations

Partners can also be subject to another set of limitations known as the **at-risk** rules. These rules can limit the losses that a partner can deduct to the amount the partner is considered to have risked by investing in the partnership. This can include cash, property, and partnership debt on which the partner is liable.

Family Limited Partnerships

To understand the use of partnerships by family businesses, and the taxation of partners and partnerships generally, an overview is necessary. A family limited partnership (FLP) gives the partners more flexibility than a corporation gives to its shareholders. The personal use of tax benefits of the partnership, such as tax losses, is permissible in a family limited partnership. This flexibility is not available with a C corporation, however, and is significantly curtailed in an S corporation. From a tax perspective, moreover, it is far easier to distribute money or property from a partnership than from a corporation.

EXAMPLE: Family limited partnerships are often used for asset protection and estate planning benefits. Instead of owning assets directly, you could transfer them to a family limited partnership and gift ownership interests to your children as limited partners. You could still control the entire partnership by serving as the general partner. The children would have some of the value of the partnership assets transferred to their names. This would remove the value of what you have given your children from your estate even though you still control it. These gifts are often made at discounted values. Finally, the family limited partnership offers protective features that make it difficult for creditors to obtain rights to the assets and economic benefits of the partnership. An LLC can often provide similar benefits.

EXAMPLE: FLPs can be used as a substitute for trusts. Often, a parent will establish an irrevocable trust for the benefit of a minor child.

FLPs and LLCs

Every family business owner must become familiar with this newest form of business operation. An LLC can offer many of the same advantages as an FLP in a much more streamlined fashion, and it does not expose additional assets to the liability of the enterprise. An LLC can offer control by designating the manager (analogous to the general partner in an FLP for control purposes), severely restricting the interests of the other members (analogous to the limited partners in an FLP), and achieving limited liability of the owners.

Conclusions about Partnerships

Every partner in a general partnership is personally liable for all partnership debts. This is a substantial disadvantage of a general partnership compared with either a corporation or an LLC.

A limited partnership can offer limited liability to its limited partners. The limited partnership requires at least one general partner, meaning that at least one owner must agree to remain personally liable on all partnership debts. This is a major disadvantage of the limited partnership form and is frequently unacceptable. An LLC does not suffer this detriment.

Thus, in most instances a limited partnership is structured with a corporation as general partner. This structure requires forming two entities and having legal documentation, tax returns, and fees for both. Not only is this approach costly, it is complex to understand and administer. Since all members of an LLC have limited liability, it avoids this additional complexity.

The LLC can offer the advantages of the limited partnership structure, for less cost, in a simpler manner, and with less tax risk. The LLC will minimize the assets exposed to the liabilities of the entity.

Finally, members of an LLC have the right to participate in management, unless the operating agreement or articles of organization provide otherwise. The ability to limit a member's participation in the LLC's management is only a contractual limitation. In contrast, limited partners in an FLP cannot participate in management without losing their personal liability shield. This is a statutory feature of limited partnerships, not merely a contractual restriction (although the FLP agreement may contain restrictions as well).

An LLC may have some advantages not available to limited partnerships that are especially relevant to real estate investors and business owners. A limited partner always will receive passive losses or income because he cannot participate in the active management of the partnership's business. However, a member of an LLC who is actively involved in the management of the LLC's business will have an easier time satisfying the material participation rules and thus may be able to use LLC losses to offset other income. In an LLC format, business owners may have an easier time arguing that certain earnings of the business should not be subject to payroll taxes. Limited partnerships and LLCs are taxed in the identical manner for federal income tax purposes. Thus, unless there are state level income tax differences, the choice between using some type of partnership or an LLC will often depend on legal nuances, or estate or asset protection planning differences. In some situations, neither the partnership nor LLC form of conducting a business or investment activity is appropriate, or another form of entity already exists. Thus, you need to understand the other options to best make a decision or to work with the specific circumstances you face. In the next sections, forms of structuring business and investments other than a partnership or LLC are discussed and contrasted with LLCs.

C CORPORATION COMPARED WITH AN LLC

In the vast majority of situations, a C corporation will not be a choice if you are planning an entity for any type of investment assets or closely held business. If a C or regular corporation (explained later) is appropriate, an LLC will not be. A corporate or business attorney can help you identify the few situations when a C corporation may be worth considering. In most situations, a family or closely held business only uses a C corporation because it was formed long ago and changing it to an LLC is too costly. Conversion is sometimes possible; and if not, the information about LLCs in this book can help you plan new expansions and endeavors in ways that obtain the advantages of being owned by LLCs. The following discussion contrasts

C corporations with LLCs and prepares you to discuss with your advisers the limited times when a C corporation may be worth considering.

How a C Corporation Is Formed

Any corporation (no matter what its classification for tax purposes) is a legal entity formed under the laws of a particular state. Although the names and procedures vary from state to state, a corporation is generally formed by a person, called the *incorporator* signing a legal document typically several pages long, called a *certificate of incorporation*. This contains certain key facts about the soon-to-be-formed corporation: the number of shares (certificates that prove ownership), number of directors (persons responsible for certain overall management decisions), the name of the corporation, the name and address of the **registered agent** (a person designated to receive legal notices), and so on. To form the corporation, the incorporator files the certificate of incorporation with the secretary of state. Next, a key tax decision must be made, whether the corporation should choose (elect) to be taxed as an S corporation (discussed later in this chapter). If no action is taken, the corporation will be a C or "regular" corporation for tax purposes.

How a C Corporation Is Taxed

General Income Taxation

A C corporation is a regular corporation, which must pay a corporate level tax. C corporations and their owners are subject to two layers of income taxation. First, a corporate tax is charged on the corporation's earnings (on IRS Form 1120). Then, to the extent that the earnings are distributed to the shareholders as dividends, each shareholder must report that dividend income on his personal tax return (IRS Form 1040) and pay any income taxes due. A C corporation does not receive an income tax deduction for its distribution of dividends. Thus, the income is taxed twice and is called *double taxation*.

Salary and Fringe Benefits and C Corporations

Many closely held corporations (those owned by a small number of owners or shareholders) use a common method of avoiding double taxation. It is feasible when the shareholders are also employees of the corporation. In this capacity, they withdraw most or all of the earnings of the corporation as salary, leaving little or nothing to pay out as dividends. The corporation then claims a deduction for the salaries paid, and the shareholders report the salary received as income on their personal income tax returns. This strategy eliminates the double taxation, but it presents risks. The IRS often challenges salary payments as being excessive compensation if they are larger than a nonowner (i.e., an unrelated person) would receive. If successful, the IRS would require the corporation to treat a portion of the salary as really being a dividend, thus forcing the corporation and its owners back to the unfavorable situation of double taxation.

Many closely held businesses also pay personal expenses of their shareholders. For example, a shareholder takes friends out to dinner and pays with a corporate business card claiming that the expense was a business deduction. These distributions bypass the double taxation on the dividends the corporation pays to its shareholders. If the IRS disallows these expenses, the same result occurs as with a disallowed excess salary—double taxation.

Numerous fringe benefits for employees of a C corporation enjoy tax-favored status. By contrast, fringe benefits provided to LLC members who own greater than 2 percent of the membership interests in the LLC are taxable as income to the members. Examples of such fringe benefits are term life insurance and medical benefits.

Double Tax on Liquidation

A C corporation is subject to double taxation on the sale of its assets and its subsequent liquidation.

EXAMPLE: Wally Widget forms a C corporation to manufacture widgets. Ten years later, Wally decides to end the corporation and sell out. The buyer does not want to buy Wally's stock because she is afraid the corporation might have liabilities that she was not able to identify during her investigations before agreeing to purchase the business. So she insists on buying the assets of Wally's corporation. To do this, Wally has to end (liquidate) the corporation and have the corporation distribute its assets to him personally as the shareholder. Wally will then sell the assets to the purchaser. On receiving the distribution of corporate assets, Wally will likely face a tax. The corporation may also have to pay a tax on the distribution. Thus, even in liquidation, Wally and the C corporation could face double taxation.

Prior to 1986, if a C corporation that was planning to liquidate sold appreciated assets, it did not have to recognize a gain on such a sale and there would only be a subsequent gain or loss to the shareholders on liquidation of the corporation. The Tax Reform Act of 1986 substantially modified this law so that there will be double taxation when the C corporation sells its assets and then liquidates.

Special Tax Problems

Corporate taxation has the following complications and potentially costly tax traps:

Personal Holding Company (PHC) Tax.   This is a tax on the unreasonable accumulation of income in the corporation (i.e., nonpayment of dividends to avoid the second level of tax at the shareholder level) called an **accumulated earnings tax.** The personal holding company (PHC) tax is in addition to the regular tax on corporate income. It is a special tax imposed on the "undistributed personal holding company income" of a personal holding company at the highest rate for individual taxpayers. The personal holding company tax is aimed at *incorporated pocketbooks* (corporations that are established to receive and hold investment income or compensation of their shareholders). The tax is assessed on the PHC's undistributed income. This is PHC income reduced by dividends paid and federal income tax. A PHC is a corporation with at least 60 percent of its adjusted ordinary gross income for the year consisting of PHC income, and during the last half of the tax year five or fewer shareholders have owned more than half of the value of its stock. PHC income consists of dividends, interest, royalties (excluding copyright and computer software royalties); annuities; rents (an exclusion is provided for real estate businesses where more than half of the adjusted ordinary gross income is rents); mineral, oil, and gas royalties (an exclusion is provided for where royalties are more than half of the adjusted ordinary gross income); rents for film exhibition and distribution (an exclusion is provided for where rents are more than half of the adjusted ordinary gross income); amounts received under contracts for personal services; and so on.

Accumulated Earnings Tax.   If your corporation accumulates too much money (beyond the reasonable needs of the business), the IRS may seek to apply a penalty tax called the accumulated earnings tax. This is a penalty imposed on a C corporation that the IRS determines has retained too much earnings, instead of paying such earnings to the shareholders as dividends, with the purpose of avoiding taxes on shareholders. The rate of tax on improper accumulations, applicable to all corporations subject to the tax, is imposed at the highest individual tax rate on "accumulated taxable income."

An overview of how this tax works can illustrate its severity. Where an accumulated earnings tax is assessed, it is charged at the highest individual tax rate on accumulated taxable income. This is a special term that for most corporations includes **taxable income** of the corporation subject to several special adjustments:

Taxable Income

- Federal income taxes.
- Charitable contributions which could not be deducted for purposes of the regular tax as a result of the limitation that contributions cannot exceed 10 percent of taxable income.
- No deduction allowed for dividends received. Most corporations can receive a deduction equal to a large portion of dividends they receive from other corporations. This special deduction is added back.
- Capital loss carryovers not permitted. These are amounts that are not deductible in certain years because of the limitation on capital losses; however, they can be carried over to and perhaps deducted in other tax years.
- Deduction permitted for net **capital gains**/losses (see Chapter 11). However, this amount must be adjusted by a special factor.
- The accumulated earnings credit. This is the amount of income that the corporation can retain for the reasonable needs of its business. A minimum amount is permitted to most corporations (other than personal service corporations) of $250,000 (from the combination of both past and current earnings). The courts will often consider whether the liquid assets of the corporation are excessive when compared with the reasonable business needs of the corporation. Reasonable business needs can include maintaining reasonable working capital, replacing plant and equipment, redeeming stock of a deceased shareholder, and paying down debt.

The accumulated earnings tax is again a concern for every closely held corporation. The corporation should document (e.g., in the minutes of the board of directors) the commercial business reasons for retaining funds. These could include working capital needs, proposed expansion plans, and contingent liabilities.

Alternative Minimum Tax (AMT).   An **alternative minimum tax** also may be imposed on a C corporation. This tax ensures that if corporations take substantial advantage of tax benefits provided under the Internal Revenue Code, they still pay a minimum tax.

Advantages of an LLC Compared with C Corporations

The Bottom Line

In most cases when a new entity is formed, an LLC will be a better choice than a C corporation. However, there are some notable exceptions when special tax circumstances exist.

C Corporation Becomes an S Corporation

If the entity has existed for many years, conversion to an LLC will rarely be practical because of the tax that will likely be triggered on liquidation of the C corporation (see earlier discussion). In such cases, new activities (e.g., a new division or new building) may be established as an LLC from inception. Existing operations will generally remain in the C corporation and be planned for based on the tax considerations noted earlier. In some instances, making an **election** to be taxed as an S corporation will be beneficial, although a 10-year time period must elapse to realize the full S corporation benefits.

Where a regular C corporation elects to be taxed as an S corporation, two special tax traps must be considered. The first is the built-in gains tax. A tax will be imposed on the S corporation on any gain that arose prior to its conversion from a regular corporation. This special tax applies during the 10-year period following the election to be taxed as an S corporation. The tax is assessed at the highest corporate tax rate. The maximum gain that can be subject to this special tax is limited to the net unrealized built-in gain that existed at the date the corporation became an S corporation.

NOTE: If a corporation owned a building with a depreciated book value of $1 million that was worth $2 million at the date the corporation was converted to an S corporation the built-in gain would be $1 million. If the S corporation was sold or liquidated within 10 years, a corporate tax would have to be paid on a portion of that built-in gain.

As a result of this built-in gains tax, it is best to have the assets of any regular corporation valued in a written and independent appraisal as of the date an election is made for it to become an S corporation. A mitigating factor is that the corporation can use any operating loss carryovers to off-set any built-in gains tax it incurs.

A second problem that a regular C corporation can face in converting to an S corporation is a limitation on passive income. A regular corporation that has earnings and profits when it elects to be an S corporation could face a corporate level tax and possible loss of its S corporation status if it earns excessive passive income. The rule is that if more than 25 percent of the taxable income for an S corporation subject to these rules is passive, a tax will be charged on excess net passive income. If this 25 percent thresh-old is exceeded for three consecutive years, the S corporation status will be terminated.

S corporations are pass-through entities so that the passive loss limita-tion rules generally do not apply directly to them. Instead, each share-holder will separately characterize income or loss as passive, active, or portfolio by considering the shareholder's ownership interest, participa-tion, and so forth. An S corporation shareholder can only deduct losses passed through up to the amount of his tax basis. Only the **basis** in the shareholder's stock, such as the price paid and amounts directly due to the shareholder from the corporation are included in the tax basis. The S corporation shareholder cannot include a pro rata share of entity level debts (a nonrecourse mortgage on the property) in his basis as can a part-ner. Where real estate assets are owned, this dichotomy greatly favors the partnership form.

How Much Income Is Anticipated and How Much Will Be Distributed Affects Your Choice

From a tax perspective, if a substantial portion of a C corporation's in-come is to be distributed to its shareholders as dividends, the corporation will have to pay a corporate tax and the shareholders will be taxed on the distributed dividends, resulting in double taxation. Under this scenario, it would be preferable to be an LLC, where there is only one level of tax, which is at the members' level.

Unlike a C corporation, an LLC is not subject to double taxation on the sale of its assets and its subsequent liquidation. Most LLCs are taxed as partnerships, which are not subject to federal income tax. Instead, income, deductions, gains, losses, and credits flow through to, and are reported on, the members' tax returns.

The pass-through nature of LLCs can be a major advantage because losses, as well as gains, pass through the LLC to its members. In this fash-ion, the members can use losses of the LLC against other income they may have, depending on the character of such losses.

However, if the entity's income is not to be distributed to its owners, then it may be more advantageous to be a C corporation.

EXAMPLE: You are a successful businessperson and pay tax at the highest federal, state, and local rate of approximately 48 percent. Your corporation earns so much money that you decide to allow funds to accumulate in the corporation. In this situation, the corporation can be an advantageous form for your business since the corporation is in a lower tax bracket than you are.

CAUTION: Watch out for the accumulated earnings tax if you plan to retain income in the corporation (see earlier discussion).

LLCs Avoid Many C Corporation Tax Traps

Using an LLC instead of a C corporation avoids the risk of being subject to the accumulated earnings tax and penalty taxes on personal holding companies. An LLC would not be subject to the alternative minimum tax that affects some corporations. However, the members may be subject to a personal alternative minimum tax. Another significant incentive for using an LLC instead of a C corporation is the potential double taxation on the liquidation of a C corporation.

Maximum Individual and Corporate Income Tax Rates Affect the Decision

Depending on the relationship of the maximum corporate and individual income tax rates, it can be advantageous to use a C corporation and subject income to a lower corporate tax, instead of the higher marginal rate applied to the owners individually. Through much, but far from all, of past history, corporations have been taxed at lower tax rates than individuals. Regular corporations (not S corporations or other forms of corporations that have a flow-through tax structure) are taxed at rates from 15 percent to 38 percent. Professional service corporations (e.g., law, accounting, and medical corporations) are taxed at a flat 35 percent rate. The result is that under the income tax rate structure, corporations will probably be taxed at higher rates than individuals. Thus, a planning strategy for many will be to try to distribute income out of the corporations in a tax-deductible manner (such as salaries) so that the income will be realized at the individual rates instead of being retained in the corporate entity. This will also mean (which had really been the case before the Tax Relief Act of 2001) that limited liability companies and family limited partnerships (and other flow-through entities) will be even more preferred.

Special Tax Benefits of C Corporations Should Be Considered

Although an LLC has many advantages over a C corporation, the latter has certain tax incentives.

EXAMPLE: There is a tax incentive for individuals (i.e., investors other than corporations) who have held qualifying stock in a qualifying small business (QSB) and have sold it at a profit. This benefit applies whether the stock owned is common stock or preferred stock. If an owner meets the requirements, he can exclude up to 50 percent of the taxable gain when he sells, or otherwise disposes of, the stock. The half of the gain that is not excluded is taxed at favorable capital gains rates (20 percent compared with individual tax rates of up to 38.6 percent). Therefore, if you can exclude one-half of the gain, the effective tax rate on the entire sale is only 14 percent. Be careful in evaluating the benefits of this special tax incentive. If you are subject to the alternative minimum tax, the tax benefit could be less than expected. To qualify for this favorable benefit, the entity must be a C corporation. An S corporation, partnership, or LLC will not qualify. Thus, if this benefit could be important, choosing to organize the business as an LLC could be a mistake.

Also, the C corporation offers greater flexibility in selecting a **fiscal year;** generally, an LLC must use a **calendar year.** Using a fiscal year means ending the corporation's tax year at the end of any month other than December.

S CORPORATION COMPARED WITH AN LLC

Formation of an S Corporation

S corporations are entities formed under a state's laws by a person called an incorporator filing a certificate of incorporation. This process is identical to that described earlier for C corporations. For legal purposes, the S corporation is treated identically to a regular corporation.

Income Tax Consequences of S Corporations

The "S" designation in an S corporation refers to the special tax treatment that such corporations have under specific provisions of the tax laws contained in Subchapter S of the Internal Revenue Code. An S corporation is taxed like a partnership for federal tax purposes (and tax purposes of most, but not all states). This means the income and deductions flow through to the shareholders and are taxed on their personal tax returns. In contrast, a regular C corporation pays tax on its income; if it then distributes a dividend, its shareholders must pay a second tax on this same income.

Requirements to Qualify for S Corporation Treatment

A corporation must meet several requirements to obtain the benefits of S corporation status. If these requirements are violated, the corporation could lose its tax-favored status.

There Can Be Only One Class of Stock

An S corporation can have only **one class of stock.** This means that each share of stock must give its owner (shareholder) the same rights as every other shareholder to receive corporate profits and corporate assets if the corporation is liquidated. The shares are allowed to have differences as to voting rights, and transfer, repurchase, and redemption rights. Therefore, a distribution of profits to a shareholder requires a simultaneous proportionate distribution to all of the other shareholders.

EXAMPLE: Widget Corporation is an S corporation owned by three equal shareholders—A, B, and C. If the corporation is going to make a $50,000 distribution to A, there must be a simultaneous $50,000 distribution to each of B and C. However, shareholders A and B might have the right to vote, and shareholder C might not have that right.

There Can Be No More than 75 Shareholders

This limitation only applies to a single S corporation. If multiple S corporations are formed to hold interests in a partnership created to operate the business, there can be more than 75 shareholders. For this limitation, a husband and wife are treated as one shareholder.

Certain Trusts and Estates Can Own Stock in S Corporations

Only specified persons can own stock in an S corporation. This includes only certain trusts and estates that are expressly allowed to be shareholders.

Qualified Subchapter S Trust as a Shareholder.   One way that a trust can be a shareholder is for it to be a special trust called a **Qualified Subchapter S**

Trust (QSST). For a corporation to qualify as an S corporation, it can only have qualified shareholders, including only certain types of trusts. The **beneficiary** must be treated as the owner of the portion of the trust that consists of S corporation stock. This means that you can have a trust with S corporation stock as an asset as well as other assets. In effect, such a trust will be treated like two separate trusts: (1) a qualified S corporation trust (QSST), which meets all the requirements outlined here; and (2) a regular trust, which can accumulate or sprinkle income in any manner. To qualify as a QSST, the trust must meet the following requirements:

- If the trust terminates during the life of the person who is then receiving the trust's income, all of the assets must be then distributed to that beneficiary.

- During the life of the current income beneficiary, only that person can receive income from the trust. All of the trust's income must be distributed, or at least required to be distributed, to only one individual beneficiary. This beneficiary must be a citizen or resident of the United States. This latter requirement helps assure that the United States will tax the beneficiary. The IRS can forgo the corporate level tax but cannot forgo the corporate level tax and then have to chase a foreign resident for taxes. These requirements can significantly infringe on your planning. Typical children's trusts, where several children are beneficiaries of a single trust, will not qualify. A charitable remainder trust cannot also qualify as a QSST.

- If any principal of the trust is distributed while the current income beneficiary is alive, the principal must be distributed to that beneficiary. The trustee cannot have the power to sprinkle trust income or make discretionary principal distributions to different beneficiaries, or to accumulate income that is not distributed (because all income must be distributed currently).

- The interest that the current income beneficiary has in receiving current income distributions from the trust must end on the earlier of the death of that beneficiary, or the termination of the trust. If the trust ends during his life, the trust assets must all be distributed to the current income beneficiary.

ESBTs: Electing Small Business Trusts.   Electing small business trusts (ESBTs) can be shareholders of S corporations after 1996. The ESBT is another exception to the general S corporation rule that only a U.S. person may be a shareholder and must pay the tax. The ESBT can be any subchapter J trust that is not a QSST. For a trust to qualify as an ESBT, all of its beneficiaries must be individuals or estates (partnerships, corporations, and so on cannot be beneficiaries). An ESBT can have a special needs trust as a beneficiary. Certain charities can be contingent remaindermen (the beneficiaries who receive trust income or assets if all prior beneficiaries die or cease to qualify as beneficiaries). Most commonly, it is a sprinkle trust created by necessity. ESBTs can provide greater flexibility than QSSTs in that they can have many current income beneficiaries. This means several people can receive income each year from the trust. QSSTs require a separate trust for each beneficiary.

If you make the ESBT election, the trust is taxed. The ESBT, however, is a tax-inefficient trust. The ESBT pays tax on income at the 39.6 percent maximum rate without any deductions and without any lower marginal rates. ESBT gets almost no deductions other than state and local taxes and administrative expenses. There is no charitable deduction for an ESBT. However, there is no distributable net income (DNI) concept in determining ESBT taxable income. All distributions to beneficiaries are tax free.

NOTE: How will an ESBT pay income tax if the S corporation it owns makes no distributions because all its earnings are being reinvested?

When counting the general 75-shareholder limit for S corporations when an ESBT is a shareholder, you must look through the ESBT to identify and count the individual ESBT beneficiaries. Anyone who is a potential distributee from an ESBT sprinkle trust is a person counted in adding up the shareholders for compliance with the 75-shareholders test. For example, if the ESBT trustee can distribute income among all of your descendants, then all of your descendants are included. If a beneficiary can only receive ESBT distributions following the exercise of a power of appointment, that beneficiary is not counted as an S corporation shareholder until the power of appointment is exercised.

There are numerous filing requirements. You must file voluminous information with the Service to comply with ESBT requirements within specified time periods.

Grantor Trust. A so-called **grantor** trust qualifies as an S corporation shareholder. A grantor trust is a trust whose income is taxed to the grantor. A trust over which a person other than the grantor is treated as the owner of the trust also qualifies. This is a trust where such other person (often the current beneficiary) has the power to vest the trust corpus or income in himself. These are trusts in which the income is taxable fully to an individual. An example is the revocable living (loving) trust.

It is not enough that your lawyer merely include the necessary provisions in your trust agreement for it to qualify as a QSST and to hold S corporation stock. Several important filing requirements must be made with the IRS for your trust to qualify as a QSST and thus be able to own S corporation stock without tainting the tax status of the corporation. This election must be made separately by the current income beneficiary for each S corporation stock that the trust holds.

EXAMPLE: Grandfather made gifts of S corporation stock to trusts for each of his grandchildren. Each grandchild, as the current income beneficiary of each trust, must make the required election. The election must be filed with the IRS office where the S corporation files its income tax returns.

The election must clearly indicate that it is an election (choice indicated by filing appropriate documents with the IRS). The election should demonstrate that the beneficiary, or other person, making the election is in fact entitled to make the election.

CAUTION: The election must generally be made within 2½ months of the date on which the trust first becomes a shareholder. Also, the election must be filed before the QSST election is effective. Although you should make every effort to ensure a timely and proper election, the IRS has shown compassion to some of those missing the deadline. This doesn't mean miss the deadline. It means, if you inadvertently do so, try letting your tax adviser pursue the IRS's gratitude with a request for a waiver of the particular provision (whether it is the election or something else). You might just have some luck.

If the trust has successive income beneficiaries, there is no need to make a new election.

EXAMPLE: John is to receive all income until age 35, whereupon all income will then go to Jane. Jane is a successive income beneficiary and need not make the election again. Jane, however, could refuse to continue the election by affirmatively electing not to consent to the continued application of the election.

NOTE: Carefully review with your tax adviser whether to make the S election. Once you have made the election, you cannot change it.

The beneficiary of a QSST should be given the necessary information for tax filing. This can become somewhat confusing because of the legal entities involved, and because guidance from the IRS is a bit sparse. The S corporation should distribute income to the trust and provide the trust (i.e., the QSST) with a Form 1120S, Schedule K-1, reflecting all income or loss to the trust from the S corporation for the year. The trust could then attach a copy of this form to Form 1065, Schedule K-1, which the trust then gives the beneficiary.

Common Trusts That Don't Qualify to Own S Corporation Stock. The typical credit shelter or bypass trust used in many estate plans can create serious problems if the **decedent** owned shares in an S corporation. A trust to which S corporation stock is transferred pursuant to the terms of a will can only be an S corporation shareholder for 60 days, or the S corporation status will be lost.

CAUTION: S corporation shareholders must review their estate plans to avoid future problems. Representations should probably be obtained in the shareholders' agreement that estate plans will be reviewed and changed if necessary.

Nonresident Aliens Cannot Own Stock

A nonresident is a person who lives outside the United States. An alien is a person who is not a United States citizen. Thus, foreign persons cannot own an interest in an S corporation. Caution must be exercised.

TIP: Have every shareholder represent in the shareholders' agreement of the S corporation that they are not nonresident aliens and that they will not sell or transfer their stock to one.

Corporation Must Elect to Be Taxed as an S Corporation

For a corporation to be taxed as an S corporation, it must make a filing with the IRS on Form 2553, signed by the shareholders. The election must be filed within 2½ months of the beginning of a particular tax year if the election is to be effective for that tax year. Tax choices must always be made with care. Whenever you form any entity, be certain to follow up immediately with your accountant to be sure you have made any necessary tax elections and have filed them with the appropriate formality. State law requirements can differ.

Restrictions on Owning Other Corporations

An S corporation may not own 80 percent or more of another corporation. This restriction can create problems for holding company structures. A holding company is an arrangement in which one corporation owns stock in one or more other corporations. If you require a more complex structure, the S corporation may not work. Although an LLC has more flexibility in this regard, C corporations often seem the most common.

An S corporation, however, can own corporations that elect to be treated for tax purposes as qualified S corporation subsidiaries (or QSSS or Q-Subs).

Domestic Corporation

The S corporation must be a domestic corporation. This means the S corporation must be organized under the laws of one of the U.S. states. For most people, this is not an issue.

Comparing S Corporations with Other Entities

Difference between S Corporation and C Corporation

The only difference between an S corporation and a C corporation is its tax status. This difference, however, is very important.

S Corporations Remain the Most Common Business Entity

Although LLCs have become the favored method of structuring new business and investment endeavors, S corporations remain the most common organization for existing closely held businesses. This is because prior to the creation of LLCs, S corporations were the most popular format for closely held businesses. It is too costly to change most of these S corporations into LLCs. The S corporation became so popular because it provides the limited liability associated with a corporation and the flow-through tax treatment associated with a partnership (one level of taxation, not two as with a C corporation). As such, the corporation may be held liable to the extent of corporate assets in the event of a claim, but the personal assets of the shareholders will generally not be at risk. Only the amount invested by the shareholder in the S corporation will be obtainable by the corporation's creditors. These two attributes made the S corporation the entity of choice. However, LLCs provide the same benefit with far less income tax complexity and fewer income tax traps. This is why the LLC has become the new entity of choice. The reason so many S corporations remain is that to change an S corporation into an LLC requires the liquidation of the S corporation, and that can trigger a corporate level tax.

S Corporations and Partnerships

In a general partnership, all partners are personally liable for entity debts and claims. In a limited partnership, the general partner (and there must always be one) is personally liable for entity debts and claims. To address this issue, many partnerships are structured using S corporations as general partners. The individuals who ultimately control the partnership, instead of directly being general partners, form an S corporation to serve in that capacity. They then control the S corporation, and hence the partnership, indirectly.

Before LLCs, the use of a limited partnership with an S corporation general partner had been common for real estate, business, or other family limited partnerships to protect the general partner/family business owner from personal liability. With the advent of LLCs, all members and managers have limited liability, avoiding the need for a second entity to achieve this goal. However, this older approach is still used in cases where a limited partnership is preferable to an LLC (e.g., state laws may favor the limited partnership).

Advantages of LLCs Compared with S Corporations

S Corporations Face More Restrictions Than LLCs. Unlike an S corporation, an LLC is not subject to restrictions on the number of owners (members). This contrasts favorably with an S corporation, which may have no more than 75 shareholders. In addition, there are no restrictions on the nature and character of those who can be owners of an LLC, as opposed to an S corporation. S corporations are subject to substantial restrictions that can wreak havoc with the best of plans. For example, S corporation shareholders are limited to individuals, decedent's estates, bankruptcy estates, and specific types of trusts; nonresident aliens are not permitted to be shareholders; and an estate can only hold stock in an S corporation for a limited time period.

NOTE: Many people desire to set up trusts for their children to be the owners of stock in an S corporation. These trusts must be specially tailored to be eligible to hold stock in an S corporation. They must require mandatory distributions of income to the child, and the trust can only provide for distributions of principal to that same child. Therefore, if the trust involves a minor child, the parents would have no alternative but to distribute all of the income to that child, which generally would be contrary to their objectives.

With an LLC, the trust can be restructured in any fashion desired by the parents and still be a member in an LLC.

An S corporation requires an election to enjoy pass-through tax treatment. An LLC does not require such an election to enjoy pass-through tax treatment.

Terminating an S Corporation Can Cause Problems.   S corporations are subject to many restrictive rules (untimely filing of the tax election, transfer of stock to someone not permitted to be a shareholder, violation of the prohibition against two classes of stock, etc.) that would have the effect of terminating the S election. This would result in the corporation being taxed as a C corporation. Once an S corporation's S election is terminated, then that corporation cannot reelect S status for five years. Using an LLC avoids these potential problems.

NOTE: Although the IRS may permit the entity to immediately reelect to be taxed as an S corporation if the event that caused the favorable S corporation status to terminate was "inadvertent," the IRS may require the payment of a significant tax penalty to do so. Further, the IRS may decide not to accept the shareholders' excuse, in which case the five-year period would apply.

Any shareholder of an S corporation can cause a termination of the S corporation's "S" status by transferring stock to someone not permitted to hold stock in an S corporation. No such problem exists with an LLC.

LLCs Provide More Flexibility to Allocate Income.   An LLC can provide for almost any type of allocation of its **cash flow,** income, expense, and gains among the members. An S corporation, on the other hand, is inflexible. Each share of stock must be entitled to identical distribution and liquidation rights. This can be an important drawback where owners make different contributions to the business. It is common for the owners of a start-up company to desire different allocations of income among the owners when one owner contributes land, another a building, and a third owner contributes other assets. This is almost impossible to do in an S corporation, and cumbersome efforts often cannot achieve the desired objectives. The LLC can provide tremendous flexibility to reach these goals.

EXAMPLE: If an S corporation is owned 50 percent by Parent and 25 percent each by child A and child B and the corporation makes a $50,000 cash distribution to the Parent, then the corporation must make a simultaneous $25,000 distribution to each of child A and child B. There is no flexibility for the Parent to receive the $50,000 distribution without corresponding distributions to the other shareholders. With an LLC, there is the flexibility to make a $50,000 distribution to Parent with no requirement to make distributions to the children.

PLANNING TIP: Consider using both an LLC and an S corporation, or two (or more) LLCs, for the situations previously described. If your business will own real estate and valuable equipment, have one LLC own the building and rent it to your business (which may be organized as an LLC or S corporation, or perhaps a C corporation to take advantage of one of the special tax benefits available to C corporations). A second LLC could own your equipment and rent it to the business. This is useful from an asset protection perspective. If the creditors, customers, or other plaintiffs sue the business entity, they should have no rights to reach the valuable real estate or equipment assets because the business does not own them.

LLC Owners Can More Readily Use Tax Losses.   Tax losses can often be used to obtain more valuable income tax benefits if incurred by an LLC than if incurred by an S corporation. This is because an S corporation shareholder's deductible losses are limited to each shareholder's basis in his stock plus any loans he has made to the S corporation. In contrast, an LLC member, like a partner in a partnership (since LLCs are generally taxed as a partnership), can deduct losses up to the sum of his basis in his LLC membership interest plus his allocable share of the LLC's debt.

EXAMPLE: Ten investors contribute $100,000 each to a newly formed entity to acquire an office building. The entity borrows an additional $500,000 as the balance of the building's purchase price. If the entity is an S corporation, each shareholder's deductible loss is limited to $100,000. However, if the entity is an LLC that is taxed as a partnership, each member can deduct losses up to $150,000 ($100,000 basis plus $50,000 share of the entity's debt).

This distinction relating to the deductibility of the entity's losses is very important when financing a business with a loan. Even if the shareholders in the S corporation guarantee the S corporation's debt, they cannot deduct losses against their share of the S corporation's debt. The tax basis of the investors for purposes of determining deductible losses can differ substantially between an LLC and an S corporation and, more often than not, will benefit the LLC owners.

EXAMPLE: Assume two S corporation shareholders contributed $10,000 each in cash to the corporation, and the corporation borrowed $200,000. As S corporation shareholders, their basis, and thus their deductible losses, is limited to the $10,000 invested. LLC owners, however, will each have a basis of $110,000 because they can include in their basis their pro rata share of entity level debt ($100,00 each) plus their initial contributions ($10,000 each). Basis is a tax term that is roughly translated as investment, and it is used to determine gain on sale and the amount of losses that can be deducted.

EXAMPLE: The S corporation acquired a building for $500,000 and the shareholders made no capital contributions to the S corporation, but instead the S corporation borrowed $500,000, which was personally guaranteed by the shareholders. The shareholders would not be entitled to deduct any losses on their individual tax returns because they have no basis in their stock and are not entitled to take losses against the liabilities of the S corporation even if they personally guarantee them. On the other hand, if the entity were a partnership or an LLC, the partners or members could deduct losses up to their allocable share of the liabilities of the entity. Thus they would be permitted to take another $500,000 in deductions allocated among the members and partners on their tax returns.

Tax Consequences of Company Sale Favor LLC.   If a purchaser acquires stock in an S corporation, the basis of the assets of the S corporation remains the same despite the purchase price paid by the purchaser. For example, assume an S corporation has two equal shareholders and the corporation's assets include a piece of machinery that has been depreciated to $10,000. If a purchaser buys the stock of one of the shareholders for a purchase price of $100,000, the corporation's basis in the machinery remains at $10,000.

With an LLC, the entity can make an election to increase (step up) the basis of the LLC's assets attributable to the purchasing member to correspond to the purchase price paid for membership interests. Assuming the same example, but using an LLC, the LLC's basis in the machinery would be increased to $105,000 ($100,000 for one-half of the machinery based on the purchase price of the membership interests and one-half of the old basis in the machinery, which would equal $5,000).

TRUSTS COMPARED WITH AND USED WITH LLCs

The trust could own assets directly connected with the family that the parent gives to the trust as gifts for the benefit of the child. The trust can control the child's use of and access to the assets, protect the child's assets from a failed marriage or creditors, and pass income to the child at a lower tax bracket (once the child has reached age 14 so that he is no longer subject to the **Kiddie Tax**). An FLP can also accomplish these goals, in some instances with greater flexibility. The child's interests are protected from divorce or creditors because of the restrictions on transfer of a partner's interest in the limited partnership agreement (see discussion of asset protection in Part Five). The parent, as general partner, has substantial control over the assets, and subject to certain tax restrictions, significant control over distributions out of the partnership.

Trusts and partnerships can also be combined for even greater protection and control. A parent can establish an FLP and gift partnership interests to a trust for a child. This will give the parent a double element of control in that the parent will select the trustee of the trust and the general partner of the partnership (or serve as the general partner himself).

By owning a general partner interest, the parent has control over the FLP (e.g., power to make management decisions, sell assets, and determine the time and amount of distributions to partners) regardless of the overall ownership percentage reflected by that interest. The general partner interest is usually small (i.e., 1 percent) because the objective is to transfer the value to younger generations.

Limited partnership interests usually are given to younger members of the family. In valuing those interests for gift tax purposes, discounts are generally available for lack of control (a limited partner is not entitled to participate in management) and lack of marketability. These discounts, which are discussed in detail in Chapter 12, usually range from 20 percent to 50 percent and create a leverage that allows the FLP technique to produce significant transfer tax savings.

If a trust is set up to own the limited partnership interest on behalf of a child, the parent can assert even greater control. The parent could serve as the sole general partner of the partnership and control the partnership from that perspective. Then by selecting the trustee to manage the trust, the parent can indirectly control the trust.

EXAMPLE: A husband and wife own $2 million of General Motors stock that they want to gift to their three children. The **annual exclusion** allows the parents to gift up to $22,000 per year to each child without having to pay a gift tax. This would allow the parents to gift an aggregate of $66,000 of stock each year (based on the New York Stock Exchange trading price) without gift tax consequences. If the parents decide to use an FLP, they can contribute the entire block of General Motors stock to the FLP. It would initially be established with each spouse owning a 1 percent general partnership interest and a 49 percent limited partnership interest. They would give the children (or trust for their benefit) a limited partnership interest. That converts the gift from one of stock with a readily determinable value into a closely held business interest that may be discounted, thereby allowing the parents to transfer more General Motors stock to their children free of gift tax.

If a valuation discount of one-third can be justified for the limited partnership gifts, a 1.65 percent limited partnership interest could be gifted to each child (or their trust) each year. This results in a gift of an interest allocable to $33,000 of FLP assets (i.e., 1.65% × $2 million) for a gift tax value of only $22,000 because of the discounting. Thus, gifts of interests allocable to $99,000 (instead of $66,000) of stock could be transferred, fully covered by the gift tax annual exclusion.

LEASES AND LLCs

A lease is not typically viewed as a method of structuring a business, but it can be an important means of arranging transactions. Real estate or valuable **tangible property** (e.g., construction equipment, medical equipment) can be given as a gift, or part gift/part sale, to family members, children, or trusts for children. These assets can then be leased back to assure the business the use of the assets. Lease arrangements can be structured as gift-leasebacks by the children, trusts, or others purchasing the assets directly.

LICENSES AND LLCs

Concepts similar to the lease arrangement in the preceding paragraph can be used to carve out the rights to important intangible assets, vest ownership in another person or entity, and then pay a license fee to obtain the use of these assets.

EXAMPLE: The name and logo for a restaurant or other business could be owned by a family trust or partnership. The restaurant can then license the right to use the name and logo. In the event of a suit or challenge to the restaurant business, these assets could have some measure of protection. This same technique can facilitate the transfer of income to lower tax bracket family members, remove assets from the estate of an older generation family member, and so forth. If the concept for the restaurant "takes off," the children, through the family limited partnership or other entity will own the license to the name, logo, and related intangibles. These could be licensed to future restaurant locations. Thus, any future appreciation would be outside the business owner's estate.

SOLE PROPRIETORSHIPS AND LLCs

Some states require an LLC to have at least two members. The term *persons* generally includes individuals, partnerships, limited partnerships, trusts, LLCs, business trusts, estates, and other associations. The requirement of having two members prevents the use of LLCs for sole proprietorships wanting limited liability without setting up multiple entities to become co-owners. The IRS has addressed the issue of one-member LLCs; they will be disregarded for tax purposes. The primary reason for the LLC requirement of two members is to allow the entity to be classified as a partnership for federal and state income tax purposes, which require partnerships to have two or more partners.

SUMMARY

To determine whether an LLC is the right entity for you, it is necessary to compare it with the traditional forms of doing business, the corporation (S and C corporations), the general partnership, and the limited partnership (LLP or FLP).

Compared with a C corporation, an LLC, if structured to be taxed as a partnership, has only one level of tax, which is at the member's level, and no entity level tax. Under the current tax rate structure, C corporations generally pay lower taxes than individuals. Thus, to the extent income is not being distributed to the owners of the entity, a C corporation may be somewhat more advantageous than an LLC. However, to the extent income is to be distributed to the ultimate owners, then the LLC avoids double taxation and dramatically reduces the overall tax burden. Furthermore, the LLC avoids the accumulated earnings tax, the personal holding company tax, and the unreasonable compensation issues. It may avoid a significant double taxation on the sale or liquidation of a business. The C corporation allows owners to receive fringe benefits and not have fringe benefits taxable as income to those owners.

S corporations offer the pass-through tax treatment of a partnership (like an LLC) but have severe restrictions on the type and number of shareholders and classes of ownership interests. S corporations are much less flexible than an LLC in the estate planning context. The limitation on the types of trusts that can be shareholders as well as the inability to make non-pro-rata distributions to its shareholders greatly impedes the attractiveness of this entity. Furthermore, the amount of losses that shareholders can deduct is subject to far greater limitations than for an LLC.

Using an LLC may allow the purchaser of an LLC interest to receive the benefits of increased basis for his allocable share of the assets of the LLC. An S corporation has no such increase.

Compared with a general partnership, an LLC offers identical tax benefits, if properly structured, but also offers its owners limited liability protection. A major drawback to a general partnership is that the owners (partners) are each personally liable for the partnership's liabilities.

A limited partnership is an entity that has both limited partners, who are not personally liable for the partnership's liabilities, and at least one general partner, who is personally liable for all of the partnership's liabilities. Unlike an LLC, a limited partnership does not provide true limited liability protection to all of its owners. Additionally, the limited partners may not participate in the partnership's management without risking the loss of their limited liability, whereas members of an LLC may participate in management without risking that loss. Compared with limited partnerships that have corporate general partners, an LLC avoids the need to have two entities (a corporate general partner and the limited partnership itself) with the attendant additional costs, organizational documents, and tax returns.

Part Two

FORMING AND STARTING YOUR LIMITED LIABILITY COMPANY

4 HOW TO SET UP YOUR LIMITED LIABILITY COMPANY

To gain the many benefits that an LLC can offer, you must first set up your LLC, convert an existing business to an LLC (Chapter 5), or buy an LLC. This chapter focuses on setting up an LLC. Although forming an LLC varies from state to state, the concepts and legal procedures are similar. The tax, business, and other planning processes are often based on federal tax and general legal principles that are applicable to all states. Thus, this discussion provides many useful planning ideas, tax tips, and sample documents. However, you should always have the final documents and plans reviewed by an attorney in the state where the LLC will be formed and operated.

Most state statutes provide that LLCs are created when one or more of the people organizing the LLC sign the Articles of Organization (also known as the Certificate of Formation in some states) and file them with the appropriate state filing authority, often the secretary of state. Usually, the organizers do not have to be members, or owners, of the LLC, but even so, they generally are. Sometimes, to expedite the signing and filing of the necessary certificate, a secretary, legal assistant, or attorney in your lawyer's office may sign.

STATE LAWS GOVERNING SETTING UP YOUR LLC

Each state that permits the formation of LLCs has laws (statutes) commonly called *enabling statutes*. These are a particular state's statutes under which individuals and/or entities may create an LLC (or other type of business entity, e.g., an enabling statute for a corporation). As long as the organizers properly follow the enabling statute, the LLC will be validly created. Effectively, you treat the enabling statute like a cookbook: You follow the recipe exactly, and you get an LLC.

HOW TO CREATE AN LLC

Determine Whether an LLC Is the Appropriate Entity

The differences and similarities among general partnerships, limited partnerships, limited liability companies, C corporations, and S corporations (as discussed in the earlier chapters) should be the first consideration when determining the appropriate structure for your business entity. If the end result of your analysis of business entities is that the LLC is the preferable form for the particular investment or business venture, then you should document the basis for such decision in writing, especially if several co-owners are involved. Then follow the procedures for implementing the LLC that are outlined in this chapter.

CAUTION: The decision to use an LLC can be complicated. Although every effort has been made in this book to provide guidance for when and how to choose the right entity, it is impossible to anticipate the particular or unique elements of every investment, business, or estate. Even if you are trying to go it alone to keep your costs down, you should consider confirming your decision to use an LLC with an attorney and/or an accountant. If you have read and thought through the many points in this and preceding chapters, you will have accomplished your goal of minimizing professional fees because the professionals' clocks won't be ticking to cover basic issues and fact-finding. But don't be penny-wise and pound-foolish; get professional confirmation of your decision. When hiring the professional, retain someone who devotes a substantial portion of his time to advising owners of closely held businesses.

Be Sure All People Involved Understand the Key Arrangements

Before forming an LLC, the prospective owners could enter into a formation agreement that spells out and puts in writing decisions regarding the choice of entity, the internal affairs, and the operation of the business. This agreement is an excellent way to put together a record that the participants were properly advised on the formation of the entity, that their choice was made after a proper analysis, and that the risks and potential problems, as well as any requirements, were known to all. The formation agreement may contain the general business purpose and plan of the LLC, the job description of the management, and the identities and duties of the members (see the sample Formation Agreement in the "For Your Notebook" section at the end of this chapter).

Draft and File the Articles of Organization or a Certificate of Formation

To form an LLC, the Articles of Organization or Certificate of Formation (which is similar to a certificate of incorporation and a certificate of limited partnership) must be filed with the appropriate state agency, and the filing fee must be paid. To properly file any certificate, including the Articles of Organization, one or more authorized persons (the organizers) must execute it. Unless state law or the operating agreement provides to the contrary, any authorized person or agent may execute the Articles of Organization.

PRACTICAL NOTE: It can be convenient, especially if there are many members, to include a provision in the LLC's operating agreement stating that the members designate and appoint a certain named individual as their attorney-in-fact (agent) to sign and file the LLC's Articles of Organization and certain types of amendments to the Articles of Organization that are mere formalities and not changes in the substantive relationship of the members. In many situations, the operating agreement is not signed until long after the LLC is formed and business begun (not the recommended approach), which would make this provision only useful for future amendments.

PLANNING TIP: You may be able to form an LLC by yourself online in your state. Before doing so, however, at least consult with a professional to assure that you have made the correct decisions and identified any problems. The cost savings of filing online yourself can be several hundred dollars. The cost of making an error and filing improperly can be in the thousands.

General Rules Concerning Certificates

As described in this chapter, in most states, the statutory requirements for forming an LLC are minimal. Usually, a brief certificate must be filed with the appropriate state agency. The filing of the Articles of Organization is generally effective to create the LLC, but the effective date of its formation may be later (or in some cases may be retroactive), as set forth in the articles. In many cases, substantial compliance with the pertinent state-enabling statute is sufficient to effect the formation of the LLC.

Information to Include in the Articles of Organization

Every state's LLC statute sets forth a list of information that must be provided in the Articles of Organization. The basic requirements are discussed later in this chapter. Each state's statute can vary, however, in the items it requests. If the drafter of the Articles of Organization fails or intentionally omits information, the particular state statute provides default rules that would apply to the LLC with respect to the omitted topic.

The Name of the LLC

The requirements for what must be set forth in the name of an LLC have few variations from state to state. An LLC's name generally must include either the phrase Limited Liability Company or LLC. Some states, however, require the phrase Limited Company or LC. The name may, but is not required to, include the name of a Manager.

The name must be distinguishable from the name of any other corporation, limited partnership, business trust, or LLC reserved or registered with the state's records, unless the other party provides written consent to use a name that is indistinguishable. A name may be reserved in advance of formation.

TIP: Pick a name that has something in it that is not extremely common. For example, "Consultants International" is probably too simple and nonspecific to be acceptable. If you can use "YOUR-NAME Consultants International," you will be far more likely to have the certificate approved. You generally cannot use a word in your LLC's name that relates to a regulated industry (unless you have met the appropriate requirements). These terms could include "bank," "securities," and so on.

Don't assume that just because you file an LLC certificate using a particular name that you have the legal right to conduct business under that name. Someone else may own a trade name or trademark that your LLC name may infringe on.

The Address for the Registered Office and Registered Agent for Service of Process

Every state requires that the Articles of Organization set forth a registered agent for the LLC and a registered office. Each state has different rules for this requirement. A registered agent and office ensure a name and address where service of process (notice) of a lawsuit or other important matter can be given. Generally, the registered office does not have to be a place of business of the LLC. In some states, the registered agent must sign a written consent to appointment that is filed with the articles.

The registered agent, with notice to the LLC, may change the registered office by filing a certificate with the appropriate state authority. In addition, where there is a change in the identity of the LLC's registered agent, a certificate must be filed with the appropriate state authority. Usually, the new registered agent, and not the replaced agent, files such a certificate. Moreover, many states provide a specific procedure for the resignation of a registered agent. Generally, the registered agent accomplishes this by sending a notice of resignation to the LLC. An affidavit of such service and a copy of the notice of resignation must then be filed with the appropriate state agency. In many states, the LLC has two years to appoint a new registered agent after its current registered agent resigns. If it fails to do so, the LLC's name may be transferred to an inactive list and the LLC may be subject to monetary penalties.

NOTE: Some lawyers routinely list themselves or their firms as registered agents. Your lawyer may be the first person any notice should be sent to, but if you decide to change lawyers, you will incur legal fees to have your new lawyer change the listing of the previous lawyer's name and address as registered agent. Lawyers have services provided by national organizations that specialize in filing certificates for all types of entities, monitoring notices issued to LLCs and corporations, and so on. By paying an annual fee, you can list such a service as registered agent to assure that you get every notice you should receive. The cheapest choice is to list yourself as agent. However, if you have partners in the LLC, you may not want your partner to be the agent, and he may not want you to be the agent. Also, if you move to a new home, you will incur legal fees to amend the certificate to the new address.

The Purpose of the LLC

Some state laws require a statement of the LLC's business purpose. This is often a broad general statement that the LLC can do anything permitted by law; however, in many cases a more limited and specific delineation may be appropriate.

Dissolution Date

A limited liability company must specify, in its Articles of Organization, a specific date for the LLC's dissolution, if that date is to differ from the statutory termination period (if any). Dissolution is when the business of the LLC will be wound up and the LLC terminated, and its assets liquidated. Although the members can, at that future date, decide to continue the business of the LLC, a dissolution date must still be provided in some cases. The statutory, or default (i.e., in the absence of a statement to the contrary) termination period is usually the earliest of the following five events:

1. The occurrence of an event specified in the operating agreement.

2. The voluntary, written consent of the members. Most states require unanimous consent of the members in this regard, whereas other states only require majority consent.

3. Expiration of the limited liability company's specified period of duration (either by the default rule set forth in the statute or at some other date set forth in the Articles of Organization). Since the enactment of **check-the-box regulations** for determining how an LLC will be taxed for income tax purposes (discussed earlier), you are assured that your LLC will be taxed as a partnership for federal income tax purposes regardless of its duration. As such, most LLC certificates don't include a termination date. This had been necessary under prior tax rules.

4. The entry of a decree of judicial dissolution. This could occur, for example, if a manager applies to the court where it is not reasonably practical to carry on the LLC's business in conformity with the operating agreement.

5. The death, retirement, resignation, expulsion, bankruptcy, or dissolution of a member or the occurrence of any other event that terminates the continued membership of a member in the LLC. Termination can be avoided in such cases if the business of the LLC continues either by the consent of all of the remaining members, or pursuant to a right to continue the business of the LLC as stated in the operating agreement.

Other Information That May Be Required in the Articles of Organization

It may be necessary to provide one or more of the following seven items:

1. A provision stating that the LLC may carry on any lawful business or purposes permitted under state law. The purposes clause can be very broad since LLCs can be used for a wide variety of activities. It may be advantageous in some situations to provide a more restrictive definition. This may be appropriate where a noncontrolling member wants to restrict the possible activities of the LLC.

2. A statement that the LLC has at least two or more members (in states that require this).

3. Any other permitted matters that the members want to include. For example, members holding noncontrolling interests may want to include in the articles certain restrictions on the transfer of membership interests or control by members or managers to protect their interests.

4. If required by the state, a provision stating a principal office where the LLC will conduct its business or location where its records will be kept.

5. The management structure of the LLC. In some states, the articles must provide whether members or managers will manage the LLC and must list the names and addresses of such individuals. Even if state law does not require this information, there may be benefits to stating that managers will manage the LLC.

TIP: Be certain to address the management issue in detailed terms in the operating agreement since the Articles of Organization is a short and sketchy document.

---

6. Capital structure of the LLC. Some states require the disclosure of the description of contributions received by the LLC and a description of any promised future contributions.

7. Every state's LLC statute enables the organizers to include any additional information in the articles that is not inconsistent with law. Some experts believe that there is no benefit in providing more than the required information in the articles. Others feel that it can be beneficial because then changes or oversights in the operating agreement governing the LLC won't change the provision included in the articles.

TECHNICAL REQUIREMENTS OF SETTING UP YOUR LLC

In most states, the enabling statutes address the following issues.

TIP: Since the laws differ from state to state, you should at a minimum obtain a copy of the your state's LLC laws. Most public libraries have books containing all state laws. Find out how the books are updated so that you can be sure you are looking at the most current law. Many statute books have what are called *pocket parts*. On the inside of the back cover of each book in the set is a slot for inserting the most current update. It is often necessary to read the book, and then check the pocket part to see whether any changes have been made to the law as presented in the main part of the book. Since LLC laws for many states are so new, you may only find them in the pocket part. Because they were not enacted when the statute book was published, the entire LLC statute appears in the update. The contents to the LLC law section will probably have an entry similar to "formation" that will direct you quickly to the appropriate provisions. Many legal publishers print state-specific forms that you can use. These may include instructions as well. In addition to books, many states' statues can be found on the Internet.

CAUTION: There are many form books with titles like *How to Set Up Your Own LLC*. These books, which are generally pitched as giving you all of the forms and instructions you need, vary tremendously in quality. Many, if not most, only reprint the same laws you can find in the library or on the Internet (and which may be more current considering publishing time requirements). The forms you need may be on your state's Web site or available for a few dollars from legal publishing companies in your state (or perhaps from the state's office where the forms are filed). Be careful. You are always safest hiring a lawyer, but if you try to go it alone, don't rely on a how-to book without reading the current law and contacting the secretary of state (or other appropriate department) for forms and instructions.

Who May File the Articles of Organization

All state laws list the requirements for an LLC's Articles of Organization. As mentioned earlier, the LLC's organizer files the Articles of Organization (sends them with the appropriate fees) to the appropriate state authority. Some statutes require only one organizer to form the LLC, whereas others require at least two. Also, in some states, the organizer must be a member, and in others there is no such requirement. Some states require that only "natural persons" may act as organizers, whereas others allow entities as well as natural persons to serve in this capacity.

The organizer is the person who signs the Articles of Organization and files (referred to as *delivers* in some states) that document with the appropriate state authority.

TIP: In most simple situations, you and—if you have one or a few partners (members)—perhaps all the other members can or should sign the form. Apart from the legal requirements that you must meet, it is probably politic for all of you to sign all key legal documents if you have only a few members. Not only does this avoid having one or more members feel left out, but it assures that all of your names are in the public record as owners and that no member can claim he did not know the contents of the certificate.

Filing and Other Fees

Each state has its own filing fees and other charges with respect to forming an LLC. Some states require annual license taxes, entry taxes, or franchise taxes. Filing fees usually range between $50 and $200+. Some states require LLCs to notify the public of its existence by publication in a newspaper of general circulation, which may add a substantial cost to the formation process.

CAUTION: The failure to publish, where required by your state, could prevent you from obtaining the benefit of limited liability, a key reason for using the LLC. Worse, if your state requires publication (i.e., it is an essential requirement of the LLC enabling statute), failure to publish will mean that you do not have a properly formed LLC. In some cases, the consequences of not publishing may simply be that you cannot bring a suit in that state.

When an LLC's Existence Begins

The exact time at which an LLC's existence begins may vary from state to state. Depending on each state and the information contained in the Articles of Organization, your LLC will come into existence at different times. This can be important for income tax and legal reasons. If the LLC was not in existence, the status of contracts or other legal arrangements may be uncertain. One of the following four events is commonly used to determine when an LLC comes into existence:

1. Retroactively on the date the Articles of Organization were executed (signed by the organizers), as long as the Articles of Organization were submitted within a specified period after the date of execution.

2. On the date of submission to the appropriate state authority. This is the date it is stamped as having been received by the state.

3. On the date of official approval. This may be deemed the date of receipt, or a later date when the submitted certificate is approved.

4. On some date within ninety (90) days (or later if your state's laws permit) after the date of the filing.

To have an effective date other than the filing date, the Articles of Organization for your LLC must state that its formation will be effective at that date. Some states insist that the LLC can only legally begin with the issuance of a certificate by the state authority.

Before the appropriate state authority files the Articles of Organization, it will review that document to make sure it complies with the state statute. Generally, this review involves ensuring that the information the state statute requires in the Articles of Organization is actually in the document. Additionally, the review will include the determination of whether the name for the LLC is permitted, which is discussed later in this chapter.

CAUTION: If your LLC begins doing business before the state completes its review and the state rejects the filing because it finds a defect, your members may be subject to personal liability as if they were doing business on behalf of an entity that was not yet formed. Their liability would be similar to that of general partners or corporate organizers who undertake prein-corporation transactions. This means that every personal asset of the LLC's members (their houses, cars, personal bank accounts, etc.) could be in jeop-ardy if the LLC is sued before the situation is remedied.

If the state authority does not approve the filing of the Articles of Orga-nization, the LLC will not be created. If this happens, the organizers may simply make the necessary technical adjustments to the Articles of Orga-nization so that it will comply with the state statute and thus be acceptable to the state filing authority. Some states allow for an appeal process with respect to Articles of Organization that are not accepted for filing.

TIP: Many times, the state rejects the LLC Certificate of Formation or Arti-cles of Organization because of a minor technicality. If you file the certificate yourself, ask the clerk why it was rejected. The problem might be something you can fix and initial right then and there to finish the filing. For this rea-son, many attorneys send paralegals to the appropriate government office to personally file the documents. Where the government office is not nearby, some attorneys use companies that, for a modest fee, file LLC forms (and many other certificates) with the various state authorities. Although this ser-vice may increase your bill by a small amount, it is often worthwhile since it assures a timely and accurate filing.

What Happens When Your LLC Is Formed

With the official formation of your LLC, four things happen:

1. The LLC becomes a separate legal entity.
2. The members become protected from liabilities and obligations of the LLC.
3. A presumption arises that all of the requirements (conditions prece-dent) to the existence of the LLC have been satisfied. This means that if anyone wishes to claim the LLC was not properly formed, he would have to prove the error.
4. The Articles of Organization may constitute notice (in certain states) of all information required by statute to be set forth in the articles.

TIP: In many states, you can file two certificates and ask the secretary of state (or other appropriate government agency) to stamp the second copy and return it to you for your files. Although this may add to the cost of the process, it is an important step. The stamped copy of the certificate that you receive provides proof that the LLC was properly formed and establishes the date of formation. You should keep this original with important LLC records. You may need to send photocopies of the certificate that has the stamps indicating when it was filed to the county clerk (or other local government property office) if you try to record a deed to real estate being transferred into your LLC. Your bank may want a copy to complete a loan to the LLC or open an account in the LLC's name, and so on.

Defective Formation and Its Consequences

One of the primary goals of creating an LLC is to have an entity that provides limited liability protection to its owners. This protection is not available until the LLC is formed. Accordingly, if individuals begin doing business before formation takes place, those individuals risk being personally liable for the actions of the not-yet-formed LLC. As mentioned, this is a possible scenario when businesspeople or investors believe they have created an LLC but a technical defect in the formation documents has caused the LLC to not be officially created.

If the LLC was not technically created but individuals have done business on its behalf, arguments might still be made for its protection. These arguments, which are based on corporate law, may offer liability protection to the individuals for actions committed before technical formation of the LLC.

The first approach to address this issue is to argue that although the LLC was not technically formed, it should be treated as if it had been. This is known as *De Facto Formation*. The personal liability protection would shield the individuals if the following three items are satisfied:

1. An enabling statute permitting the creation of LLCs exists.

2. A good-faith effort has been made by the acting individuals to comply with the state's LLC statute.

3. The individuals have conducted themselves and their business as if the LLC had been formed. This de facto argument has been applied to corporations but not yet to LLCs. Its rationale, however, would seem to apply to LLCs as well.

CAUTION: Proving a good-faith effort is a question of fact for a court to interpret. It is not worth the risk. You will generally be better off waiting for the state to confirm your LLC's proper formation than to risk undertaking transactions before it is confirmed.

The second approach is to argue a legal concept called *estoppel.* The legal doctrine (concept) of estoppel, historically applied to corporations, may be argued in the LLC context. Estoppel would bar creditors who have entered into contracts believing that the LLC was formed. In such cases, part of the bargain was that just the liability of the entity was available to the creditors. This doctrine would only apply to contract and not tort creditors.

EXAMPLE: This situation is typical of many LLC situations. Since LLCs are so new compared with other forms of business entities, the laws have simply not had the opportunity to develop to the extent that they have for partnerships and corporations. This is in fact an important drawback to using an LLC—what the courts will say is still unknown. A good-faith effort may depend on how a judge views your efforts to properly form the LLC, not how you view it. Therefore, you are always better off being careful to assure proper formation. Don't rely on a good-faith attempt to form your LLC to get off the hook. You may not succeed.

Steps That Occur Immediately Following Formation

Once the LLC is formed, it is common to transfer assets to the LLC, often in exchange for membership interests in the LLC. This might be the transfer of real estate by a deed; the transfer of personal property, such as equipment, by a bill of sale; or other items. Some of these are illustrated in the "For Your Notebook" section of this chapter.

SUMMARY

The first step to benefiting from an LLC is forming the entity that will serve as your LLC. This requires the filing of a formal document with your state. This chapter has explored many of the points to address in this process as well as some of the issues that may arise.

For Your Notebook

LLC FORMATION AGREEMENT

NOTE: This sample form illustrates the document you and other members about to form an LLC should consider signing. The goal is to avoid problems at a later date by assuring that everyone involved is fully informed and understands the decisions made. In some situations, especially if you want to control legal costs, you may skip this document and sign a comprehensive operating agreement that includes many of these items.

AGREEMENT dated as of _____ between and among [List the name and address of each prospective LLC Member here] (collectively the "Prospective Members"); and LLCNAME, and LLC in the process of formation (the "LLC") (collectively, the "Parties").

RECITALS

a. The Prospective Members hereto have evaluated the benefits, risks, and requirements of causing an LLC to be formed for the purpose of engaging in the trade or business of DESCRIBE BUSINESS (the "Business").

b. The parties hereto wish to confirm their decision to form an LLC to operate the Business.

AND, THEREFORE, AGREE TO THE FOLLOWING TERMS AND CONDITIONS:

1. *Decision Regarding the Choice of Entity*

The Prospective Members have evaluated individually, and with their individual legal, tax, accounting, and business advisers, the benefits, costs, risks, requirements, and other relevant considerations of using an LLC rather than other types of arrangements, for the purpose of organizing and conducting the Business. Each Prospective Member based on such evaluation concurs in the use of an LLC for the Business.

2. *Internal Affairs and Operation of the Business*

The Prospective Members agree that the Business shall have its affairs and operations conducted in generally the following manner:

DESCRIBE KEY POINTS AGREED TO.

3. *Preliminary Agreement; Operating Agreement to Be Signed*

The Prospective Members acknowledge that this LLC Formation Agreement is only a preliminary agreement and that the parties intend and shall execute a comprehensive Operating Agreement at some future date. The terms and provisions of this LLC Formation Agreement shall govern until such Operating Agreement is executed.

4. *Business Purpose and Business Plan of the LLC*

In addition to the description above of the intended Business of the LLC, the Prospective Members acknowledge and agree that the

DESCRIBE ADDITIONAL BUSINESS DETAILS.

The Prospective Members further acknowledge that they have received, reviewed, and generally accepted the draft Business Plan and Projections attached to this LLC Formation Agreement.

5. *Description of the Management of the LLC*

The Management of the LLC shall be conducted by

DESCRIBE IN GENERAL TERMS.

6. *Voting Rights of Members*

The Membership Interests anticipated to be issued to LIST VOTING MEMBERS shall be voting Interests. The Membership Interests issued to LIST NONVOTING MEMBERS (if any) shall be nonvoting Interests.

7. *Limitation on Other Activities of Prospective Members*

Except for MEMBER NAME, who shall serve as DESCRIBE DUTIES, nothing in this LLC Formation Agreement shall be deemed to restrict in any way the freedom of any Prospective Member to conduct any other business or activity whatsoever at any location other than the Business, so long as such business or activity does not directly compete with, or conflict with the Business of the LLC.

8. *Identities and Duties of the Prospective Members of the LLC*

Member Name	Member Address	Tax ID Number	Intended Duties	Intended Contribution

9. *Independent Advice of Counsel*

Each party hereto has been advised to seek the advice of independent legal, tax, business, and accounting counsel prior to executing this LLC Formation Agreement. Each party, by executing this LLC Formation Agreement, acknowledges that he has been advised to seek independent counsel and that the execution of this Agreement can affect their legal rights, that reasonable time to consult with independent counsel has been afforded, and that he or she has consulted with independent counsel, or has of his or her own volition decided not to do so.

10. *Arbitration*

Any dispute under this LLC Formation Agreement shall, upon notice to the parties be submitted to binding arbitration, in LOCATION, in accordance with the rules of the American Arbitration Association.

IN WITNESS WHEREOF, the parties hereto have hereunto set their hands and seals the day and year first-above written.

_____

NAME-1, Prospective Member

_____

NAME-2, Prospective Member

_____

NAME-3, Prospective Member

For Your Notebook

UNANIMOUS CONSENT
CONCERNING FORMATION

NOTE: The following form is a consent to be signed by all members indicating their agreement to the contribution (investment) of noncash assets. This consent is in the form of an amendment to what is assumed to be an existing operating agreement. If property is invested at the outset, when the LLC is first formed, the nature of the property and the LLC membership interests received in exchange, should all be spelled out in the original operating agreement.

NOTE: You may not need all members to sign. It depends on the terms of your Certificate of Formation and operating agreement. The safest and preferable approach in all cases where there are a limited number of members in your LLC is to have all members sign off as agreeing on any contribution to capital of the LLC as well as any other significant transaction. This avoids the problems later of any member claiming he did not agree with a particular transaction or was not advised of it.

LLCName
Action Taken by Unanimous Written
Consent of All Members
to Accept Property Contribution and
Issue Membership Interest of the LLC
and Amend the LLCNAME Operating Agreement

The undersigned, being all of the Members of LLCNAME, hereby take the following action:

RESOLVED, Authorize the issuance of the following Membership Interests in the LLC to the Members listed below, at the price and for the consideration listed:

Member Name	Membership Interests	Contribution
Member-1 NAME		$15,000
Member-2 NAME		2 pickup trucks
Member-3 NAME		lathe and other equipment
Member-4 NAME		$4,000 and office equipment

NOTE: Attach detailed descriptions of all noncash assets to the consent, including vehicle registrations, sales receipts evidencing the members' earlier purchase of the equipment, and so on. The descriptions attached should include, at minimum: (1) contributing member's name; (2) description of property contributed; (3) agreed value of property contributed; (4) agreed membership interests issued for such property.

RESOLVED, that the LLC accept the transfer of the above assets under the Bill of Sale, and Assignment of Contract forms attached hereto.

NOTE: If the LLC is run by one or more managers as opposed to by all members, the language in this form would have to be changed. However, it is still ideal to have members sign off. Where a member is also a manager, the signature lines at the end of this form should be revised to indicate that person is signing in both capacities.

RESOLVED, That the aforesaid offers of contributions to the capital of the LLC in exchange for Membership Interests in the LLC are agreed as being fair, adequate, and reasonable, and should be and are hereby accepted by the LLC and its Members and Manager.

RESOLVED, That the entire amount of the above payments be credited on the LLC's books and records in the manner designated by the LLC's accountant as contributions to the LLC's capital.

RESOLVED, that the Managers of the LLC are directed and authorized to take all necessary actions to implement the above resolutions.

RESOLVED, that this Unanimous Consent, signed by all Members, is hereby deemed an amendment to the LLCNAME Operating Agreement, originally signed on MONTH, DAY, YEAR.

Dated: SIGNDATE

_____

MANAGER-1NAME, Manager

_____

MEMBER-1NAME, Member

_____

MEMBER-2NAME, Member

_____

MEMBER-3NAME, Member

_____

MEMBER-4NAME, Member

For Your Notebook

CERTIFICATE OF FORMATION TO ORGANIZE AN LLC

Certificate of Formation
of
LLCNAME

The undersigned, each over the age of majority, and in order to form a limited liability company pursuant to Article 42:2B of the New Jersey Statutes Annotated, under Section 11 of the New Jersey Limited Liability Company Act, hereby certifies as follows:

1. The name of the LLC shall be:

LLCNAME

2. The address of the initial registered office of the LLC shall be LLCADDRESS, and the name of the registered agent of the LLC at that address is MANAGER-NAME.

3. The LLC has one member [at least two or more members].

NOTE: There may not be any fixed date for termination of the LLC. Since the check-the-box regulations, there is no need to have a limited duration to assure characterization as a partnership for income tax purposes.

---

4. The LLC shall dissolve and terminate at the earliest of the following events:

a. The occurrence of the termination events specified in the operating agreement of the LLC.

b. Written consent of all members.

c. The entry of a decree of judicial dissolution.

d. The death, retirement, resignation, expulsion, bankruptcy, or dissolution of a member or the occurrence of any other event which terminates the continued membership of a member in the LLC unless the business of the LLC is continued either by the consent of all of the remaining members within the time period, and in accordance with the requirements, provided in the operating agreement.

5. The LLC may carry on and engage in the DESCRIBE-BUSINESS, and all activities related or incident thereto.

6. This Certificate of Formation shall be effective upon the initial filing and recording with the Secretary of State of the State of STATE-NAME.

7. The undersigned persons executing this Certificate of Formation are properly authorized persons to do so as such term is defined under STATUTE-REFERENCE.

IN WITNESS WHEREOF, We the undersigned sign our names this _____ MONTH, YEAR and I affirm under the penalties of perjury that the statements in this Certificate are true.

_____   _____
MANAGER-NAME   MEMBER-1NAME

_____   _____
MEMBER-2NAME   MEMBER-3NAME

_____   _____
MEMBER-4NAME   MEMBER-5NAME

[Witness and notary forms omitted, check with an attorney in your state for applicable requirements.]

For Your Notebook

BILL OF SALE TO TRANSFER
PROPERTY TO LLC

NOTE: This form is used to transfer personal property (e.g., furniture, equipment, a car, but not real estate) to an LLC.

CAUTION: Where personal property is transferred, check with your accountant to see if a sales or other local tax may be due. Also, check with your lawyer to see if any other documents also have to be prepared. For example, if you use a bill of sale to transfer ownership (title) to a car or truck to your LLC, you must also sign and transfer the vehicle's official registration issued by your state.

KNOW ALL MEN BY THESE PRESENTS, that MEMBER-1NAME an individual who resides at MEMBER-1ADDRESS (the "Transferor") for and in consideration of the sum of $1.00 and _____ Membership Interests in the LLC, to LLCNAME, doing business at LLC-ADDRESS (the "Transferee"), has granted, transferred, and conveyed and by these presents does grant, transfer, and convey unto the said Transferee, and said Transferee's successors and assigns property as hereinafter described:

ALL THE RIGHT, TITLE, AND INTEREST in the following asset ("Asset"):

DESCRIBE ASSETS TRANSFERRED

including all Transferor's right, title, and interests in the Asset.

Transferor hereby represents and warrants that he or she has good and marketable title to the Asset name hereinabove, subject to no liens, mortgages, security interests, encumbrances, or charges of any nature.

This Bill of Sale has been executed to complete the transfer as a contribution to capital of LLCNAME, in accordance with the provisions of Section 721 of the Internal Revenue Code of 1986, as amended, and as contemplated herein. Nothing herein contained shall be deemed or construed to confer upon any person or entity other than Transferee any rights or remedies by reason of this instrument.

TO HAVE AND TO HOLD the same unto the said Transferee and the Transferee's successors and assigns forever; and the Transferor covenants and agrees to and with the said Transferee to warrant and defend the said described Asset against all and every person or persons whomsoever.

IN WITNESS WHEREOF, the Transferor has set his or her hand and seal to be hereto affixed this DAY day of MONTH, YEAR.

Sworn, Signed, Sealed, and Delivered

_____

MEMBER-1NAME, Transferor

in the Presence of:

_____

Witness

For Your Notebook

ASSIGNMENT OF CONTRACTS TO TRANSFER CONTRACT RIGHTS TO AN LLC

EXAMPLE: Use this form to transfer existing contracts to your LLC. For example, you may have an equipment or property lease, a service contract for you to provide services for certain customers, and so on. In many cases, filling in and signing this general assignment of contract forms is only the start. Each contract right you assign has to be reviewed and special documents prepared where required. For example, say you operated a retail store as sole proprietorship. You want to limit your liability exposure. You must review the lease for the requirements you must meet. You will almost always need the landlord's approval. Most likely the landlord will insist that you sign a personal guarantee of the new LLC's performance under the lease (paying rent, keeping the premises clean, etc.). The landlord should insist on this because otherwise the transfer to an LLC with limited assets (the LLC will have less assets than you did personally, e.g., your house will remain in your name) will leave the landlord less protected in the event of a default or other problem under the lease. You will thus probably have to sign a personal guarantee, and either an assignment of lease (where you assign all your rights and interests in the lease to the LLC), or a sublet agreement (where you remain the main tenant and your LLC is a subtenant under you). This is less desirable from a liability perspective.

THIS AGREEMENT made as of the DAY day of MONTH, YEAR, between LLCNAME, doing business at LLC-ADDRESS ("Assignee"); and MEMBER-1 NAME, an individual who resides at MEMBER-1 ADDRESS ("Assignor").

NOTE: While you must at minimum attach a listing of the contracts, you should also attach a copy of each contract signed in its entirety.

WHEREAS, the Assignor wishes to assign all his right title and interest in those certain contracts more particularly set forth and described in Schedule "A" hereto (hereinafter called the "Contracts"); and Assignee wishes to accept the assignment of the Contracts.

NOW, THEREFORE, THIS AGREEMENT WITNESSETH that the parties hereto covenant and agree as follows:

1. In consideration of One Dollar ($1.00) and _____ Membership Interests in the LLC, Assignor hereby assigns, transfers and sets over unto Assignee the said Contracts and all rights, titles, and interests of Assignor therein and thereto, together with all rights, benefits, privileges, and advantages of Assignor to be derived therefrom, subject to the rights of certain third parties to approve, or consent to such assignments, as provided in the Contracts.

2. The Assignor covenants and agrees with the Assignee that Assignor shall at the request of the Assignee, do and perform all such acts and things, and execute and deliver

all such consents, documents, and other writings as may be required to give full force and effect to the assignment herein contemplated.

3. Assignee accepts the within assignment to it of the said Contracts and agrees with Assignor to assume, carry out, observe, perform, and fulfill said Contracts in accordance with their terms.

4. This Agreement shall, subject to the terms and conditions of the individual Contracts, enure to the benefit of and be binding upon the parties hereto and their successors and assigns.

5. This Assignment of Contract has been executed to complete the transfer as a contribution to capital of LLCNAME, in accordance with the provisions of Section 721 of the Internal Revenue Code of 1986, as amended, and as contemplated herein.

IN WITNESS WHEREOF, the parties hereto have executed and delivered this Agreement as of the day and year first above written.

NOTE: Although the form is not set up to be notarized, where a transaction is between related parties (i.e., a member and the LLC he owns an interest in) having a form notarized, even if not required by law, is a desirable step. It helps prove to the IRS (and others) that the documents were really signed when they indicate that they were. Also, if the LLC is controlled by its members instead of a manager, the signature line for the LLC should be revised below. Again, it is ideal to have all members sign off if possible. If every member signs the Assignment of Contract form and you follow the suggestion to attach a copy of the entire contract involved, no member can later claim that the contract assigned was a bad deal for the LLC.

WITNESSES:

ASSIGNEE:
LLCNAME, Assignee

_____

By: _____
MANAGER-NAME, Manager

ASSIGNOR:

_____

_____
MEMBER-1NAME, Assignor

5 CONVERTING YOUR EXISTING BUSINESS INTO A LIMITED LIABILITY COMPANY

Many investors or business owners own an existing business or investment that is a C corporation, S corporation, limited partnership, or general partnership. Although organization as an LLC offers many benefits, it is necessary to evaluate whether conversion of an existing entity into an LLC would be worthwhile.

Before converting an existing entity, such as a corporation, into an LLC, make sure that you will really benefit. Will the conversion into an LLC result in a tax cost? Depending on the type of entity being converted and the manner in which you may have to handle the conversion, it could trigger an income tax that might outweigh any potential benefits. When determining the desirability of converting an entity into an LLC, the business planner must keep the following factors in mind:

- *The nature and purpose of the business.* Some businesses lend themselves to specific types of entities. For example, real estate is generally best held in a partnership or LLC form, not in a corporation.
- *The states where business will be conducted.* Different entities may be better to use in some states than in others.

You must closely scrutinize several other issues before moving forward with an entity conversion into an LLC. This chapter reviews these issues and explains how to work best with your advisers to determine whether to convert your existing business to an LLC.

Sometimes it may also be advantageous to consider converting an LLC into another type of entity. For example, it may be possible for a limited liability company to convert out of LLC status into a partnership. This often can be done on a tax-free basis. This chapter, however, does not focus on such situations.

INCOME TAX CONSEQUENCES OF CONVERTING AN ENTITY INTO AN LLC

The key threshold issue to consider, usually before all others, is whether the conversion of an existing entity into an LLC will cause a significant current income tax cost. In many instances, the tax cost resulting from changing a corporation into an LLC is so substantial that it obviates any other analysis. It is simply unaffordable.

PLANNING TIP: Have your accountant prepare a hypothetical (pro forma) income tax return illustrating the results if the conversion occurred. A sample tax return is often the best way for you to identify the actual tax cost and be certain that you have not overlooked any potential problems. The computer income tax programs may identify issues that your advisers missed or did not quantify.

Generally, a conversion to an LLC will involve a general partnership, a limited partnership, a corporation, or a sole proprietorship. The conversion from the partnership format or the sole proprietorship to an LLC usually can occur on a tax-free basis (with certain exceptions), but a conversion from a corporation to an LLC will involve a liquidation of the corporation, which may result in severe tax consequences and expenses. Since the determination of whether there will be a large income tax cost will depend initially on the type of entity being converted, the rest of this chapter addresses this factor on an entity-by-entity basis. Many other income tax issues, such as the method of accounting for income taxes, are noted in the following discussion.

LEGAL CONSEQUENCES THAT MAY EFFECT THE CONVERSION OF ANY ENTITY TO AN LLC

There are numerous legal aspects to consider before deciding to convert an existing entity into an LLC. Although the legal questions will often be unique to your business, investment, or entity (which is why legal advice is essential), many conversions involve several common legal issues. For example, will the conversion trigger "due on sale" clauses contained in any loan documents? If there were loans or other obligations, personal guarantees, or similar financial assurances, the conversion of the entity into an LLC can affect these obligations. Not only can the conversion affect the legal status of the loan, but also changes in who is liable personally on a loan can have significant income tax consequences. If the business liabilities that are transferred to the LLC exceed the basis (in rough terms, your investment increased and decreased by various adjustments) in the business assets of the sole proprietor, the sole proprietor might have to recognize gain equal to the difference. These effects are discussed in more detail in the context of converting partnerships into LLCs.

Will the conversion cause the entity to default under any contracts to which it is a party? There is the potential for the entity to incur severe conversion costs (or adverse legal consequences).

TIP: Identify and organize copies of all contracts to which the business or investment is a party. These should include mortgages, notes, and other loan documents; equipment and real property leases; license agreements; and employment agreements. Have your attorney review each document to determine the consequences of conversion (could conversion cause a loan to be accelerated, a lease to be violated, etc.?). You should have your attorney obtain the necessary approval from the other side to each agreement that is affected. The cost of this process often can be more than legal fees. A landlord or lender who is asked to approve a transfer may look on the request as an opportunity to extract some type of concession from you.

You should also address with a business attorney whether the conversion from the existing entity into an LLC is permitted under state law. If it is not expressly permitted, then conversion may be possible, but may require a multistep process with different legal and tax consequences. If you can convert your existing entity into an LLC under an express provision of state law (e.g., you may only have to file a single document with your state to effect the conversion), there may be no need to complete the documents generally used to transfer legal title from one entity to another (e.g., a deed). If such a law does not exist, your attorney may have to formally transfer every asset from the old entity to the new LLC.

As part of the conversion, an interest in the LLC may be issued to the new second member in exchange for services to be rendered by the new incoming partner (member). The new partner then may have taxable consequences if the membership interest is an interest in the LLC's capital and/or profits.

If your existing entity has used an assumed or fictitious name (e.g., your corporation is called Joe's Sweat Shop, Inc., but you operate under the name Joe's Sauna), you may intend that your new LLC will operate using the same assumed or fictitious name. In that case, your attorney may need to file a document (certificate) to permit such use by your LLC. You should carefully calendar the date of filing since these certificates may have to be refiled every five years in some states. If the name is important to your business, seek the assistance of intellectual property counsel concerning any trade name, trademark, or related issues. Merely filing certificates may not be sufficient.

Your accountant should determine whether the new LLC can use the old entity's tax identification number or must obtain a new one from the IRS.

Insurance issues must be addressed in any conversion. If your partnership or corporation owns real estate, you should notify the title insurance carrier in advance of the transaction. Although ordinarily carriers require a full additional premium to insure a new entity, they may (depending on state law and the method you convert into an LLC) accept the LLC as a successor in interest to the corporation or partnership and continue the title insurance coverage. You should notify the casualty/property insurance company in writing in advance of the transaction. They will have to change the policy to reflect the LLC as the new insured. You should also coordinate this with any commercial umbrella liability insurance you carry to assure that the policy is amended as necessary, and the umbrella and underlying coverage are properly coordinated.

Always retain legal, insurance, accounting, and other appropriate advisers. Every conversion has its own nuances that no general book, or even legal treatise, can identify.

CONVERSION OF A SOLE PROPRIETORSHIP INTO AN LLC

The most common and simple method of conducting business is as a sole proprietor. You simply begin business, without any legal entity. This is easy and cheap, but usually not particularly smart. There is no liability protection, and the sole proprietor method implies to colleagues and customers that you are less sophisticated than owners who organize their businesses properly. Conversion to an LLC is an important step to consider.

NOTE: Tens of millions of home-based businesses are sole proprietorships. Converting to an LLC, especially if there are no significant or problematic mortgages or legal contracts to assign, is relatively simple and inexpensive. If you remain a one-member LLC (only one owner, like your sole proprietorship), there are no federal income tax consequences. Many home-based businesses should consider this step.

The conversion of a sole proprietorship into an LLC could happen simply by you, the sole proprietor, contributing all of your business assets (subject to business liabilities) to an LLC. You "contribute" assets by transferring them into the name and tax identification number of the LLC once it is formed. For a bank account, you can write a check from your business checking account (never commingle business and personal funds!) into the new LLC bank account that is set up under the LLC's tax identification number. Always have an attorney assist you, not only in setting up the LLC, but also approving the methods or steps to transfer assets to the new LLC, assuring that any contract rights are transferable, and so on.

TIP: It may be feasible to gift some portion of the interest in the LLC to your spouse. There is no gift tax cost on the transfer to a spouse (where the spouse is a U.S. citizen). If you have two owners (members) instead of one, however, a partnership tax return will have to be filed unless you formally notify the IRS that you won't be treated as a partnership. Many small or home-based businesses are set up to be owned by husband and wife, or partners, because of personal or psychological reasons (both want to feel like owners). The resultant legal and tax complications can be excessive.

CONVERSION OF A PARTNERSHIP INTO A LIMITED LIABILITY COMPANY

One of the most common forms of conducting business has been the partnership. Partnerships have always been the entity of choice for real estate transactions (based on favorable income tax consequences) and have become a common tool for many families in estate and personal planning. Partnerships are the most likely entity for conversion because they are so popular and are easier to convert into LLC format than corporations.

The consequences of converting the two types of partnerships (general partnerships and limited partnerships) may differ somewhat.

Converting Partnerships into an LLC

Why Convert a General Partnership into an LLC?

There may be many reasons to convert a general partnership into an LLC. An LLC will provide limited liability protection to certain owners, which a general partnership will not. The LLC form facilitates gift-giving transfers to children or other beneficiaries by making gifts of non-voting equity in the company without relinquishing any control. If a building, business, investment, or other asset is owned in a general partnership format, many of the benefits of a limited partnership can be obtained by converting the general partnership into a limited partnership. The primary reason for converting a general partnership into a limited partnership is to provide the family business owners with limited liability although there must always be at least one general partner with unlimited liability. An LLC does not require this and is thus usually a better end result than a limited partnership.

General Income Tax Consequences of Conversion

Since almost every LLC with more than one member will be treated as a partnership for income tax purposes, the terms *partnership* and *LLC* are interchangeable in the tax aspects of the discussions. If the IRS considers the conversion of a partner's general partnership interest into an LLC membership interest to be a "sale or exchange" of the partnership interest or the termination of the partnership, this determination could have adverse tax consequences. The IRS, fortunately, has decided that converting a general partnership into an LLC should not trigger adverse income tax consequences.

There remain, however, some troubling tax points so that where significant dollars are involved, the organizers must exercise caution and consult a tax expert.

Impact of Conversion on Debt

Another potential tax problem can arise on conversion of a general partnership interest into an LLC membership interest if the conversion reduces a partner's share of partnership liabilities. This means that as a partner (or member in the LLC) you are personally liable for less partnership debts than you were before the change. A reduction in a partner's share of liabilities will be treated as a cash distribution to the partner with all the tax consequences of an actual cash distribution (called a *deemed* distribution). Thus, the IRS will treat a reduction in your responsibility for partnership debt as if you had received a distribution of cash from the partnership equal to the amount of debt for which you are no longer responsible. If the reduction in your share of the partnership debt exceeds your investment (basis) in your partnership interest, you may be taxed on that amount. The determination can be tricky. If the partnership debt had recourse against you (the lender could sue you personally if the partnership didn't pay), but after converting the partnership to an LLC, you were no longer liable personally on the debt, the conversion could trigger tax.

The IRS will generally treat a conversion of a partnership into an LLC as a tax-free transaction if the conversion does not excessively reduce any partner's share of partnership liabilities. By this, the IRS means that no partner's share of liabilities should be reduced by an amount that would cause a deemed cash distribution in excess of that partner's basis.

Similar problems can arise where any changes occur in a partner's interest in the partnership capital (how much of the partnership/LLC value he owns) or profits (how much of the partnership/LLC earnings he is entitled to receive).

The following few paragraphs explain this tax problem in greater detail. (If the preceding discussion did not convince you to get the help of a tax professional, the following will.)

Under the tax laws if a partner's share of partnership liabilities is decreased, such decrease generally is treated as a distribution of money from the partnership to the partner. If a partner's share of partnership liabilities is increased, such increase is treated as a contribution of money by the partner to the partnership. Moreover, while the deemed distribution of money to a partner will decrease the partner's basis in the partnership, but not below zero, a deemed contribution of money from the partner to the partnership would cause the partner's basis in the partnership to increase. These basis adjustments are important because a distribution (or deemed distribution) of money to a partner from the partnership will not cause the partner to recognize gain unless the distribution amount exceeds the partner's basis (investment) in the partnership.

The analysis of a reduction or increase in a partner's share of partnership liabilities may depend on whether a liability is a **recourse liability** or a **nonrecourse liability.** A liability is a recourse liability to the extent that any individual partner bears the economic risk of loss for that liability. A liability is a nonrecourse liability to the extent that no individual partner bears the economic risk of loss for that liability. A discussion relating to the effects of nonrecourse versus recourse liabilities on shifts of partnership liability among partners is beyond the scope of this book.

Effect of Conversion on the LLC's Method of Accounting

It is important for a partnership that uses the cash receipts and disbursements method of accounting not to convert its method of accounting to the **accrual method** on the conversion to an LLC. Such a change in the accounting method could force the partnership/LLC to accelerate the recognition of income, which could be a very unfavorable outcome.

This situation is especially prevalent and must be considered when converting a professional practice (i.e., law and accounting firms) from a partnership to an LLC. Several IRS letter rulings have held that the conversion of a professional practice partnership to an LLC would not in fact force a conversion from the cash method of accounting to the accrual method of accounting.

More Tax Traps May Await

Before you decide to convert your partnership into an LLC, the partners should consider whether there will be any other adverse consequences as a result of the conversion. Converting the partnership's tangible personal property may result in a transfer tax or sales and use tax. In many states, statutory conversions will not trigger sales taxes.

TIP: Most taxpayers base their planning on federal income tax, and to a lesser extent on federal estate and other transfer taxes. Do not underestimate the potential costs of local transfer and recording fees. They can be surprisingly large.

License fees and miscellaneous state level statutory provisions could cause adverse tax ramifications on a conversion. Some states have issued notices and/or rulings relating to the applicability of real estate transfer taxes. In other states, however, the conversion to an LLC will involve a deed for the transfer of real property and a realty transfer tax may be due.

EXAMPLE: General Partnership (GP) is formed under the laws of State X and owns two parcels of real property. The owners of the GP wish to convert to an LLC to obtain liability protection. GP's state does not have a statute that expressly provides for the conversion of a general partnership into an LLC. Therefore, GP wants to proceed with the conversion by having the partners form an LLC to which they contribute their respective partnership interests in exchange for membership interests in that LLC. The partnership would then have only one partner—the LLC—and thus would be dissolved, with the two parcels of real property being distributed to the LLC in liquidation of the GP. State X, however, imposes a realty transfer fee on all transfers of real property and does not provide any exceptions for conversions of existing entities into LLCs. Therefore, the conversion is not totally cost-free because a realty transfer fee will be due on the transfer (by deed) of each of the two parcels of the real property from GP to LLC. Some states, however, have ruled that the transfer in this case would be exempt from the realty transfer tax.

How Do You Convert a Partnership into an LLC?

There are several ways to change a partnership, whether general or limited, into an LLC. The following are the most common methods.

*Method 1: Your State Law Includes a Specific
Rule for Conversion*

When available, this method is often the best. It achieves the conversion in the most direct, tax-efficient, and legally simple (read less problems and lower fees) method. Some states have a specific statute in their partnership statutes and/or LLC statutes permitting a general or limited partnership to convert (change) directly into an LLC. The partnership generally accomplishes this conversion by filing a legal form with the state called *Articles of Conversion, Certificate of Conversion,* or a similar name. Filing means sending the document to the appropriate state agency, properly prepared and signed, along with the required fee. Articles of Conversion typically contain a statement that the partnership is converting into an LLC, the names of each general and/or limited partner and the effective date of the conversion. Once the Articles of Conversion have been filed with the appropriate state filing authority, the conversion will become effective on that date, unless you have specified some allowable later date in the Articles of Conversion. On the effective date, the partnership's assets and liabilities will be treated as if they have been formally transferred to the LLC.

Generally, statutes permitting the direct conversion of a partnership into an LLC require the unanimous vote of the partners, including limited partners, before a conversion can occur. A conversion accomplished in this manner should generally not result in the partners/members recognizing taxable income or loss.

Like all tax rules, however, the tax-free conversion rule is subject to exceptions. A shift in liabilities among partners (members) that causes a partner/member to recognize gain for income tax purposes is one example.

*Method 2: Contribution by Partners of Their Partnership Interests to an
LLC in Exchange for LLC Interests*

If you cannot convert your partnership into an LLC under your state's laws (e.g., simply by filing a Certificate of Conversion), the conversion method discussed here may be the simplest way to convert a partnership into an LLC. Under this method, the partners of the existing partnership form a new LLC. In exchange for ownership (i.e., membership) interests in the new LLC, each partner contributes his partnership interests to the LLC. The partnership would then have only one partner, the LLC, and thus would be dissolved, wound up, and terminated, because a partnership must always have at least two partners.

In this case, the LLC would be a continuation of the partnership because the business of the partnership would continue after the conversion. Moreover, even though the partners contribute their partnership interests to the LLC, the partnership is deemed to continue (in the form of the LLC) after the conversion. The contribution by the partners of their partnership interests to the LLC should generally not be an event that can cause a partner to recognize gain or loss.

CAUTION: To the extent that there is a shift among the partners of their respective shares of partnership liabilities, the partners/members may have to recognize a taxable gain.

Method 3: Partnership Transfers Assets to the LLC for LLC Membership Interests

Under this conversion method, the partnership would transfer its assets and liabilities to the new LLC and would receive LLC membership interests in exchange. The partnership would then distribute those same membership interests to the partners, and the partnership would be liquidated. The net result is the partners would own interests in the new LLC and hence would be owners (members) of the LLC.

The technical tax problem of this conversion method is that initially the partnership would be the only member of the LLC and would thereafter transfer membership interests to the partners. This can be avoided by having the existing partners of the partnership form the LLC along with the partnership, followed by a liquidation of the partnership of its membership interests. In this fashion, there would always be at least two members of the LLC, if state law required.

Method 4: Liquidation of Partnership Followed by Contribution of Partnership Assets to the LLC

The final method to convert a partnership into an LLC is for the partnership to liquidate and distribute all partnership assets and liabilities to the partners in complete liquidation of the partnership. The partnership begins the process of ending its existence by giving all assets to its owners, its partners.

Generally, this would not result in any gain or loss recognition to the partners. Taxable gain may be recognized, however, in the following situations:

- If cash is distributed to a partner that exceeds the partner's investment (tax basis) in the partnership.
- If there is a deemed distribution of cash to a partner as a result of a reduction in your share of partnership liabilities that exceeds your

investment (tax basis) in the partnership (this concept was explained earlier in the general discussion, but is very complex and should always be reviewed by a tax adviser).

- There could also be gain recognition to a partner who had contributed appreciated property to the partnership within the five-year period prior to its liquidation and received in the liquidation a distribution of property with a **fair market value** exceeding that partner's basis (investment) in his partnership interest.

Even though this liquidation approach to converting a partnership into an LLC will generally not have adverse income tax consequences, it is not usually advisable. From a practical standpoint, liquidation followed by a contribution involves two transfers of assets and liabilities—one transfer on liquidation of the partnership to the partners, and the second on the contribution by the members to the LLC. The second transfer could result in additional costs as other methods of conversion may require only one transfer. If real property is involved, several deeds may be required to effectuate this conversion. Many states impose a realty transfer fee on each transfer, and individuals would be in the chain of title.

Conclusions about a Partnership Conversion

Partnerships, both limited and general, can convert to LLCs tax free. In tax parlance, the conversions are generally treated as nontaxable events. This means that the partners (members) won't recognize any taxable gain or loss on the transaction. There are, however, instances when substantial gains, or perhaps deductible tax losses might be recognized. The most common of the taxable situations occurs if there is a reduction in a partner's share of liabilities that exceeds his investment (**adjusted basis**) in his partnership interest. To avoid inadvertently stepping into a costly tax trap, you should always have an accountant carefully review the conversion.

CONVERTING A CORPORATION INTO AN LLC

The majority of closely held businesses remain corporations, which for many years were the common method of forming closely held businesses. Prior to the enactment of LLC statutes in most states, S corporations were the most popular entity for small or closely held (i.e., few owners) businesses. Corporations have a host of tax and other problems that can make LLCs a better choice. Although corporations can also be converted into LLCs, the tax results are potentially much more costly.

Legal Considerations When Converting a Corporation into an LLC

If you want to convert a corporation into an LLC, you should first obtain the required vote of the shareholders.

NOTE: To ascertain what portion of shareholders must approve the transaction, always review the following with your attorney: applicable state laws, the corporation's bylaws, and certificate of incorporation, and any shareholders' agreement.

Method and Tax Consequences of Converting a Corporation into an LLC

The most common form of a corporation conversion into an LLC involves liquidating the corporation and distributing its assets to its shareholders. These actions are followed by the shareholders' contribution of the assets to an LLC in exchange for membership interests. The liquidation of a corporation is generally a taxable event for both the corporation and its shareholders. If the liquidating corporation distributes appreciated assets to its shareholders, it usually will recognize a gain in a manner similar to what the corporation would have recognized if the assets were sold at their fair market value.

Both C corporations and S corporations must undergo this taxable liquidation if they want to convert into an LLC. The tax treatment for an S corporation, however, is generally more favorable on liquidation than for a C corporation. A C corporation that liquidates its assets generally recognizes gain on the assets distributed. In addition, the shareholders recognize a gain on receiving a distribution from the company of an amount equal to the fair market value of the assets distributed to a shareholder less the shareholders' basis in their stock.

Accordingly, a C corporation has two levels of taxation on liquidation. An S corporation may essentially avoid one of these levels because the gain that the S corporation recognizes on the liquidation of its assets will flow through to the shareholders. This will increase their basis (investment) in their stock, which effectively alleviates the second level of tax. There will be two levels of tax on the liquidation of an S corporation, however, to the extent that the S corporation had built-in-gain on property distributed in liquidation that had appreciated at the time when the corporation switched from a C corporation to an S corporation. These latter rules are complex and should encourage you to review any conversion with your accountant and tax adviser.

CONVERSION OF LIMITED LIABILITY COMPANIES TO OTHER TYPES OF ENTITIES

Although it is not yet a common scenario for an LLC to convert into a partnership, the possibility of such a conversion should be addressed. As LLCs become more common and the potential problems and issues more focused, some investors who established LLCs may wish to convert back to another type of entity. The IRS held that if a conversion of an LLC (that is classified as a partnership for federal tax purposes) into a partnership occurs, the rules discussed previously about the conversion of a partnership into an LLC will apply. Therefore, the conversion of a partnership into an LLC will likely be income tax free if the issues described earlier do not apply. As in all conversions, your tax advisers should analyze the facts in the context of the specific transaction to avoid any unexpected tax traps.

MERGERS AND LLCs

A *merger* occurs when two or more business entities combine into one. This differs from a conversion, which folds an old entity into a new entity. In a merger, two or more existing entities join forces in a new entity.

In addition to the nonstatutory conversion methods described previously, some states permit the merger of a partnership and/or corporation into an LLC with the LLC being the remaining (surviving) entity. The IRS explicitly provides that it does not matter how a conversion from a partnership into an LLC is accomplished under state law. The analysis of a statutory merger from a partnership with and into an LLC should have the same tax consequences as a conversion from a partnership to an LLC.

Two or more businesses may choose to merge for many reasons. For example, several companies under common control or ownership may want to merge to centralize operations or management or to avoid multiple regulatory requirements. The merger of a corporation with and into another entity requires approval by the shareholders (but always have your attorney review the Certificate of Incorporation, bylaws, and shareholders' agreement).

In states that allow partnerships to merge with and into LLCs, the merger requires the unanimous consent of the partners unless the partnership agreement provides otherwise. In other states, partnerships have no merger provisions, and thus, a merger involving a partnership may result in the dissolution of the partnership under state law.

Some state LLC statutes explicitly permit LLC mergers with other entities and/or LLCs, whereas other states do not expressly provide guidance relating to mergers. LLCs in those states that do not provide for mergers must look to partnership law regarding mergers. You can start your review by looking up merger in your state's LLC laws. You can find these at your local library or online on your state's Web site. Once you have completed your review, you should consult with a business lawyer in your state. Merely reading the state law cannot alert you to its many nuances and practical issues.

The special merger rules of the tax laws for partnerships should apply to the mergers of LLCs and partnerships. The tax laws provide that the merger of two or more partnerships will not trigger termination of the partnership if: (1) the members own an interest in the partnership of 50 percent of the capital and profits of the resulting partnership (in this case, the LLC); and (2) no portion of any business, financial operation, or venture of the partnership continues to be carried on by any of its partners. If a conversion of a partnership into an LLC is accomplished by a merger of the partnership with an LLC, the merger/conversion will occur through operation of law instead of through the coupling of distributions and contributions, as was the case for the nonstatutory conversion methods discussed earlier. The details of a merger vary by state. Some states only allow mergers of partnerships with domestic LLCs (LLCs formed under that state's laws, not formed under another state's laws). Other states allow mergers with foreign LLCs (LLCs formed under the laws of other states) as well.

The main advantage of converting your partnership to an LLC using merger statutes is that existing partnerships may be converted without exchanging assets. This can avoid sales, transfer, and use taxes because the transfer of assets to the LLC (conveyance) occurs by operation of law, and nothing else has to be done (no contract documents, etc.). State laws must still be reviewed to determine if transfer taxes apply even by a conversion through merger or statute. Another advantage is that a conversion through these statutes assures that the conversion is legally valid.

EXAMPLE: General Partnership (GP) is formed under the laws of State Y and owns two parcels of real property. The owners of GP want to convert to an LLC to obtain limited liability protection. GP's state does not have a statute that expressly provides for the conversion of a general partnership into an LLC. GP does not want to do a nonstatutory conversion because it would have to pay the realty transfer taxes that would result from transferring the parcels of real property to the LLC. State Y does have a statute expressly authorizing the merger of general partnerships and LLCs. Therefore, the partners of GP form an LLC and cause GP to merge with and into the LLC with the LLC being the surviving entity. By operation of law, all assets and liabilities of GP become owned or assumed by LLC, and no deed transferring the real property to LLC is required. Therefore, this transaction does not trigger a realty tax.

SUMMARY

If you think that your existing corporation or partnership (or some other entity) should operate as an LLC, consider converting it into an LLC. However, before taking any steps toward this process, find out whether the transaction is permitted under state law and what legal method will have to be used to effect the change. Also determine whether the change will result in any tax costs or other expenses that might outweigh the benefits of operating in the LLC format.

General partnerships, limited partnerships, corporations, and sole proprietorships all can be converted into LLCs. The conversion of a corporation into an LLC, however, will generally be a taxable event and the liquidation of the corporation may have adverse tax consequences. By contrast, the conversion of a partnership or sole proprietorship into an LLC generally can be accomplished on a tax-free basis. There are exceptions to this general rule, so always get professional advice.

The LLC is an excellent form of transacting business, and thus existing companies may desire to convert into an LLC. Nevertheless, each conversion must be thought out to determine whether the benefits of the conversion outweigh the costs.

Part Three

OPERATING AND TERMINATING YOUR LIMITED LIABILITY COMPANY

6 NEGOTIATING AND DRAFTING THE OPERATING AGREEMENT

WHAT IS AN OPERATING AGREEMENT?

Shareholders in corporations have shareholders' agreements that define the relationship between the shareholders and the corporation, and among the shareholders. Similarly, members of an LLC should have an operating agreement defining the relationship between the members and the LLC, and among the members.

Relationship of State Law and Operating Agreements

Although most state laws provide rules (default provisions) to govern the relationship between the members of an LLC, once an LLC is formed, the members should have an attorney prepare and enter into a written *operating agreement*. In some states, it is referred to as *regulations* or the *limited liability company agreement*. The operating agreement is a contract that governs the operation of the LLC and the relationship of the members and managers (those who run the LLC if the LLC has managers), to each other and to the LLC. Although an operating agreement is not required in most states, it is certainly advisable to enter into one every time you form or invest in any LLC.

CAUTION: In most states, the Articles of Organization or Certificate of Formation used to create the LLC are short, general, and vague documents. They are mere formalities and will not disclose or discuss much of the agreed-on relationship among the members/managers and the LLC. Therefore, the operating agreement is the document that will most likely be relied on to memorialize such agreements.

Most LLC statutes require a unanimous consent of the members to adopt the operating agreement. In states that do not expressly require unanimity, general contract principles may imply such a requirement. Whatever the law, have every member and manager sign.

States vary in whether they require the operating agreement to be in writing. Some states do not require putting the overall operating agreement in writing; only the particular items that the members agree to must be in writing. Moreover, if an operating agreement is to modify the rules of any particular state's statute, then there must be a written version of that agreement. Even if you are doing business in a state that expressly permits oral operating agreements, not having a written agreement is unwise. People and their relationships can change over time and individuals may have different understandings and perceptions of oral agreements that were made several years in the past. Whatever the law, get it in writing.

Changing the Operating Agreement

What happens if the members decide to amend the operating agreement? Who can make the amendment? Generally, state law requires the unanimous consent of the members to amend the operating agreement. Under other state laws, only a majority of the members are required to amend the operating agreement. A few states' laws even permit the managers to amend the operating agreement if the power to do so is expressly given in the Articles of Organization. Other statutes permit both the managers and the members to have control over amending the operating agreement if provided by the Articles of Organization. Again, whatever the law, it is better to have all members and managers in a closely held LLC agree to any changes in writing than to risk later disagreements or misunderstandings.

General Issues to Address in the Operating Agreement

LLC operating agreements, like most legal contracts, should be carefully tailored to the specific circumstances involved. Using a form (boilerplate) may be fine for some provisions, but even form or standard language must be tailored. The following discussion addresses some of the common issues that might warrant inclusion. Since almost all LLCs with two or more members are treated as partnerships for income tax purposes, the operating agreement must discuss the members' understanding of the formula for distributions and the allocation of profits and losses. What income, gain, or loss should be distributed to which members, and when? Your tax adviser will have to include many technical provisions to comply with partnership income tax requirements. The agreement may also provide for other aspects of business transactions among the members. It should address the transfer of membership interests to other members and third parties, as well as the relative classes, rights, powers, and duties of each class or group of members. The operating agreement should address the voting rights of members. It may provide that certain actions by the LLC require a certain percentage of votes, and other actions may be taken either without a vote or may require a different percentage of votes. It may provide for classes or groups of members having the rights, powers, or duties of managers. In some states, if the operating agreement does not specify who has management control, the management powers of the LLC will be vested in all of the LLC members with voting rights in proportion to each member's respective share of the LLC's profits.

EXAMPLE: Joe and Jane are members in an LLC. Joe owns 60 percent of the LLC and Jane owns 40 percent. Profits are distributed in the same proportions. The operating agreement does not specify the voting arrangements. Therefore, Joe has 60 percent voting rights and Jane has 40 percent.

The operating agreement may provide that the LLC has a manager or group of managers that functions like a general partner of a limited partnership in managing the affairs of the partnership. Whether the management of the LLC operations will be vested in a manager or in the members should always be addressed in the operating agreement. If a manager is selected to manage the LLC, the rights and obligations of the manager and members should be discussed in detail. It may be practical to include penalties or other provisions in the event that a manager or member fails to comply with the terms of the operating agreement. Operating agreements must be drafted carefully to avoid future management problems, abuse by majority owners, and potential operational deadlock.

Subsidiaries

An LLC may have subsidiaries, thus an LLC can serve as a holding company for different investments. This is a flexible and important characteristic.

EXAMPLE: The Smith family set up the Smith Family LLC to hold most family investments. Although initially the investments were composed solely of marketable securities, the family decided to diversify into rental real estate holdings. Instead of setting up new LLCs which would require separate tax returns, the Smiths set up a new LLC for each rental property they acquired, but had each new LLC owned 100 percent by Smith Family LLC. Thus, the Smith Family LLC served as the main or holding company LLC for all investments.

When an LLC owns 100 percent of another LLC, that wholly owned LLC is sometimes referred to as a *subsidiary*. Since the **subsidiary LLC** has only one owner, it is ignored for income tax purposes (treated as a **disregarded entity**). Thus, no additional tax return is required.

Provisions Governing Members in Your LLC Operating Agreement

Many of the most important provisions in an operating agreement detail the rights and obligations of members. The following detailed discussion covers these provisions.

Who Can Be a Member of the LLC?

Any individual or entity may be a member of an LLC, as long as such individual or entity has the capacity to enter a contract.

EXAMPLE: Someone who is incompetent (as a result of disease, age, retardation, etc.) may not legally be able to be a member of an LLC.

A minor child may have his membership interest held in a trust or under a state's **Uniform Gift to Minors' Act (UGMA)** or **Uniform Transfers to Minors' Act (UTMA)** account.

To become a member of an LLC, a person or entity must be admitted to the LLC. An LLC's membership may include many types of persons or entities not permitted to be owners of other entities. Nonresident aliens, partnerships and corporations, trusts, foreign LLCs (i.e., an LLC organized under the laws of another state or foreign country), custodian, nominee, or any other individual or entity, generally may own membership interests in an LLC.

This lack of restrictions on membership may be a tremendous advantage to the LLC over the S corporation.

Rights and Obligations of Members

Generally, members are not personally liable for an LLC's debts, liabilities, and other obligations, which is a similar outcome as limited partners of a limited partnership and shareholders of a corporation. Unless the operating agreement or Articles of Organization provide otherwise, all members are of the same class and have equal rights, unlike a limited partnership, which has two classes of partners, limited and general.

CAUTION: This is an important drawback to the use of an LLC. For corporations, the shareholders, and for limited partnerships, the limited partners, are likely to be treated as having limited liability automatically. For an LLC, you may still have to "do things right" to qualify to be a member.

Allocating Profits

There are many different ways to allocate profits. The LLC law in every state provides for a method. The rules differ considerably depending on the state:

- Profits and losses of an LLC can be allocated according to the value of capital contributed to the LLC and not yet returned (called *adjusted capital*).

EXAMPLE: The best way to explain the concept of allocation is with an example. Say you are one of four members in an LLC. The other members are Member B, C, and D (you are A). You (Member A) contribute land to the partnership worth $20,000. Member B contributes $20,000 in cash. Members C and D both work full time in the business and receive salary and/or distributions on their membership interests for services. A and B share profits and losses equally.

- Profits can be allocated per capita. If there are five members, each gets one fifth of the profits.
- Profits can be allocated according to capital contributions until capital is returned.

EXAMPLE: Tom, Sam, and Fred form the TSF Management, LLC. Tom contributes a building worth $100,000. Sam contributes cash of $50,000. Fred contributes computers and office equipment, and cars worth $50,000. If profits are to be allocated based on initial capital contributions, Tom is allocated 50 percent and Sam and Fred both are allocated 25 percent.

Once capital is returned, profits might then be allocated per capita.

- Profit allocation can be based on book value of contributions.

EXAMPLE: Tom, Sam, and Fred form the TSF Management, LLC. Tom contributes a building worth $100,000, but which has been depreciated to $50,000. Sam contributes cash of $50,000. Fred contributes computers, office equipment, and cars worth $50,000. If profits are to be allocated based on the book value of these initial capital contributions, one-third of profits will be allocated to each of Tom, Sam, and Fred.

- Profits can be allocated based on the agreed value of contributions. The members may agree among themselves as to the values for allocations.

Because of the many options, and the potentially significant economic differences between them, it is essential to address the method for allocating profits in the operating agreement. Some LLCs have special allocations (i.e., a disproportionate allocation) that may differ from the general allocations previously mentioned. For example, in the preceding examples, Tom contributed a building to the LLC. The members might agree that some percentage of the rent received on the building may be specifically allocated back to Tom. For the IRS to respect such special allocations, they must meet additional tax law requirements (they must have "substantial economic effect). This means that the allocation must be realistic and must affect the actual economic returns of the people involved (not just provide tax benefits).

Loans to/from LLCs

In most states, any member of an LLC may, but is not obligated to, lend money to, borrow money from; act as a surety, guarantor, or endorser for; guarantee or assume one or more specific obligations of; provide collateral for; and transact other business with the LLC unless provided to the contrary in the operating agreement. Accordingly, the operating agreement of every LLC must address which of these rights a member should, or should not, have.

For many new businesses, the right to demand that all members make loans, may be essential for the business to survive economic hardship. If abused, this right could enable a wealthier member to force out less wealthy members who do not have the financial ability to loan funds.

Accounting

Every member, pursuant to most statutes, has the right to demand and receive true and full information regarding the status of the business and financial condition of the LLC; a copy of the LLC's federal, state, and local tax returns; a current list of all members and managers; true and full information regarding the amount of members' contributions; and a description of the agreed value of any property or services contributed by each member. This information availability statute is a valuable protection, particularly for noncontrolling members. It does not, however, mean that the accounting, disclosure, audit right, and related provisions typically included in the governing agreement for a business transaction can be ignored when drafting an operating agreement. Thus, the operating agreement should address in some detail the content of accounting reports to members, when they will receive the reports, and what rights they have to challenge and investigate the reports.

Classes and Groups of Members

LLCs may have different classes or groups of members, each with different rights, powers, and duties. To do this, however, the Articles of Organization and the operating agreement must list these distinctions.

When Is a Person Admitted as a Member?

An individual or an entity (e.g., another LLC, partnership) becomes a member of an LLC by receiving a membership interest from that LLC. This can occur when the LLC is formed and the individual or entity transfers cash or other assets to the LLC in exchange for a membership interest. If a member is to obtain membership interest by direct issuance from the LLC, several issues need to be considered. The default rule provided by the state law or the operating agreement will provide a requisite consent that must be obtained before an additional member may be admitted to an LLC. The members who have the ability to participate in any such consent requirement will vary by each particular state law and each LLC's operating agreement. Generally, a new member obtains his membership interest in exchange for making a contribution to the LLC. The members whose consent for admission is required must be satisfied with the proposed contribution. The state law must also permit the particular type of contribution.

An individual can also gain admission by assignment of an existing member's interest after obtaining the necessary consent required under statute or the operating agreement from the nontransferring members.

Voting Rights

The operating agreement may provide for different classes or groups of members and/or managers, with different rights, powers, and duties. For example, certain groups or classes of members may take specified actions without the vote or approval of other members. The operating agreement may grant certain members the right to vote separately or as a group. Where a business comprises active participants and less active investors, the investor-members could compose a group that is authorized to make certain financial decisions without the consent of the active members. Similarly, the active members could be empowered to make all daily operating decisions without consultation with the investor-members group.

Where voting rights are provided, the operating agreement should state the minimum number of members required to have a vote (called a quorum), the notice members must receive prior to a vote, time a vote shall occur, proxies, and so on.

EXAMPLE: Multiple rules for different types of voting issues can sometimes be useful in resolving disputes.

Recording Membership Status

Most state statutes require the LLC to record the admission of an additional member. In fact, most states require that the LLC maintain a record of all members. The value of a member's contribution to the LLC is particularly important under the LLC statutes of states that use the value of a member's contribution (investment) to determine that member's voting power, as well as the allocation of profits and losses and rights to distributions from the LLC. You can change this only if the Articles of Organization or the operating agreement for your LLC state that the member will have a different vote.

EXAMPLE: You contribute property worth $50,000 to your LLC. Your friend contributes $50,000 of cash. However, it is your knowledge and know-how, and the unique property you are contributing, that will make your new LLC profitable. You and your friend agree that you should have 60 percent of the vote and profits. Unless this is in the Certificate of Formation or the operating agreement, it may not be valid.

When Does a Member Cease Being a Member?

A member who does any of the following may have his membership terminated:

- Makes an assignment for the benefit of creditors.
- Files a voluntary petition in bankruptcy.
- Is adjudicated bankrupt or insolvent.

- Files a petition or answer seeking reorganization.
- Transfers all of the underlying economic rights to his interest in the company.

CHECKLIST FOR DRAFTING TERMS FOR AN OPERATING AGREEMENT

The following checklist of 23 items will help you identify other issues to address with your attorney for inclusion in your LLC's operating agreement:

1. What decisions require the unanimous consent of the members versus a majority or other percentage vote of the members? Perhaps such situations as selling the entire business or major business assets, serving as a guarantor on debt, settling major litigation claims, and so on, should require the unanimous consent of the members. A unanimous consent or *major decisions* clause, as it is sometimes called, can be critical to protecting the interests of a noncontrolling member.

2. What decisions can be relegated to the manager with respect to daily business operations that do not require member approval? For example, should the managers have unfettered discretion to make all but major decisions? Such parameters can help avoid potential problems.

3. Carefully define in specific terms the nature and extent of the LLC's business. It is essential that the requisite percentage of members approve extensions beyond the primary business purpose. For a new business, this requirement can assure that all participants agree on the business approach being taken by the LLC. Often reducing this to writing exposes different views on where and what the business should be and the direction it is moving. This can be helpful to solve fundamental problems at a later date.

4. What types of notice provisions should be given to members and managers for meetings and other matters that may arise under the agreement?

5. Under what conditions, if any, may a manager be permitted to resign?

6. When and how may a member resign/withdraw from the LLC?

7. Should the operating agreement provide penalties or other specified consequences where a member or manager does not comply with its terms?

8. Should the manager be permitted to withhold and not disclose certain confidential data (i.e., trade secrets) to the members; or alternatively, should the operating agreement specifically override this right?

9. Should different groups of members be provided for in the operating agreement? What relative rights and obligations and duties should the members of each particular group have?

10. Should the operating agreement include precautionary language concerning each member's purchase of interests in the LLC, such as purchase of an investment, without intent to resell, and so on? Alternatively, does it appear safe enough to avoid such language, based on an analysis of applicable law and the particular facts in the situation at hand?

11. Should penalties be levied on a manager who fails to perform as required under the operating agreement? Should the statutory default standard relating to liability of managers be changed by the operating agreement so that a manager can be held liable for acts or omissions at a lesser standard than "gross negligence" or "willful misconduct"?

12. Since a member and manager are generally protected by a state's statute for relying in good faith on the LLC's records, who should be responsible for maintaining such records and what specific provisions, if any, should be included in the operating agreement concerning such records?

13. Generally, member contributions may be in cash, property, or services; a promissory note; or the obligation to contribute other cash, property, or services. Should any such contributions be accepted, or should contributions be limited to cash? Where services are to be contributed, the operating agreement should specify the specific services to be rendered, a standard to approve the quality of the services rendered, the terms of the services, and an agreed value for the services.

14. How should profits and losses be allocated among the members? If incentives for different performances or contributions for specific assets are to be provided for, be certain that the operating agreement complies with the LLC requirement to state that services are to be treated as contributions if this is the intent.

15. How should compensation of the members and managers be determined? How can it be changed? Are perks permitted and how should they be determined? In a family business where certain children or family members are to receive salaries and be active in the business and other family members are not, it is essential to set forth the items in detail in the operating agreement. The formula for compensation of members must be carefully structured or the family members in the business might not be fairly compensated for their work if nonparticipating family members control the membership vote. On the other hand, if a specific formula is not imposed, those active in the business could potentially remove all profits from the business in the form of salaries, leaving nothing for the nonparticipating family members to receive as distributions of profits.

16. How much vacation time should be allowed for each member and how much notice should be given to the LLC and other members before vacation dates? If several members would like to take a particular vacation time, perhaps a rotational basis should be provided for in the operating agreement.

17. Who should be a manager of the LLC? In the event of the permanent disability or death of a manager, how should successors be selected (i.e., by remaining managers or by the members)? How should tie votes or deadlocks of managers and/or members be resolved?

18. Several statutes provide that if a person is required to execute a certificate (i.e., a Certificate of Amendment to the Articles of Organization) on behalf of an LLC and fails or refuses to do so, any person who is adversely affected by such failure or refusal may petition the court to direct the execution of any such certificate. A similar provision is contained in some state statutes relating to a person who may be required to execute an operating agreement but refuses to do so. As a result, consideration should be given to include specific instructions in the Articles of Organization as to when a court can and cannot require a member or manager to execute a particular document.

19. What should happen if a member becomes disabled? Will disability income insurance be purchased by the LLC so that it may continue to pay salary to the disabled member? Will the business self-insure (i.e., pay out of its own pocket) for a period of time (e.g., six months) to obtain lower premiums on its disability income insurance? After what length of a disability may a member return to his former position with the LLC? One year, two years, or perhaps a longer time period? How long should benefits other than salary (i.e., health, pension) be continued during disability? What should happen to voting rights of a member during disability? At what point, if any, should there be a mandatory buyout of a disabled member's interest in the LLC? In the event of a buyout of a disabled member's interest, who will be the purchasing party—the LLC or

the nondisabled members? Will the purchase price be funded with disability buyout insurance?

20. What should happen if a member dies? Will the legal representatives of the deceased member's estate be obligated to sell the deceased member's membership interest? Who will be the party required to purchase such interest—the LLC or the surviving members? Would the purchase price for such deceased member's interest be funded with life insurance?

21. If there is a buyout on a member's death or permanent disability, how should such buyout be structured? Different types of buyout arrangements may be used for different circumstances. If a buyout is provided for on the death or permanent disability of a member, the LLC could be appraised to determine the purchase price (with the purchase price equal to the appraised value of the LLC divided by the interest in the LLC being purchased). This would prevent the surviving and nondisabled members from taking advantage of the deceased or disabled member's family by setting an artificially low purchase price. A stated or agreed on value for the LLC that the members determine annually can sometimes be used. It must be determined whether a formula method, an agreed-on value method, or an appraisal method is more appropriate to determine the purchase price. If a member receives a third-party offer to purchase his membership interest, should the LLC and/or other members have a right of first refusal to purchase such member's interest in the LLC? If so, on what terms? In some businesses, such as certain real estate ventures, it is important to give a member the right to "put" or offer the entire property and business to a third party. That might be the only way to realize a fair value. Would a person purchase one tenth of a real estate venture for exactly one tenth of the appraised value of the company when the purchaser would have no control over distributions to the members or management of the business?

22. Should expenditures on the LLC's behalf in excess of a certain amount (i.e., $5,000) require more than one member's or manager's signature?

23. How should an LLC that needs more capital obtain it? Should the operating agreement require mandatory loans to the LLC on prearranged terms from existing members? Should membership interests be offered to recruit new members after a right of first refusal for additional membership interests is given to existing members to contribute capital for additional membership interests?

SUMMARY

An operating agreement governs the internal operations of an LLC. Once an LLC is formed, the members should enter into an operating agreement, in writing, so that there will be no uncertainty as to the agreement among the members at a later date. The operating agreement should address the management structure of the LLC; set forth the contributions of each member to the LLC; set forth the allocations of profits, losses, and so on for the members; provide for scenarios relating to the death or disability of a member; and address the transfer of membership interest to other members and third parties.

For Your Notebook

SAMPLE LLC OPERATING AGREEMENT

NOTE: The following is a sample LLC operating agreement for a hypothetical LLC formed by a small group of investors for the sole purpose of investing in a particular parcel of land. The LLC vehicle was used to limit their liability exposure from owning the land. Many of the provisions governing the management and operation are tailored to reflect this limited purpose. Because complex allocations of income and gain are not relevant to the particular deal, many more sophisticated tax-related provisions are not included.

OPERATING AGREEMENT
FOR
BIG-DEAL PROPERTIES LLC
A Some-State Limited Liability Company

THIS OPERATING AGREEMENT is made and entered into as of DATE by and among BIG-DEAL Properties LLC, a Some-State Limited Liability Company (the "Company") and the persons executing this Operating Agreement as members of the Company and all of those who shall hereafter be admitted as members (individually, a "Member" and collectively, the "Members") whose names and signatures shall appear on "EXHIBIT A MEMBER LISTING; CAPITAL CONTRIBUTIONS," below, hereby agree as follows:

WITNESSETH:

NOTE: From a tax perspective, the investors in this LLC want to make it clear that they are merely holding land as an investment, which should qualify for capital gains treatment when sold. If the LLC developed, subdivided, or improved the land they purchased, they could be characterized as a dealer in real estate, depending on the facts and circumstances. If this occurred, the gain on sale could then be characterized as **ordinary income,** taxable at a much higher tax rate.

---

a. Whereas, the Members desire to enter into this operating agreement ("Operating Agreement" or "Agreement") for the purposes of governing the Company, to and for the purpose of investing in, purchasing, selling, granting or taking an option on raw land solely for investment purposes and not as a trade or business ("Business"). The Company shall not conduct any other business unless related to the Business, unless approved by unanimous consent of all Members.

b. Whereas, the Members intend to operate the Business, appoint a person or persons to assume responsibility for certain management matters (the "Manager") and provide for the restriction on the transfers of ownership interests in the Company ("Interests").

NOW, THEREFORE, in consideration of the mutual premises below, and other good and valuable consideration receipt and sufficiency of which is hereby acknowledged, it is agreed as follows:

1. *ORGANIZATION.*

a. *Formation.* The Company has been organized as a Some-State Limited Liability Company under and pursuant to the Some-State Limited Liability Company Act (the "Act") by the filing of Articles of Organization ("Articles") with the Department of Commerce of the State of Some-State as required by the Act.

b. *Name.* The name of the Company shall be the "BIG-DEAL Properties LLC." The Company may also conduct its business under one or more assumed names.

c. *Purposes.* The purpose of the Company is to engage in any activity for which Limited Liability Companies may be formed under the Act for purposes only of advancing the Business as defined above. The Company shall have all the powers necessary or convenient to effect any purpose for which it is formed, including all powers granted by the Act.

NOTE: The duration for the LLC should be consistent with the duration specified in the Certificate of Formation.

---

d. *Duration.* The Company shall continue in existence for the period fixed in the Articles of Organization, or until the Company shall be sooner dissolved and its affairs wound up in accordance with the Act or this Operating Agreement.

NOTE: The following provision assures a continuation of a Registered Agent if the first named Agent resigns, without the need for an approval of the Manager or Members. This can be a useful precautionary step.

---

e. *Registered Office and Resident Agent.* The Registered Office and Resident Agent of the Company shall be as designated in the initial Articles or any amendment thereof, MANAGER-NAME, who resides at MANAGER-ADDRESS. The Registered Office and/or Resident Agent may be changed from time to time. Any such change shall be made in accordance with the Act. If the Resident Agent shall ever resign, the Company shall promptly appoint REPLACEMENT AGENT, who resides at REPLACEMENT-AGENT ADDRESS, as the successor. If he is unable or unwilling, then he shall designate a successor Manager by giving written notice to the Members.

f. *Intention for Company.* The Members have formed the Company as a Limited Liability Company under and pursuant to the Act.

NOTE: The following statement makes clear that the intent of the members is for the LLC to be taxed as a partnership. Even if the IRS permits a simple check-the-box approach for an LLC to designate on its tax return how it wants to be taxed, every operating agreement should clearly state the members' intent concerning tax classification: partnership or corporation.

The Members specifically intend and agree that the Company shall not be, for legal and tax purposes, a partnership (including a limited partnership) or any other venture, but a shall be a Limited Liability Company under and pursuant to the Act.

No Member or Manager shall be construed to be a partner in the Company or a partner of any other Member, Manager, or person; and the Articles, this Operating Agreement, and the relationships created thereby and arising therefrom shall not be construed to suggest otherwise.

2. BOOKS, RECORDS, AND ACCOUNTING.

a. *Books and Records.* The Company shall maintain complete and accurate books and records of the Company's business and affairs as required by the Act and such books and records shall be kept at the Company's Registered Office.

NOTE: There is no requirement to designate a specific accountant. In this transaction, several of the members were comfortable with a particular accountant and felt that it would give stability to the venture, and help avoid disputes, to assure that a particular accountant was involved. This is simply an example of the many ways any agreement can be tailored to meet the specific needs you and your partners have for your LLC, the investment involved, and so on. The key point is do not simply fill in the blanks on a form and assume you have obtained reasonable protection. Every document should be tailored to the specific situation. The more effort you expend in the beginning on addressing and resolving likely issues in the operating agreement, the less likely it will be that significant, costly, and disruptive disputes will arise later.

---

b. *Fiscal Year; Accounting.* The Company's fiscal year shall be the calendar year. The particular accounting methods and principles to be followed by the Company shall be selected by the accountant for the Company ("Accountant") who is hereby designated as JOE ACCOUNTANT & CO., CPAs, Accounting Road, BIG CITY, Some-State, its successor or assigns. The Accountant may be changed by written Notice of the then-serving Manager, consented to in writing by at least Two (2) Members.

NOTE: Since this particular deal is only raw land an annual accounting report is adequate. If you have a retail business, you may want to insist that you (and all members) receive some type of monthly report. Tailor the provision to meet the reasonable needs and expectations you have for the business, without creating undue cost or administrative burdens.

---

c. *Reports.* The Managers shall provide reports concerning the financial condition and results of operation of the Company and the Capital Accounts of the Members to the Members in the time, manner, and form as the Managers determine. Such reports shall be provided at least annually as soon as practicable after the end of each calendar year and shall include a statement of each Member's share of profits and other items of income, gain, loss, deduction, and credit.

d. *Member's Capital Accounts.* Separate Capital Accounts for each Member shall be maintained by the Company. Each Member's Capital Account shall reflect the Member's capital contributions and increases for the Member's share of any net income or gain of the Company. Each Member's Capital Account shall also reflect decreases for distributions made to the Member and the Member's share of any losses and deductions of the Company.

NOTE: Many of the following technical definitions are helpful to the LLC in meeting tax law partnership requirements. Similar provisions in your operating agreement should be reviewed with your tax adviser and not dismissed as mere standard, form, or boilerplate language.

---

(1) *Definition of Capital Account.* A separate capital account shall be maintained for each Member or Assignee in accordance with the provisions below ("Capital Account").

(2) *Increases in Capital Account.* Each Member's Capital Account shall be increased by:

(a) The amount of money contributed by the Member to the Company.

(b) The fair market value of property contributed by the Member to the Company (net of liabilities secured by such contributed property that the Company is considered to assume or take subject to under Code Section 752). If any property, other than cash, is contributed to or distributed by the Partnership, the adjustments to Capital Accounts required by Treasury Regulation Section 1.704-1(b)(2)(iv)(d), (e), (f), and (g) and Section 1.704-1(b)(4)(i) shall be made.

(c) The Member's share of the increase in the tax basis of Company property, if any, arising out of the recapture of any tax credit.

(d) Allocations to the Member of Profit.

(e) Allocations to the Member of income or gain as provided under this Agreement, or otherwise by Regulation Section 1.704–1(b)(2)(iv).

(3) *Decreases in Capital Account.* Each Member's Capital Account shall be decreased by:

(a) The amount of money distributed to the Member by the Company.

(b) The fair market value of property distributed to the Member by the Company (net of liabilities secured by such distributed property that such Member is considered to assume or take subject to under Code Section 752).

(c) Allocations to the Member of Losses.

(d) Allocations to the Member of deductions, expenses, Nonrecourse Deductions, and Net Losses allocated to it pursuant to this Agreement, and the Member's share of Company expenditures which are neither deductible nor properly chargeable to Capital Accounts under Code Section 705(a)(2)(B) or are treated as such expenditures under Treasury Regulation Section 1.704-1(b)(2)(iv)(i). "Nonrecourse Deductions" shall have the meaning set forth in Treasury Regulation Section 1.704-2.

(e) The Members' share of the decrease in the basis of the Company's property under Code Section 48(q) arising from the allowance of any tax credit.

(4) *Capital Account of Transferee.* In the event of a permitted sale or exchange of an Interest in the Company, the Capital Account of the transferor shall become the Capital Account of the transferee to the extent it relates to the transferred Interest in accordance with Regulation Section 1.704-1(b)(2)(iv).

(5) *Capital Accounts Shall Comply with Code Section 704(b).*

NOTE: A paragraph similar to the following should appear in every LLC operating agreement where the LLC is to be taxed as a partnership. The purpose is to assure that the LLC meets the tax rules for maintaining capital accounts. If they are not maintained properly, the consequences can be dire. Problems are far less likely if your deal has all members receiving only distributions that are proportionate to their membership interests (e.g., a 10 percent member receives 10 percent of all income, losses, gains, distributions; a 42 percent member receives 42 percent of all items). In that case, a general provision like the one in this sample agreement could suffice (but have your tax adviser review the operating agreement to be sure). Where distributions are nonproportionate (e.g., you are a 25 percent member but receive 45 percent of the profits from the sale of a particular parcel of property the LLC purchased), be certain to get competent tax advice and use a more sophisticated agreement.

CAUTION: Where members of the LLC are family members (e.g., you give membership interests to your children as gifts to reduce your estate) additional tax provisions, called the family partnership rules under Section 704(e) of the Internal Revenue Code, should be discussed with your tax adviser. These rules are addressed in a provision of this sample agreement.

The manner in which Capital Accounts are to be maintained pursuant to this Agreement is intended to comply with the requirements of Code Section 704(b) and the Regulations thereunder. It is the specific intent of the Members that all such further or different adjustments as may be required pursuant to Code Section 704, and any Regulations thereunder be made, so as to cause the allocations prescribed hereunder to be respected for tax purposes. Therefore, if in the opinion of the Accountant (or if the Accountant is unable or unwilling to act, the Manager, the manner in which Capital Accounts are to be maintained pursuant to this Agreement should be modified to comply with Code Section 704(b) and the Regulations thereunder, then notwithstanding anything to the contrary contained in this Agreement, or any other agreement between the Parties, the method in which Capital Accounts are maintained shall be so modified. However, any change in the manner of maintaining Capital Accounts shall not materially alter the economic agreement between or among the Members. Each Member hereby appoints the Manager the Tax Matters Member and agent for the purpose of making any amendment to this Agreement solely for purposes of complying with this provision.

3. *CAPITAL CONTRIBUTIONS.*

NOTE: It is best for all investments to be made at the outset since it is simplest. If a member will make a contribution at a later date, see the Amendment and related forms in the "For Your Notebook" section of this chapter.

---

a. *Initial Commitments and Contributions.* By the execution of this Operating Agreement, the initial Members hereby agree to make the capital contributions set forth in the attached Exhibit A. The interests of the respective Members in the total capital of the Company (their respective "Sharing Ratios," as adjusted from time to time to reflect changes in the Capital Accounts of the Members and the total capital in the Company) are also set forth in Exhibit A. Any additional Member (other than an assignee of a membership interest who has been admitted as a Member) shall make the capital contribution set forth in an Admission Agreement. No interest shall accrue on any capital contribution and no Member shall have any right to withdraw or to be repaid any capital contribution except as provided in this Operating Agreement.

b. *Additional Contributions.* In addition to the initial capital contributions, the Managers may determine from time to time that additional capital contributions are needed to enable the Company to conduct its business and affairs. Upon making such a determination, notice thereof shall be given to all Members in writing at least Ten (10) business days prior to the date on which such additional contributions are due. Such notice shall describe in reasonable detail, the purposes and uses of such additional capital, the amounts of additional capital required, and the date by which payment of the additional capital is required. Each Member shall be obligated to make such additional capital contribution to the extent of any unfulfilled commitment. Any Member who has fulfilled that Member's commitment, shall have the right, but not the obligation to make the additional capital contributions needed according to that Member's Sharing Ratio.

c. *Failure to Contribute.* If any Member fails to make a capital contribution when required, the Company may, in addition to the other rights and remedies the Company may have under the Act or applicable law, take such enforcement action (including, the commencement and prosecution of court proceedings) against such Member as the Managers consider appropriate. Moreover, the remaining Members may elect to contribute the amount of such required capital themselves according to their respective Sharing Ratios. In such an event, the remaining Members shall be entitled to treat such amounts as an extension of credit to such defaulting Member, payable upon demand, with interest accruing thereon at the federal mid-term rate provided for under Code Section 1274(d), plus Two (2%) percent until paid, all of which shall be secured by such defaulting Member's interest in the Company, each Member who may hereafter default, hereby granting to each Member who may hereafter grant such an extension of credit, a security interest in such defaulting Member's interest in the Company.

4. ALLOCATIONS AND DISTRIBUTIONS.

a. *Allocations.* Except as may be required by the Code as amended or this Operating Agreement, net profits, net losses, and other items of income, gain, loss, deduction, and credit of the Company shall be allocated among the Members in accordance with their Sharing Ratios.

CAUTION: Distributions can be a tough area to address. Some partners who need funds will want to have all available cash distributed. Others, who have a longer term interest in the business may prefer to play it safe and leave more funds in the business for an emergency, to fund future repairs, and so on. Every operating agreement must include some mechanism that establishes rules for making distributions. If the LLC has two or three active members, you may simply hash it out at year-end. Where there are many passive members who are not involved in management, the decision may be assigned to the manager. In-between situations are tougher to call, but it is important to negotiate something workable to avoid fights later.

CAUTION: When the LLC is taxed as a partnership, every member will have to report his share of income on his tax return regardless of the income distributed. For example, assume you are a 10 percent member and the LLC earns $58,000 for the year. Because of anticipated repairs to the roof of the LLC's rental property, no distributions are made. You have what tax experts call *phantom income.* You will have to report your share, or $5,800 [10 percent × $58,000] on your personal tax return and pay tax. Your tax cost could be $2,436 [$5,800 × 42 percent marginal federal and state tax rate]. You are now out of pocket $2,436 and have received no distributions from the LLC. This is why the $5,800 is called phantom income. You have to report it, but did not receive it. Be sure to discuss this issue with other members. If you are a nonvoting member or a voting, but noncontrolling, member, you may want to negotiate a requirement that the manager or other members must distribute not less than say 40 percent of taxable income to the members unless 75 percent or more of the members agree otherwise.

---

b. *Distributions.* The Manager may make distributions to the Members from time to time. Distributions may be made only after the Managers determine in their reasonable judgment, that the Company has sufficient cash on hand which exceeds the current and the anticipated needs of the Company to fulfill its business purposes (including needs for operating expenses, debt service, acquisitions, reserves, and mandatory distributions, if any). All distributions shall be made to the Members in accordance with their Sharing Ratios. Distributions shall be in cash or property or particularly in both, as determined by the Managers. No distribution shall be declared or made if, after giving it effect, the Company would not be able to pay its debts as they become due in the usual course of business or the Company's total assets would be less than the sum of its total liabilities plus the amount that would be needed if the Company were to be dissolved at the time of the distribution, to satisfy the preferential rights of other Members upon dissolution that are superior to the rights of the Members receiving the distribution.

c. *Family Partnership Savings Provision.* Notwithstanding anything in this Operating Agreement to the contrary, should any provision of this Operating Agreement, or any act of the parties, result in a violation of the family partnership provisions of Code Section 704(e) or the regulations and cases thereunder, the Managers may amend this Agreement, or take any other actions reasonably necessary to prevent such violation, or to correct such violation.

5. *DISPOSITION OF MEMBERSHIP INTERESTS.*

NOTE: The following provision is quite tough and may make it impossible for an unhappy member to sell his interest. These provisions are a balancing act: You want any member who is very unhappy, or with whom the other members are unhappy, to be able to leave. On the other hand, you don't want to make it so easy for any member to dispose of his membership interest that an outsider can get involved. Where you and a limited number of close friends or business associates own the LLC, you would not wish an outsider to own shares. Many approaches can address this. A right of first refusal, for example, gives the LLC or other members the right to purchase any membership interests that any member wants to sell. Only if the LLC and other members turn down the opportunity, can the selling member sell his interests to a third party. An advantage of this method is that an independent sale to a third party sets the price, not a battle of who has greater clout in the LLC. This method has its own problems, however. A right of first refusal for a noncontrolling interest in an LLC is often difficult, if not impossible, to sell.

---

a. *General.* Every sale, assignment, transfer, exchange, mortgage, pledge, grant, hypothecation, or other disposition of any Membership Interest shall be made only upon compliance with this Article. No membership interest shall be disposed of if the disposition would cause a termination of the Company under the Code Section 708, as amended; without compliance with any and all state and federal securities laws and regulations; and unless the assignee of the membership interests provides the Company with the information and agreements that the Manager may require in connection with such disposition, including but not limited to an executed counterpart of this Agreement. No Member shall be entitled to assign, convey, sell, encumber, or in any way alienate all or any part of its Membership Interest in the Company and as a Member except with the prior written consent of a majority of all other Members, which consent may be given or withheld, conditioned or delayed (as allowed by this Agreement or the Act), as the remaining Members may determine in their sole discretion. Transfers in violation of this provision shall only be effective to the extent of an assignment of such interest with only the rights set forth in the following provision "Permitted Dispositions."

b. *Permitted Dispositions.* Subject to the provisions of this Article, a Member may assign such Member's Membership Interest in the Company in whole or in part. The assignment of a Membership Interest does not itself entitle the assignee to participate in the management and affairs of the Company or to become a Member. Such assignee is only entitled to receive, to the extent assigned, the distributions the assigning Member would otherwise be entitled to, and such assignee shall only become an assignee of a Membership Interest and not a substituted Member.

NOTE: An *assignee* of an LLC interest is entitled to only the income and distributions of that membership interest. He is not entitled to the other rights of being a member unless he becomes a "substitute Member." Requiring unanimous consent makes this an important restriction on who can become a member and have the rights of a member. Also, this restriction is an important issue in asset protection planning since it can prevent a creditor from obtaining full rights of your interest in an LLC to satisfy a lawsuit.

---

c. *Admission of Substitute Members.* An assignee of a membership interest shall be admitted as a substitute Member and shall be entitled to all the rights and powers of the assignor only if the other Members unanimously consent. If admitted, the substitute Member has, to the extent assigned, all of the rights and powers, and is subject to all of the restrictions and liabilities of a Member.

6. *MEETINGS OF MEMBERS.*

NOTE: Every operating agreement must address voting and control issues. In more complex business or investment transactions, you may have a series of different requirements as to what each member can vote on, different percentages of membership interests required to pass various matters, and so forth. The key point is to identify the major concerns of the members, the most important issues that are likely to affect a particular LLC, and the mechanisms that can be used to protect the LLC and members as a whole. For example, a vote that exceeds 80 percent may be required to sell an LLC's only rental property, whereas just a 51 percent vote of membership interests may be necessary to approve a lease to a tenant in one of the apartments in the LLC's building.

---

a. *Voting.* Except to the extent provided to the contrary in this Agreement, all Members shall be entitled to vote on any matter submitted to a vote of the Members. Notwithstanding the foregoing, the Members shall have the right to vote on all of the following: (a) the dissolution of the Company pursuant to the provisions of this Operating Agreement that permit a dissolution of the Company upon the unanimous consent of all Members; (b) the merger of the Company; (c) a transaction involving an actual or potential conflict of interest between a Manager and the Company; (d) an amendment to the Articles; or (e) the sale, exchange, lease, or other transfer of all or substantially all of the assets of the Company other than in the ordinary course of business.

b. *Required Vote.* Unless a greater vote is required by the Act or the Articles, the affirmative vote or consent of a majority of the Sharing Ratios of all the Members entitled to vote or consent on such matter shall be required.

c. *Meetings.* An annual meeting of Members for the transaction of such business as may properly come before the Meeting, shall be held at such place, on such date and at such time as the Managers shall determine. Special meetings of Members for any proper purpose or purposes may be called at any time by the Managers or the holders of at least Ten (10%) percent of the Sharing Ratios of all Members. The Company shall deliver or mail written notice stating the date, time, place, and purposes of any meeting to each Member entitled to vote at the meeting. Such notice shall be given not less than Ten (10) and not more than Sixty (60) days before the date of the meeting. All meetings of Members shall be presided over by a Chairperson who shall be a Manager. A Member may participate and vote at such meeting via telephone conference call.

d. *Consent.* Any action required or permitted to be taken at an annual or special meeting of the Members may be taken without a meeting, without prior notice, and without a vote, if consents in writing, setting forth the action so taken, are signed by the Members having not less than the minimum number of votes that would be necessary to authorize or take such action at a meeting at which all Membership Interests entitled to vote on the action were present and voted. Every written consent shall bear the date and signature of each Member who signs the consent. Prompt notice of the taking of action without a meeting by less than unanimous written consent shall be given to all Members who have not consented in writing to such action.

7. *MANAGEMENT.*

a. *Management of Business.* The Company shall be managed by MANAGER-1 NAME ("Manager"), so long as she is able and willing to serve. If MANAGER-1 NAME shall ever resign, or be unable or unwilling to serve as Manager, then MANAGER-2 NAME, who resides at FANCY STREET, BIG CITY, Some-State, shall serve as the successor. If MANAGER-2 NAME is unable or unwilling to so serve, then MANAGER-3 NAME, who resides at 123 Main Street, Anytown, Some-State, shall serve as Manager. If he is unable or unwilling, then he shall designate a successor Manager by giving written notice to the Members. The terms, duties, compensation, and benefits, if any, of the Managers shall be as follows: shall receive compensation for serving as Manager as follows: DESCRIBE COMPENSATION. The duties of the Manager shall be those duties reasonably necessary to conduct the Business of the Company, and shall include, but not be limited to: DESCRIBE DUTIES.

b. *Removal of Manager.* Any Manager may be removed at any time, with or without cause, by the affirmative vote of Seventy Five (75%) Percent of the Membership Interests in the Company then entitled to vote.

c. *General Powers of Managers.* Except as may otherwise be provided in this Operating Agreement, the ordinary and usual decisions concerning the business and affairs of the Company shall be made by the Manager. The Manager has the power, on behalf of the Company, to do all things necessary or convenient to carry out the business and affairs of the Company, including the power to: (a) purchase, lease, or otherwise acquire any real or personal property; (b) sell, convey, mortgage, grant a security interest in, pledge, lease, exchange or otherwise dispose or encumber any real or personal property; (c) open one or more depository accounts and make deposits into and checks and withdrawals against such accounts; (d) borrow money, incur liabilities, and other obligations; (e) enter into any and all agreements and execute any and all contracts, documents, and instruments relating to the Business; (f) engage consultants and agents, define their respective duties and establish their compensation or remuneration; (g) obtain insurance covering the Business and affairs of the Company and its property; (h) commence, prosecute, or defend any proceeding in the Company's name; and (i) participate with others in partnerships, joint ventures and other associations and strategic alliances only where same are directly in pursuit of the Business, as defined above.

As an express limitation on the nature of the Business and the powers granted the Manager herein the Company is intended to hold real estate for investment purposes only, and no activities inconsistent with such limited purposes shall be undertaken.

d. *Limitations.* Notwithstanding the foregoing and any other provision contained in this Operating Agreement to the contrary, no act shall be taken, sum expended, decision made, obligation incurred, or power exercised by any Manager on behalf of the Company except by the consent of Seventy Five (75%) Percent of all Membership Interests with respect to (a) any significant and material purchase, receipt, lease, exchange, or other acquisition of any real or personal property or business; (b) the sale of all or substantially all of the assets and property of the Company; (c) any mortgage, grant of security interest, pledge, or encumbrance upon all or substantially all of the assets and property of the Company; (d) any merger; (e) any amendment or restatement of these Articles of this Operating Agreement; (f) any matter which could result in a change in the amount or character of the Company's capital; (g) any change in the character of the business and affairs of the Company; (h) the commission of any act which would make it impossible for the Company to carry on its ordinary business and affairs; or (i) any act that would contravene any provision of the Articles of this Operating Agreement or the Act.

e. *Standard of Care; Liability.* Every Manager shall discharge his or her duties as a manager in good faith, with the care an ordinarily prudent person in a like position would exercise under similar circumstances, and in a manner he or she reasonably believes to be in the best interests of the Company. A Manager shall not be liable for any monetary damages to the Company for any breach of such duties except for receipt of a financial benefit to which the Manager is not entitled; voting for or assenting to a distribution to Members in violation of this Operating Agreement or the Act; or a knowing violation of the law.

8. *EXCULPATION OF LIABILITY: INDEMNIFICATION.*

NOTE: Consider whether, and to what extent, a manager or member performing management functions, should be held harmless (indemnified) from lawsuits or claims. The compensation and relationship (e.g., brother) of the persons performing management functions will be important considerations.

---

a. *Exculpation of Liability.* Unless otherwise provided by law or expressly assumed, a person who is a Member or Manager, or both, shall not be liable for the acts, debts, or liabilities of the Company.

b. *Indemnification.* Except as otherwise provided in this Article, the Company shall indemnify any Manager and may indemnify any employee or agent of the Company who was or is a party or is threatened to be made a party to a threatened, pending, or completed action, suit, or proceeding, whether civil, criminal, administrative, or investigative, and whether formal or informal, other than an action by or in the right of the Company, by reason of the fact that such person is or was a Manager, employee, or agent of the Company against expenses, including attorneys' fees, judgments, penalties, fines, and amounts paid in settlement actually and reasonably incurred by such person in connection with the action, suit, or proceeding, if the person acted in good faith, with the care an ordinarily prudent person in a like position would exercise under similar circumstances, and in a manner that such person reasonably believed to be in the best interests of the Company and with respect to a criminal action or proceeding, if such person had no reasonable cause to believe such person's conduct was unlawful. To the extent that a Member, employee, or agent of the Company has been successful on the merits or otherwise in defense of an action, suit, or proceeding or in defense of any claim, issue, or other matter in the action, suit, or proceeding, such person shall be indemnified against actual and reasonable expenses, including attorneys' fees, incurred by such person in connection with the action, suit, or proceeding and any action, suit, or proceeding brought to enforce the mandatory indemnification provided herein. Any indemnification permitted under this Article, unless ordered by a court, shall be made by the Company only as authorized in the specific case upon a determination that the indemnification is proper under the circumstances because the person to be indemnified has met the applicable standard of conduct and upon an evaluation of the reasonableness of expenses and amounts paid in settlement. This determination and evaluation shall be made by a majority vote of the Members who are not parties or threatened to be made parties to the action, suit, or proceeding. Notwithstanding the foregoing to the contrary, no indemnification shall be provided to any Manager, employee, or agent of the Company for or in connection with the receipt of a financial benefit to which such person is not entitled, voting for or assenting to a distribution to Members in violation of this Operating Agreement or the Act, or a knowing violation of law.

9. *OTHER ACTIVITIES.* Any Member and the Manager may engage in other business ventures of every nature, including, without limitation by specification, the ownership of another business similar to that operated by the Company. Neither the Company nor any of the other Members shall have any right or interest in any such independent ventures or to the income and profits derived therefrom.

10. *DISSOLUTION AND WINDING UP.*
a. *Dissolution.* The Company shall dissolve and its affairs shall be wound up on the first to occur of the following events: (a) at any time specified in the Articles or this Operating Agreement; (b) upon the happening of any event specified in the Articles or this Operating Agreement; (c) by the unanimous consent of all of the Members, (d) upon the death, withdrawal, expulsion, bankruptcy, or dissolution of a Member in the Company unless within ninety (90) days after the disassociation of membership, a majority of the remaining Members consent to continue the business of the Company and to the admission of one or more Members as necessary.

b. *Winding Up.* Upon dissolution, the Company shall cease carrying on its business and affairs and shall commence the winding up of the Company's business and affairs and complete the winding up as soon as practicable. Upon the winding up of the Company, the assets of the Company shall be distributed first to creditors to the extent permitted by law, in satisfaction of Company debts, liabilities, and obligations and then to Members and former Members first, in satisfaction of liabilities for distributions and then, in accordance with their Sharing Ratios. Such proceeds shall be paid to such Members within One Hundred Twenty (120) days after the date of winding up.

11. *MISCELLANEOUS PROVISIONS.*

a. *Terms.* Nouns and pronouns will be deemed to refer to the masculine, feminine, neuter, singular, and plural, as the identity of the person or persons, firm, or corporation may in the context require. The term "Code" shall refer to the Internal Revenue Code of 1986, as amended.

b. *Article Headings.* The Article headings and numbers contained in this Operating Agreement have been inserted only as a matter of convenience and for reference, and in no way shall be construed to define, limit, or describe the scope or intent of any provision of this Operating Agreement.

c. *Counterparts.* This Operating Agreement may be executed in several counterparts, each of which will be deemed an original but all of which will constitute one and the same.

d. *Entire Agreement.* This Operating Agreement constitutes the entire agreement among the parties hereto and contains all of the agreements among said parties with respect to the subject matter hereof. This Operating Agreement supersedes any and all other agreements, either oral or written, between said parties with respect to the subject matter hereof.

e. *Severability.* The invalidity or unenforceability of any particular provision of this Operating Agreement shall not affect the other provisions hereof, and this Operating Agreement shall be construed in all respects as if such invalid or unenforceable provisions were omitted.

f. *Amendment.* This Operating Agreement may be amended or revoked at any time by a written agreement executed by all of the parties to this Operating Agreement, except where a lesser percentage of Membership Interests is permitted elsewhere in this Operating Agreement. No change or modification to this Operating Agreement shall be valid unless in writing and signed by all of the parties to this Operating Agreement.

g. *Notices.* Any notice permitted or required under this Operating Agreement shall be conveyed to the party at the address reflected in this Operating Agreement and will be deemed to have been given, when deposited in the United States mail, postage paid, or when delivered in person, or by a national overnight courier or by facsimile transmission (the receipt of which is confirmed).

h. *Binding Effect.* Subject to the provisions of this Operating Agreement relating to transferability, this Operating Agreement will be binding upon and shall inure to the benefit of the parties, and their respective distributees, **heirs,** successors, and assigns.

i. *Governing Law.* This Operating Agreement is being executed and delivered in the State of STATENAME and shall be governed by, construed, and enforced in accordance with the laws of the State of Some-State.

IN WITNESS WHEREOF, the parties hereto make and execute this Operating Agreement on the dates set below their names, to be effective on the date first above written.

WITNESSETH:

LLCNAME, LLC

By: _____
    MANAGER-1NAME, Manager

MEMBERS:

_____

MEMBER-1NAME, Member

_____

MEMBER-2NAME, Member

John Doe Investment Trust

By: _____
     Thomas Trustworthy Trustee

_____

MEMBER-3NAME, Member

Exhibit A
Member Listing; Capital Contributions

Member Name and Address	Member Social Security Number	Capital Contribution	Percentage Interest
Total			

Date: _____ ____ , 2006

7 OPERATING AND MAINTAINING YOUR LIMITED LIABILITY COMPANY

In prior chapters, you have made the decision that an LLC is the right choice for your business or investment situation. Then you have formed your LLC and put in place the most important legal document, your Operating Agreement. Finally, you have transferred cash and other assets to the LLC so it can begin operations. Now you must operate your LLC. This may require the contribution by members of additional assets. You also may need to set up bank accounts, purchase assets, hire consultants and/or employees, conduct business, and so on.

Like any other form of business entity (i.e., corporations and partnerships), LLCs must be professionally and efficiently managed and operated to be productive, generate profits, provide liability protection, and achieve your other goals. Much of the success of an LLC depends on the individuals who manage the LLC and such individuals' rights and obligations in their management capacity. It is essential to retain qualified legal, tax, accounting, and business advisers, and methodically implement their advice. An important factor in maintaining smooth, professional operations and maintaining limited liability is having the necessary legal documents in place. This chapter provides an overview of many of these important points. The "For Your Notebook" section at the end of this chapter provides several sample forms that may be helpful in operating your LLC.

CAUTION: Because every business is unique and each business transaction has its own nuances, every LLC needs different legal documents. The "For Your Notebook" section includes samples of some of the more commonly used documents. This does not mean that these are the only documents your LLC will need, or that their format is appropriate for the circumstances your LLC faces. The first step in making that determination is defining the goals and objectives of your LLC and deciding precisely how those goals should be achieved. This will give your advisers the framework they need to help you implement the appropriate documents.

MANAGING AN LLC

Members Generally Manage the LLC

In most states, the law is that the members of an LLC handle its management unless they take specific steps to have specified persons, called managers, run the LLC. No state LLC statutes, however, require that the members themselves manage the LLC. In a few states, the LLC is to be managed by managers if the members do not provide for a different management structure. Depending on which state the LLC is formed in, the LLC's Articles of Organization or operating agreement must provide that management is to be vested in managers to change the default rule of member management to manager management. If management is to be vested in managers instead of in members, it may be advisable to set forth the management structure in the Articles of Organization instead of the operating agreement. This is because the Articles of Organization is a public document that third parties can find simply by looking in the public records. Many of the standard forms for setting up an LLC do not address this refinement. Accordingly, if the management structure is set forth in the operating agreement, other people (third parties—other than members and managers) may not have easy access to such structure. This can complicate relations with third parties, who may wrongly believe that the LLC is managed by its members instead of by managers.

Member Votes on Management and Other Issues

Unless the operating agreement provides otherwise, most member-managed LLCs vote on the basis of one vote per member, and require a majority vote for most actions. Some state laws provide instead for voting by members in proportion to their contributions or in proportion to the members' shares in profits. Under most LLC laws, when a majority vote is required to approve a decision, it means a majority of all voting members, not only the members present at any specific meeting.

Certain decisions are considered so important that the state rules may require unanimous consent of all members (unless the operating agreement modifies this rule). These critical decisions include: (1) admission of new members, (2) continuation of the LLC's business after a member disassociates, (3) amending the Articles of Organization, and (4) amending the operating agreement.

In every LLC, the operating agreement should specifically address the decision-making criteria for the members. It should address the voting criteria for any particular decision, which persons or members should have management control, what types of issues should be within the purview of a manager, and which decisions should require the input or approval of some portion of the members.

Manager(s) May Be Designated to Manage the LLC

Instead of the members managing the LLC, they can designate one or more persons to serve as managers. In some states, the law—if your operating agreement does not provide otherwise (a default rule)—is that management of the LLC is to be by managers. There are no requirements relating to the number of managers that an LLC must maintain. Some states require that a manager must be a natural person (e.g., not a corporation), whereas other states do not have such a requirement. In fact, some states expressly state that the manager does not have to be a natural person. This is a distinct difference from the law of corporations, where a member of the board of directors cannot be an organization.

No LLC state statute requires that managers be members. Some states expressly permit nonmember managers and other states are silent on this issue. Moreover, it is not necessary for a manager of an LLC to be a resident of the state in which the LLC is formed.

An LLC's managers can be of the same class or group, or there can be different classes or groups of managers. Being able to create different classes of managers enables the LLC to designate authority for different types of actions among different managers.

TIP: Do not make the management structure more complex than the economics of the LLC business and the needs of the deal warrant. If the LLC owns a single residential rental property with four units, having tiers of managers for different structures not only is unnecessary, but is unworkable. Even if the property is valuable, the situation should not require a complex management structure. If, however, the four units are large commercial units in a multimillion-dollar warehouse, a more elaborate arrangement may be warranted. Not only does the economic value of this latter example justify a somewhat stronger structure, but also the decisions are likely to be more complex. But in all situations, no matter how complex or large in dollar terms, always go with the simplest approach that works. Do not complicate any deal unless the complication serves an important purpose that cannot be accomplished in an easier manner.

In some states, the Articles of Organization must provide the names of the initial managers, whereas other states omit this requirement. The general default rule for selection of managers is that the election of managers requires a majority vote of the members of the LLC. Either the Articles of Organization or the operating agreement can modify this requirement. The operating agreement should include specific guidelines for how long a manager can serve in that office. Most state LLC statutes provide default rules in this context, but the default rules may not necessarily represent exactly what the members want to have happen.

Some state statutes provide default rules for the removal of managers (with or without cause, and others do not provide such rules). If an LLC is organized in a state whose LLC statute does not contain any rules relating to the removal of a manager, the Articles of Organization should enumerate such rules. Otherwise, it may be virtually impossible to remove a manager who is also a member because unanimous consent of the members may be required in such a situation.

The resignation of a manager, whether a member or a non-member, will not cause a termination of the LLC. Instead, each particular state's statute must be examined to determine the rules for filling a managerial vacancy. An LLC's operating agreement should contain specific rules stating how to fill the vacancy when a manager retires, dies, or is terminated. The failure to include these provisions could cause the LLC to have a temporary period with no manager, or a managerial deadlock among the remaining managers.

Transactions between a Manager and the LLC

Generally, a manager may lend money to; borrow money from; act as a surety, guarantor, or endorser for; or guarantee or assume one or more obligations of; provide collateral for; and transact other business with the LLC, unless the Articles of Organization, operating agreement, or state statute provide to the contrary.

TIP: In most LLC matters, you will not want the manager borrowing or loaning money, or engaging in any of these other actions unless they are based on fair terms that an unrelated person (e.g., a bank) would charge. This criterion for conducting business is called *an arm's length basis.* Often an operating agreement will require that transactions between the LLC and manager must be approved by a large percentage of the members.

Rights of the Manager

As a member of a manager-managed LLC, you would want the operating agreement to state the manager's responsibilities in considerable detail. If you were serving as the manager of an LLC, you would also want the operating agreement to provide you with certain rights. Managers are generally given the right to demand and receive: (1) true and full information regarding the status of the business and financial condition of the LLC;

(2) a copy of the LLC's federal, state, and local tax returns; (3) a current list of all members and managers; (4) true and complete information regarding the amount of the LLC's cash; (5) a description of the agreed value of any property or services contributed by each member; and (6) any other matter as long as such disclosures reasonably relate to the person's position as manager.

In some states, the manager may even be given the right to withhold confidential information (e.g., trade secrets) from the members if he reasonably believes in good faith that disclosure is not in the LLC's best interest. Although this provision may be helpful in many instances, it may not be appropriate where the members are all actively involved in the business of the LLC. Therefore, in negotiating and drafting an LLC operating agreement, you may want to specify that the manager must disclose all information.

The manager may have the right to resign as a consequence of events specified in the operating agreement. Or the agreement may provide that the manager does not have the right to resign. Such a clause will not prevent the manager from resigning, but its presence will provide the LLC with a cause of action for damages.

Obligation and Liability of a Manager

An operating agreement can penalize a manager who does not perform the duties required by state law, the Articles of Organization, or the operating agreement. Some state laws permit a member to bring a derivative action against a manager or other members. This is a lawsuit for harm that the manager or members have done to the LLC or the LLC's business or assets.

NOTE: Although these types of rights and protective rules may sound appealing, keep in mind that if the operating agreement or Articles of Organization are too unfair or restrictive, no one will be willing to serve as manager. Even if you have a manager, it may be difficult to find a replacement should one be needed.

Other Managerial Rights

Unless provided otherwise in the articles or operating agreement, management may appoint committees and people to serve on them. Each committee may exercise the authority designated by the management. Management does not need to have meetings unless required by a particular state's LLC act, the Articles of Organization, or operating agreement. Most states do not require the managers or members to have meetings. In closely held

LLCs, a meeting should be held regularly or at least periodic written consents of all members (a formal memorandum) should be signed to demonstrate that they all have agreed to major decisions.

Consent of Members

If the members manage your LLC, they must provide some form of consent, whether majority, unanimous, or otherwise, for the company to take action. In most states, there is no requirement that the members engage in formal meetings to take managerial actions. Some states's statutes do require the written approval of the members for certain acts to be effective. For the same reasons, an operating agreement, and a meeting of the minds of the members relating their management decisions, should also be in writing. Having a written document provides a record of the agreement of the members to eliminate any future arguments about past decisions. The importance of putting agreements of the members in writing is obviously more important for decisions that have a potentially greater impact on the LLC. Some states do in fact require formal meetings of the members. This requirement may be modified through the Articles of Organization and the operating agreement.

TIP: No matter what your state's laws require, it usually is best to have any major decision approved, in writing, by all members and managers in any LLC with a relatively small number of members. The form Unanimous Consent of All Managers and Members illustrated in the "For Your Notebook" section at the end of this chapter can be adapted for approval of almost any type of action. Simply modify the form as needed to address the actions involved, attach complete copies of all relevant documents concerning the actions, and have everyone sign.

Decisions of the Managers

If more than one manager runs your LLC, you must understand your state's default rules for a vote of the managers to take managerial action. Unless there is a provision in the operating agreement to the contrary, managers may be required to act with a majority vote. In a manager-run LLC, unless the operating agreement provides otherwise, a member who is not a manager does not have the right on his own to bind the LLC to any contracts or other decisions with a third party. In many LLCs, the operating agreement states in detail the matters that managers can control and those that members control.

Contractual Relationship

The operating agreement is a contract between the managers, the members, and the LLC. State laws and court decisions establish standards for the duties of LLC managers. The operating agreement may expand or limit these duties and obligations. The operating agreement should specify the important points of the manager's relationship with the LLC and with the members. This is important to assure that both the manager and the members will have similar expectations concerning the duties to be performed.

TIP: Many people do not like long legal documents, including long operating agreements, or dismiss them as a way lawyers try to make more money. However, writing down the details about how the LLC is to operate and how decisions are to be made can focus the managers and members on matters they may not have otherwise considered. Working through these items to find a reasonable resolution of conflicting opinions early on when everyone gets along and wants the deal to work can be very productive. Thus, it is the creating of the operating agreement, not just the final paperwork, that is important. For this process to be productive, all of the people involved, including the attorneys, must realize that everyone is working toward the common good and toward the benefit of all. Antagonism is neither necessary nor appropriate.

OPERATING AN LLC

LLC Periodic Reporting and Record Keeping

Managers, or members if they are responsible for management of the LLC, must document and record information about their LLC to protect the LLC and their interests. Proper records will prevent ambiguity over management decisions. LLCs may also be subject to certain record-keeping requirements depending on each state's laws. Some states require LLCs to maintain books and provide an accounting to members; other states have more informal information requirements. Most states require that an informational report must be filed with the secretary of state at least annually.

A typical state LLC law requires the LLC to keep at its registered office or principal place of business the following information for its members and managers:

- A current list of members
- A copy of the filed Articles of Organization and any amendments
- Copies of tax returns and financial statements for the past three years

- A list of events of dissolution and other specific information depending on each state

An LLC also should maintain minutes from meetings of its members and/or managers, written documentation of actions taken without meetings, and a record of its members and their respective contributions. Failure to keep such records may create a problem when a crisis arises, and may result in penalties being charged to the LLC.

Tax Filing Requirements

An LLC will have to consider three categories of income tax filings. The decision will depend on how you have structured your LLC:

1. *Partnership tax returns.* Since almost all LLCs that have two or more members are characterized as partnerships for income tax purposes, most LLCs must file annual tax returns, IRS Form 1065. This form reports the income or loss earned by the partnership for any particular tax year. Then each member in the LLC (members are treated as partners for tax purposes) will have his share of income or loss reported on a Form K-1. The LLC will give this form to each member, who will use it in the preparation of his own tax return. The LLC must also comply with any federal and state reporting or filing requirements established for partnerships.

PLANNING TIP: Even if you want to do your own tax return, where the LLC has several members, it can be advantageous to have a professional accountant prepare the return. Not only will this assure that these important matters are handled correctly, but an accountant can often be an excellent source of ongoing business advice and can serve as a mediator or go-between if problems arise. For the accountant to be effective, a history with you, the LLC, and the business of the LLC can be extremely important. It is much harder for an accountant to help resolve problems if he is called in after problems have occurred and he has limited or no prior experience with the business. Where an accountant is engaged throughout, it avoids many problems, and when they do occur, the accountant will have the knowledge of the business, and the trust of the members, to best address them.

---

2. *Single-member LLC.* Many LLCs, such as those formed for a simple home-based business, are structured with one owner. For federal income tax purpose, these LLCs are ignored. If you have a business, you will report the income or loss from the business on your personal tax return, Form 1040, Schedule C. If your single-member LLC owns a rental property, that income or loss will be reported on Schedule E. An

advantage of having only one member own your LLC is that you avoid the extra cost and hassle of an annual partnership income tax return.

3. *All others.* Under the check-the-box regulations, explained earlier in this book, an LLC may effectively choose how it will be taxed. Few LLCs with two or more members choose to be taxed as anything other than partnerships. But should an LLC choose to be taxed as a corporation, for example, then the LLC would file the appropriate corporate returns.

Ancillary Legal Documents

Every LLC should be treated as a distinct legal entity, independent from its owners. Any legal documentation that would ordinarily be required of any business entity is required for an LLC. Failure to adhere to the formalities could jeopardize the tax or legal status (e.g., protection of non-LLC personal assets). The formalities include maintaining separate bank accounts, insurance coverage, and other common business steps. Legal documentation is also critical to the formalities and could include employment agreements, buy/sell agreements, license and other agreements, and minutes of meetings. The legal documentation you will need to operate your LLC will vary depending on the nature of that LLC's business.

PLANNING TIP: For sample legal documents, see the Web site: www .laweasy.com.

Once you have signed a necessary legal document, do not let it gather dust. Periodically, review it with your business attorney to assure that it remains current and relevant in light of any changes in the law, ownership, or nature of the business or investments involved with the LLC. The "For Your Notebook" section at the end of this chapter includes common forms that may be useful for you during the operational stage of your LLC.

AMENDING ARTICLES OF ORGANIZATION AND THE OPERATING AGREEMENT

Keep Your Documents Current

Once you have filed the documents with the state and other governmental agencies to form your LLC, and completed a detailed operating agreement governing the relationship between all the members and perhaps managers of your LLC, don't file them away in a time capsule. You must update these documents to reflect changes in circumstances, laws, tax rules, and so on. Failure to do so will eventually undermine your efforts to handle everything properly when first implementing these steps.

When and Why You Must Update Your Certificate

Businesses change. Your legal documents must keep pace. Many events may make it advisable, or even mandatory, to amend the articles or certificate that you filed with your state to form your LLC. Be careful: The rules vary considerably from state to state. Many states require amendments on the occurrence of any of the following four events:

1. *Any event that terminates or changes the membership of a member.* Your friend quit the LLC. You may have to amend the certificate. Even if the articles or certificate does not have to be amended, the operating agreement will absolutely have to be changed. In fact, the changes should be negotiated with your friend as part of terminating his membership.

2. *A change in the LLC name or purpose.* It is not uncommon to start a business under a name and then realize that it is too cumbersome for sales materials or marketing; or perhaps as the business evolves, another name becomes preferable. Several points should be considered. First, changing the name of your LLC might not be necessary. Instead, you could simply obtain for your LLC the right to operate under the additional name. This is discussed later in this chapter. Second, never assume that a mere filing of any certificate grants you the legal right to use that name, or is sufficient to protect it. You should always consult with an intellectual property (IP) attorney to assure that you have addressed all issues of trade name, trademark, copyright, and so on.

NOTE: In most cases, your Certificate of Formation will simply state that your LLC can do anything permitted by law. This is so general that you will never have to amend the certificate if the nature of the LLC's business changes. However, this is not necessarily the best approach. If you specify a more restrictive business purpose, you will limit the scope of what your partners (i.e., the other members or even the managers) can do. This can protect you by preventing them from expanding the scope of the business beyond the original agreement. For example, you may state in the Certificate of Formation that the purpose of the LLC is "To invest in residential rental properties of one to four family units, in XYZ county, only." Now everyone knows the limits.

---

3. *A change in the registered agent or office.* This is the person and place where notifications of a lawsuit against the LLC or other official matters are to be sent. In many cases, you may be able to accomplish this change for a modest fee (in some states $10.00) as part of an annual report you must file each year with your state. In other cases, you may need to retain an attorney to prepare the appropriate legal form to send to (file with) your state.

4. *When the Articles of Organization are discovered to be inaccurate.* This could be because of a mistake or omission, or a change in the facts and circumstances of your LLC. Some states have different forms and procedures for each of these situations.

In most states, a unanimous decision of the members is required to amend the Articles of Organization. Other states, however, require merely the majority consent of the members to amend them. At least one state allows the managers to amend the articles by a majority vote, yet other states require approval of amendments by both the management group and the members. Still other states are silent on the issue of the consent required to adopt an amendment. In those states, it may be proper to apply the unanimity standard to ensure that the amendment will be valid. If your operating agreement provides for requirements that have to be met before changing the articles or certificate, you must address them as well as the requirements of state law.

If one of the preceding events occurs and the articles must be amended, failure to make the amendment can have drastic consequences for the LLC. Under some state laws, the failure to amend when required may result in the involuntary dissolution of the LLC. In other states, the failure may lead to damage claims by individuals who are misled by false statements in the articles.

The filing fee for most amendments is usually minimal.

After Filing for Your LLC, What Additional Documents Are You Likely to File with the State?

There are a host of documents that you might file with your state to keep your LLC's legal documents up to date. The previous discussion told you why, the discussion following will summarize common filings. Remember, state law differs and each state will have its own unique forms. State laws will outline the procedures and contents of the forms, and filing fees will vary. Thus, the following discussion focuses on general concepts.

CAUTION: You can probably go to a Web site for your state, find a form, and prepare and file online—all without a lawyer. Well almost. It can be cheaper and quicker to file online. In fact, if you do not have a competent lawyer, the results of doing it on your own may be just as good. However, the savings rarely warrant foregoing the advice of an experienced business attorney who might identify significant problems that the change implies in areas such as taxes and planning ideas. Filling out the form should be the end result of a plan, not the sole action.

Certificate of Amendments/Correction

The filing of the form of Articles of Organization required by your state (names differ) creates your LLC as a legal entity. The articles must be amended when the information they contain is no longer correct. The information required in a certificate of amendment or correction varies from state to state, but usually include the name of the LLC, the date of filing of the original certificate or articles, and the amendment that is being made—what you are changing.

The amendment or correction can be made to be effective on filing the document, or on a later date not more than a specified number of days (i.e., 30 days) following the date of filing, which is similar to the effective date rules for the creation of the LLC. In some states, the **Certificate of Amendment** is used to update a matter that has changed from what was originally filed, while a Certificate of Correction is used when the information originally filed was incorrect.

Certificate of Ownership

Generally, it is not necessary to file evidence of ownership with your state to confirm who are the members of your LLC. A Certificate of Ownership, however, may be filed in some states if restrictions on interests or classes of members are desired.

EXAMPLE: You form an LLC to operate a widget manufacturing company (widgets are the mythical product accountants and attorneys have their mythical companies build and sell in examples). You have three active partners and six passive investors who, while contributing money, are not to participate in management decisions. You might wish to structure the investors' membership interests as nonvoting, to assure their noninterference. Further, you might file a certificate to state that their class of membership cannot vote so it is a matter of record.

Many states permit this certificate to be filed for an LLC, and some states refer to this certificate as a "Certificate of Membership." This certificate will typically include the name of the LLC and the state of organization; the percentage of ownership in the LLC that the certificate represents; the name of the individual or entity to whom or which the certificate is issued; any transfer restrictions imposed on such interest; and specific acts of termination of the ownership interests.

When used, people authorized by the LLC must sign the certificate of ownership. Restrictions of the certificate are to be placed conspicuously on the front or back of the certificate. Examples of restrictions, other than voting illustrated earlier, include the enforcement of **buy-sell agreements,** preservation of exemptions under federal and state securities laws, and a prohibition on the transfer of interests to designated parties.

Certificate of Foreign LLC Registration

Operation across state borders is common, but also brings with it a bevy of legal requirements. Before an LLC may conduct business in a state other than the state in which it was formed, it must register with the appropriate state authority by paying a fee (now that's a surprise!) and sending in a legal form (filing an application). Many state statutes provide comprehensive provisions governing the operation of a foreign LLC. In this context, foreign means an LLC formed in one state, operating in another, not an LLC from a different country. If an LLC transacts business in a foreign state without registering, it could be subject to penalties and/or fines.

EXAMPLE: ABC Shoes Limited Liability Company is formed in Idaho. ABC wants to do business in Kansas (something about ruby slippers with heels). Prior to engaging in business in Kansas, ABC should file an application to do business in that state.

Certificate of Alternate/Fictitious Name

Businesses commonly develop multiple product or trade names. Sometimes a name becomes so popular that the business begins to identify with the name and conducts business under that name. Such additional names (i.e., names other than the name under which an LLC is formed) are referred to as *alternate* or *fictitious* names. Your LLC may register and use them by filing a document known in some states as a *Certificate of Registration of an Alternate Name* with the appropriate state authority. It must include the following information: the name, jurisdiction, and date of establishment of the LLC; the alternate name to be used; a brief statement of the character or nature of the particular activities to be conducted using the alternate name; a statement that the LLC intends to use the alternate name in that state; a statement that the LLC has not previously used the alternate name.

If the LLC has used the alternate name previously, the certificate usually must state when it commenced using the name. A fee for the period in which the alternate name was improperly used may be required.

In some states, the **Certificate of Alternate Name** is effective for a period of five years and may be renewed at any time within 90 days prior to the expiration of the five-year period. The LLC may be subject to penalties if it files false information in this certificate.

CAUTION: Do not assume that the corporate attorney filing your certificate has the intellectual property law background to advise you about all the legal issues of using and protecting a name. Further, do not assume that your attorney calendars the five-year (or other) renewal deadline for filing. Protect yourself and monitor those deadlines. Consider asking your accountant to calendar it along with other tax filings.

Certificate of Name Reservation

When planning to set up a business and before forming it, it is a good idea to assure that the name you choose is available. This is important as many people try to coordinate the business name, Web site domain name, and even telephone number. While planning and coordinating, you may want to "hold" a name or two. You can reserve the exclusive use of a name for an LLC by filing a *Certificate of Name Reservation*. Any person intending to organize an LLC may file such a certificate. You can also use it to change the name of an existing LLC by filing an application with the appropriate state authority that specifies the name to be reserved, as well as the name and address of the person applying for the reservation. States vary in the amount of time they will reserve a name and the number of renewals they will permit. The right to use a particular name can be transferred to another person by filing a certificate of transfer. Obviously, only available names can be reserved.

Certificate of Merger or Consolidation

If an LLC is to merge or consolidate with another entity, a **Certificate of Merger or Consolidation** should be filed. Generally, the certificate is filed by the surviving entity of the transaction. It must provide the name and jurisdiction of formation or organization of each LLC or other business entity; a statement that an agreement of merger or consolidation has been approved and executed by each LLC or other business entity that is to merge or consolidate; the name of the surviving entity; the future effective date or time certain of the merger or consolidation (if none is specified, it is effective on filing); a statement that the agreement of merger or consolidation is on file at a place of business of the surviving or resulting LLC or other business entity, and the address; a statement that a copy of the agreement will be furnished on request; if the surviving entity is not an LLC in the state of filing, a statement that the surviving entity can be served with process in the state of filing, and the address where it can be served.

PLANNING TIP: Merging or consolidating entities involves myriad legal and tax issues. Always consult a corporate attorney and tax accountant in advance. Be certain no key legal relationships will be undermined (e.g., your lender calls your loans). Also, you will need more legal documents than just the certificate you file with the state. The documents should, at a minimum, include a merger or consolidation agreement that specifies all the details and steps of the transaction, obtains all necessary approvals, and memorializes the reasons for the transaction.

Certificate of Restatement

An LLC may file a certificate restating all previously filed certificates (i.e., Articles of Organization and amendments thereto) into a single certificate. Such a certificate restates and integrates previously filed certificates but does not act to amend the existing certificates on file. If it restates and amends (which in practice is likely to be the most common), the certificate should be labeled: "Amended and Restated Articles of Organization" or "Amended and Restated Certificate of Formation" depending on what your state refers to as its formation document. After your LLC has filed three or more amendments to prior certificates, it becomes difficult to read all the documents. Signing a new certificate that reflects the current status of all prior filings minimizes confusion because anyone reading your LLC's certificate no longer has to go back to the older certificates.

Certificate of Cancellation

A **Certificate of Cancellation** may be filed to cancel the Articles of Organization on the dissolution and completion of the winding up of an LLC. In states where there is a two-member minimum, the Certificate of Cancellation may also be filed where the LLC no longer has at least two members.

PLANNING TIP: If you set up a two-member LLC years ago, before a single-member LLC was permitted, it may be advantageous to convert to a single-member LLC and then file this certificate to avoid annual partnership tax returns. Before converting, however, be sure there are no negative estate planning implications.

Update Your Operating Agreement

The operating agreement is the key document memorializing the relationship between each manager and member and the LLC. If circumstances change, you should amend the operating agreement. Each of the items discussed in Chapter 6 for inclusion in your operating agreement, when outdated, should be reviewed with your corporate attorney to determine whether an amendment is necessary. Minor or administrative changes may be accumulated for a periodic update. More significant changes, such as the admission of a new member, a change in the manager's rights, or anything else your attorney or common sense (they might be different!) tell you, may warrant an immediate change. Preparing an Amended and Restated Operating Agreement, which is similar to the Certificate of Restatement discussed previously, will eliminate having to consult multiple documents to determine the current arrangements.

PLANNING TIP: An Amended and Restated Operating Agreement is cheaper for a lawyer to prepare than a separate amendment. The old document is retrieved on the computer, the change desired is made, the title and date are changed, and presto! Your lawyer pulls a new agreement out of the printer (or hat, depending on whom you have used!).

SUMMARY

For an LLC to be successful, it is essential to manage it efficiently, professionally, and legally. In the vast majority of states, the default rule is that an LLC is managed by its members. It is possible, however, to appoint managers for the task of running the LLC. Managers and members must all comply with the terms of the LLC's Articles of Organization and its operating agreement, as well as good business practices. The simplicity of operating a business as an LLC can lull managers and members alike into forgetting business formalities. This will be to the peril of all. This chapter has highlighted some of the legal steps you must take to keep your LLC operating in the proper manner.

For Your Notebook

UNANIMOUS CONSENT

CAUTION: The documents presented here are merely samples of common documents. Be sure that the documents you use not only are the appropriate types for any given situation, but are properly tailored to meet your needs. These samples will help you reduce legal and other professional fees by helping you think through the information you need to convey to your attorney, financial adviser, and so forth. It is best, however, to retain a professional and not merely adapt a standard form.

LLCNAME
Action Taken by Unanimous Written
Consent of All Managers and Members
To Authorize LLC Leasing Property

The undersigned, being all of the Managers and Members of the LLC, hereby take the following action:

RESOLVED, The LLC adopts and becomes a party to a lease substantially in the form of attached hereto to enable the LLC to obtain the use of certain real property necessary and useful to the operation of the LLC's business.

RESOLVED, The Managers of the LLC are directed and authorized to execute such lease, obtain any insurance necessary or appropriate to protect the LLC's interest in such leased property, and take any additional actions necessary or desirable to facilitate the LLC's using such property.

RESOLVED, The Managers of the LLC are directed and authorized to take all necessary actions to implement the above resolutions.

Executed: SIGNDATE

_____
MEMBER-1NAME, Member and Manager

_____
MEMBER-2NAME, Member

_____
MEMBER-3NAME, Member and Manager

_____
MANAGER-1NAME, Manager

[Attach lease to this page]

For Your Notebook

LOAN ARRANGEMENT

NOTE: In many businesses, especially start-up businesses, cash flow may be inadequate at different times. A common way to deal with this is for investors to loan the business money. The following consent and note are samples of documents that can be used where a member loans the LLC money. Be certain that the terms are reasonably arm's length (i.e., what a noninvolved person would charge for interest, provide for maturity date, and accept as collateral). Also, be sure that the operating agreement does not prohibit the loan itself, or its terms. To avoid problems, all members and managers should consent to this transaction. Also, be sure interest payments are made on a timely basis as required by the note.

LLCNAME
Action Taken by Unanimous Written Consent
of the
Managers and Members
To Authorize Loans to the LLC from a Member

The undersigned, being all of the Managers and Members of the LLC, hereby take the following actions:

RESOLVED, The LLC shall borrow from MEMBER-1NAME, [describe the purpose for the loan] on the terms and conditions set forth in the Promissory Note attached.

RESOLVED, The LLC enter into a loan, and accept and receive the funds, substantially in accordance with the form Note attached.

RESOLVED, The Managers of the LLC are hereby authorized to take any and all actions to effect the above.

Dated: SIGNDATE

_____

MEMBER-1NAME, Member and Manager

_____

MEMBER-2NAME, Member

_____

MEMBER-3NAME, Member and Manager

_____

MANAGER-1NAME, Manager

For Your Notebook

PROMISSORY NOTE

$00,000.00

Location: CITY, STATE

Date: SIGNDATE

FOR VALUE RECEIVED, the Undersigned promises to pay to the order of MEMBER-1NAME, or the holder hereof ("the Payee") at MEMBER-ADDRESS or at such other place as the Payee may designate in writing to the Undersigned, the principal sum of LOANAMOUNT Thousand Dollars ($0.00) in lawful money of the United States of America.

This Note shall be repaid in full upon the maturity hereof, on MATURITY DATE. Repayment shall include all then unpaid principal and any accrued but unpaid interest on this Note.

Interest shall accrue on this Note at the rate of RATE percent (00%) per annum. Interest shall be due and payable within Thirty (30) days of each anniversary date of this Note.

The Undersigned shall, at any time, have the right to prepay, without penalty or premium, all or any portion of the loan evidenced by this Note.

The Payee shall not exercise any right or remedy provided for in this Note because of any default of the Undersigned to pay the sums due hereunder, until after the expiration of a Five (5) days' grace period from the Undersigned's receipt of any demand for payment.

If the Payee shall institute any action to enforce collection of this Note, there shall become due and payable from the Undersigned, in addition to the unpaid principal and interest, all costs and expenses of such action (including reasonable attorneys' fees) and the Payee shall be entitled to judgment for all such additional amounts.

The Undersigned irrevocably consents to the sole and exclusive jurisdiction of the courts of the State of STATENAME and of any federal court located in STATENAME in connection with any action or proceeding arising out of, or related to, this Note. In any such proceeding, the undersigned waives personal service of any summons, complaint, or other process and agrees that service thereof shall be deemed made when mailed by registered or certified mail, return receipt requested to the undersigned. Within Twenty (20) days after such service, the undersigned shall appear or answer the summons, complaint, or other process. If the undersigned shall fail to appear or answer within that Twenty (20) day period, the Undersigned shall be deemed in default and judgment may be entered by the Payee against the Undersigned for the amount demanded in the summons, complaint, or other process.

No delay or failure on the part of the Payee on this Note to exercise any power or right given hereunder shall operate as a waiver thereof, and no right or remedy of the Payee shall be deemed abridged or modified by any course of conduct.

The Undersigned waives presentment, demand for payment, notice of dishonor, and all other notices or demands in connection with the delivery, acceptance, performance, default, or endorsement of this Note.

This Note shall be governed by and construed in accordance with the State of STATE-NAME applicable to agreements made and to be performed in STATENAME.

This Note cannot be changed orally.

UNDERSIGNED:

LLCNAME
LLC-ADDRESS

By: _____
     MANAGER-NAME, Manager

For Your Notebook

EQUIPMENT LEASE

NOTE: The following is a simplified equipment lease that the LLC can use to lease equipment from or to another person. If the LLC intends to lease expensive equipment, such as a car or copy machine, from a major corporation, the larger lessor will insist on using its own lease form. In such instances, the LLC does not need to use the equipment lease following, but it can use one of the consent forms in this chapter as a model for the managers and members to approve the lease.

AGREEMENT made this DAY of MONTH, YEAR, between LESSOR-NAME, doing business at LESSOR-ADDRESS, (the "Lessor"), and LESSEE-NAME, doing business at LESSEE-ADDRESS, (the "Lessee").

1. *Lease agreement.* The Lessor hereby leases to the Lessee the machinery described in Schedule A attached hereto (the "Equipment"), upon the terms and conditions set forth in this agreement.

2. *Term of agreement.* The term of this agreement shall commence as of the date hereof and ends on the last day of the month following the date of this Lease ("Termination").

3. *Rental payments.* The Lessee shall pay, as rental for the use of the Equipment, $_____ per month commencing the first day of the first full month beginning after the date this lease is executed and ending on the Termination, for an aggregate rental of $_____. Said rent is payable without notice on the first day of each month, at the Lessor's address set forth above.

4. *Title to equipment.* Title to the equipment shall remain in the Lessor. The Equipment shall at all times be and remain personal property, however it may be affixed to realty.

5. *Removal, inspection, and return of equipment.* The Equipment shall not be removed from the premises of the Lessee to which originally delivered without the prior written consent of the Lessor. The Lessor shall have the right, upon reasonable prior notice to the Lessee and during the lessee's regular business hours, to inspect the Equipment at the premises of the Lessee or wherever the Equipment may be located. Upon the termination of the lease with respect to the Equipment, the Equipment shall be returned, at the Lessee's expense, to any place reasonably designated by the Lessor.

6. *Maintenance and repair.* The Lessee shall pay all transportation and installation costs with respect to the Equipment. The Lessee shall be responsible for maintaining the Equipment in good mechanical condition and running order at all times during this Agreement, but the Lessor shall be responsible for the costs thereof. In consideration for the Lessor discharging Lessee's maintenance obligation hereunder and as full payment for Lessee's services, or the services of Lessee's employees or agents operating under Lessee's instructions and supervision, for maintaining and repairing the Equipment Lessor shall pay the Lessee $_____ per annum. Such amount shall be payable in equal quarterly installments on the last day of each calendar quarter commencing March 31. All additions, attachments, accessories, and repairs at any time made to or placed upon the Equipment shall become part of the Equipment and shall be the property of the

Lessor. The Lessor shall deliver to the Lessee a copy of any warranty agreement it may receive from the manufacturer of the Equipment, and the Lessee shall comply with all the conditions of such warranty required to be performed by the Lessor. To the extent that such compliance requires performance of normal maintenance and repairs, such compliance shall be at the expense of the Lessor to the extent provided for in this paragraph.

7. *Risk of loss and insurance.* All risk of loss or damage to the Equipment shall be borne by the Lessor. The Lessor shall, at his own expense, keep the equipment insured, at the full value thereof, against fire with extended coverage, and shall likewise insure the Equipment adequately against such other risks and in such amounts as the Lessor may reasonably deem necessary, and with insurance companies qualified to do business in the State of STATENAME or such other state in which the Equipment may, with Lessor's consent, be located. Notwithstanding the foregoing, the lessee shall be responsible for procuring the insurance and naming the Lessor as an insured as the Lessor's interests may appear, and advancing the insurance premium. The Lessor shall reimburse the Lessee for the cost for insurance promptly upon receipt of the policies or evidence of insurance obtained by the Lessee and the insurance bills.

8. *Extraordinary damage to equipment.* Notwithstanding any extraordinary damage to the Equipment, the monthly rental for the Equipment shall continue to be paid by the Lessee. The Lessee shall have the responsibility for the repair of any damaged equipment, at the Lessor's expense only as described in paragraph 6, and the Lessee shall repair or cause such equipment to be repaired promptly after the damage. In every such instance, the Lessor shall assign to the Lessee any and all rights the Lessor may have under insurance policies carried by the Lessor with respect to such damage, as well as any rights the Lessor may have to be reimbursed for such damage pursuant to insurance coverage carried by others, as reimbursement to the Lessee for any sum or sums expended by the Lessee in connection with the extraordinary repair of such equipment.

9. *Taxes, and so on.* The Lessee shall pay all use taxes, excise taxes, personal property taxes, assessments, ad valorem taxes, stamp and documentary taxes, and all other governmental charges, fees, fines, or penalties whatsoever, whether payable by the Lessor or the Lessee or others, on or relating to the use of the Equipment or the registration, rental, shipment, transportation, delivery, or operation thereof, and shall file all returns required therefor and furnish copies thereof to the Lessor. Upon demand, the Lessee shall reimburse the Lessor for any such taxes, assessments, charges, fines, or penalties which the Lessor may be compelled to pay in connection with the Equipment. The Lessor will cooperate with the Lessee and furnish the Lessee with any information available to the Lessor in connection with the Lessee's obligations under this paragraph. The Lessor has paid the applicable sales tax on the purchase of the Equipment.

10. *Indemnity.* The Lessee shall indemnify and hold harmless the Lessor from and against all losses, damages, injuries, claims, demands, and expenses (including legal expenses) of whatever nature, arising out of the use, condition (including, but not limited to, latent and other defects and whether or not discoverable by him), or operation of the Equipment, regardless of where, how, or by whom operated. The Lessee shall assume the cost and responsibility for defending any legal proceedings brought with respect to any losses, damages, injuries, claims, demands, and expenses, and shall pay all settlements or judgments entered in any such legal proceedings. The indemnities and assumptions of liabilities and obligations herein provided for shall continue in full force and effect notwithstanding the termination of this Agreement.

11. *Assignment and sublease.* The Lessee may not sublet or assign the Equipment, without the Lessor's consent, which both parties agree Lessor may withhold without regard to reasonableness. If the Lessee assigns or sublets the Equipment without the

Lessor's consent, such assignment or sublet shall be deemed to be a default under this agreement entitling the Lessor to immediately repossess the Equipment at the Lessee's expense.

12. *Lessee's default.* The following events shall constitute defaults on the part of the Lessee hereunder: the failure of the Lessee to pay any installment of rental within 30 days after the date on which the rent shall become due and breach or failure by the Lessee to observe or perform any of its other obligations hereunder and the continuance of such default for 30 days after notice in writing to the Lessee of the existence of such default; the insolvency or bankruptcy of the Lessee; the consent of the Lessee to the appointment of a trustee or receiver for the Lessee or for a substantial part of its property; the institution by or against the lessee of bankruptcy, reorganization, arrangement, assignment for, or insolvency proceedings; or the Lessee's assignment or subletting of the Equipment without Lessor's consent. Upon the occurrence of any such default, the Lessor may, at its option and without notice to or demand on the Lessee, declare this agreement in default and thereupon all Equipment and all rights of the Lessee therein shall be surrendered to the Lessor. The Lessor may, by the Lessor's agents, take possession of the Equipment wherever found, with or without process of law, and for this purpose may enter upon any premises of the Lessee without liability for suit, action, or other proceeding by the Lessee and remove the same. The Lessor may hold, use, sell, lease or otherwise dispose of the Equipment or keep any of it idle if the Lessor so chooses, without affecting the obligations of the lessee as provided in this paragraph. If the Lessee fails to deliver the equipment as provided in this paragraph, or converts or destroys the equipment, the Lessor may hold the Lessee liable for a sum equal to the fair market value of the equipment, which the Lessee shall forthwith pay the Lessor. With respect to Equipment returned to the Lessor or repossessed by the Lessor, the Lessor shall be entitled to any amounts realized by the Lessor through the sale, lease, or other disposition thereof.

13. *Purchase option.* The Lessee shall have the right to purchase the Equipment for its fair market value, as determined by appraisal, at the termination of this lease.

14. *Invalid provision.* Any provision of this agreement prohibited by law shall be ineffective to the extent of such prohibition without invalidating the rest of this agreement.

15. *Complete agreement.* This agreement and the Schedules executed by the parties contain the entire understanding of the parties, and such understanding may not be modified or terminated except in writing signed by the parties and by proper sublessee or assignee.

16. *Governing Law.* This agreement shall be governed by the laws of the State of STATENAME.

IN WITNESS WHEREOF, the Lessor and the Lessee have caused these presents to be duly executed.

Lessor:

By: _____

Lessee:

By: _____

8 SPECIAL LEGAL ISSUES AFFECTING THE OPERATIONS OF YOUR LIMITED LIABILITY COMPANY

Like any legal entity, LLCs bring with them a host of legal issues. The documents reviewed in Chapter 7 illustrated many of the legal formalities your LLC should take (filing certificates, an operating agreement, contract documents, etc.), but there are still other significant legal questions. This chapter provides an overview to help you gain background; however, to protect yourself, always consult with an attorney about these special legal issues.

PIERCING THE LLC "VEIL"

A key reason to form any LLC is to protect your personal assets from LLC liability issues (asset protection). Generally, a member in an LLC will be liable only to the extent of his investment in the LLC, thus providing members with the personal liability protection traditionally associated with corporations. This protection is not foolproof, but it is helpful to respect all LLC formalities, as advised in this book. How can a claimant suing your LLC (or other entity) in a lawsuit reach your house and other personal assets? By piercing the entity. There has long been a doctrine in corporate law called *piercing the corporate veil*. Since the vast majority of LLC statutes do not provide guidance on piercing the LLC veil, the situations that would result in the piercing of an LLC veil should probably be similar to those that pierce the corporate veil. This doctrine permits, in certain instances, a claimant to have the courts disregard, or "pierce," the entity, to reach the members' (owners') personal assets to satisfy a judgment against the entity. Courts will pierce the entity veil when the owners use the entity as their alter ego, instead of respecting its status as a separate and distinct entity. The piercing of the veil applies to the legal process of holding a member liable for the acts of an LLC. The courts have established factors (which vary from state to state) to consider when determining whether to pierce the veil. The primary factors can be divided into four categories:

1. *Fraud by owners.* If you as a manager and member of your LLC have fraudulently deceived your customers using false advertising, a court will be unlikely to allow the LLC to protect you.

2. *Inadequate capitalization of the entity.* You and the other members of your LLC should make reasonable investments of cash and other assets to permit the LLC to operate.

3. *Failure to observe company formalities.* Take to heart the advice contained throughout this book. You and your LLC are not one. Treat the LLC as if it were someone else's company.

4. *Mixing of the businesses and finances of the company with the members, to the extent that there is no distinction between them.* It is essential to keep separate business and personal bank accounts, to avoid commingling funds, and to maintain other commonsense business practices.

An LLC should be much easier to operate in accordance with the required LLC formalities since they are so much simpler than those for a corporation. However, make certain that all documents and contracts are signed in the name of the LLC, by the manager if so required under the operating agreement, and take care to make all necessary tax and annual report filings. When additional certificates (Certificate of Amendment, Certificate of Assumed Name, etc.) are required, these too should be properly filed. Leases, licenses, and other ancillary agreements should all be completed in the proper name of the LLC.

EXAMPLES:

- State A requires all LLCs formed in that state to file annual reports setting forth the names of its members and managers, its registered agent, and its registered office. A filing fee must accompany the report. If an LLC formed in State A continually and repeatedly does not file its annual report, it would be failing to comply with company formalities.

- The members of an LLC cause the LLC's cash receipts to be distributed directly into their individual checking accounts instead of first going into a company account and thereafter having the company issue a check to them. This abuse of company formalities gives creditors a better chance of piercing the LLC veil to reach the members' personal assets if LLC assets are insufficient to satisfy claims.

FIDUCIARY OBLIGATIONS OF MANAGERS

If you serve as the manager of an LLC, you must take your responsibilities seriously. You must carry out all of the responsibilities required under state law and the operating agreement. However, your responsibility and liability extend further. As the manager, you are deemed to have a general obligation to protect the interests of the other members and the LLC. In legal parlance, you have a *fiduciary obligation* that includes many specific obligations or legal duties. These are important to understand because violating them will expose you to the risk of lawsuit by the members harmed.

Most state laws address a manager's duty of care and loyalty to the LLC. Generally, a manager for this purpose could be either members or managers, whichever group has management authority. The states that have such statutes vary in their approach to the duty of care and loyalty owned by the management group. Therefore, you should review the state LLC law to determine what rights and obligations would exist in the absence of such provisions in an operating agreement.

PLANNING TIP: If you are serving as manager, periodically report your significant actions and business results to the members. Keep them informed. Document, perhaps in a unanimous written consent of the members, the members' agreement to major decisions (hiring a new accounting firm, purchasing a building, etc.). Read, understand, and follow the guidelines contained in your state's laws as to how you must operate. If you are not familiar with them, or find provisions of the operating agreement vague or unclear, consult with the LLC's attorney.

Duty of Care

A manager will generally owe, under state law, a *duty of care* to the LLC. The typical state law provides several categories of duty of care standards. As a manager, you have a duty to exercise ordinary care in your conduct. You cannot commit gross negligence or willful misconduct. You have a duty to exercise good-faith business judgment in your actions. This does not mean you cannot make a mistake, but your judgments, which will be evaluated with the benefit of hindsight, must have been made in good faith. You have a duty to not act in a manner that constitutes recklessness. You have a duty to provide information that others will rely on (e.g., periodic accounting reports).

In states that do not have express provisions concerning a manager's duty of care, the courts will still require some degree of duty of care by the management group.

Duty of Loyalty

As a manager, you owe the LLC a duty of loyalty. If, in your capacity as a manager you learn of a business opportunity, you cannot invest in it personally without first offering it to the LLC. There are myriad examples of how you owe loyalty to the LLC you are managing, many of which are common sense. You owe a duty to account for profits made in connection with the LLC's business. No side dealings are allowed.

EXAMPLE: You are the manager of an LLC that manufactures widgets. You learn from industry publications that there is likely to be a significant increase next year in the particular wood that is used in widget manufacturing. You purchase contracts to buy substantial quantities of this wood. Next year, when the price increase hits, you sell the wood contracts you own to the LLC at less than market prices. You make a handsome profit, and the LLC saves money. Have you violated your duties to the LLC? After all, the LLC was able to purchase raw materials at a lower price because of your actions. If you had not disclosed and offered the chance to purchase wood contracts to the LLC, you would have clearly violated your duties to the LLC.

There is a general duty of good faith. If a state does not have an express provision, it is most likely that the courts would require some degree of duty of loyalty by the management group.

Bankruptcy Issues and LLCs

Under bankruptcy law, the treatment of LLCs is similar to that of a corporation. The distinction between corporate and partnership treatment under the Bankruptcy Code is important because general partners of a partnership may be held personally liable if the partnership's assets are insufficient to satisfy claims of creditors in a bankruptcy proceeding against the partnership. Shareholders of a corporation are not subject to such personal liability.

USING LLCs FOR MULTISTATE OPERATIONS

In determining whether a limited liability company is the right entity for you, an analysis of the states in which your LLC will operate its business can provide key information. An LLC is known as a *domestic* LLC in the state in which it was organized and as a *foreign* LLC in a state other than the state of organization.

Each state has specific rules relating to LLCs. Because these rules vary from state to state, you must carefully review the statutes of the states in which the LLC will operate to determine how a particular state will treat an LLC. It is obviously much better to know this information in advance than to be surprised later. Accordingly, where a multistate operation is important to the company's business, you must determine what filing requirements, if any, are required for your LLC in a foreign jurisdiction (a state other than the state of organization).

State Law Permitting Registration of Foreign LLCs

Not all states expressly provide in their statutes for the registration of foreign LLCs, even though such a state may authorize their formation. Generally, registration of a foreign LLC is a matter of filling out and filing some type of registration form with the appropriate state filing authority of the foreign jurisdiction, and paying a fee. The information in such a registration form usually includes the name of the LLC, the jurisdiction of its organization, the name and address of a registered agent in the foreign jurisdiction, and under some states, the business purpose of the LLC.

It is the approval of such registration by the appropriate state filing authority, not merely the filing of a document, that authorizes the foreign LLC to transact business in the foreign jurisdiction.

Some states require a foreign LLC, as well as domestic LLCs to file annual reports with the appropriate state filing authority and pay an annual filing fee.

NOTE: Having your LLC authorized to conduct business in another state may also have important state income, and other, tax filing requirements. Be certain to review these with your tax accountant before filing. The filing may create a presumption that your LLC has to file tax returns, and even pay tax, in that new state (see discussion later in this chapter).

Registration in Foreign Jurisdictions That Do Not Have Specific Registration Requirements for LLCs

What if you want your LLC to do business in a state that does not have a law expressly dealing with the registration of foreign LLCs? In those states, it may be wise to proceed with any statutory filing procedures for foreign partnerships. If the state does not accept the registration of foreign partnerships (either general or limited), then proceeding with the foreign registration requirements for corporations may be appropriate. If an LLC follows the procedure of registration of a foreign corporation, take care that it does not in fact register as a corporation or it may risk losing the partnership tax benefits of an LLC in that state.

Not Registering Your LLC in a Foreign Jurisdiction

Generally, if your LLC is required to register in a foreign jurisdiction and fails to do so, it will be precluded from bringing a lawsuit in the courts of that state. The failure to file a registration, however, should not alone invalidate any contract that the LLC had entered into in the foreign jurisdiction. Nor will the failure to file a registration impede the LLC's ability to defend itself in a lawsuit.

EXAMPLE: Assume a foreign LLC does business in another state and fails to get authorized to do business in that state. If the foreign LLC and its members are sued in that foreign jurisdiction, the LLC would be able to defend itself in the lawsuit and the individual members would still benefit from limited liability. The LLC, however, may be limited in its ability to bring a counterclaim.

Saving the cost of a proper filing is rarely worth the risk of facing the uncertain consequences of not filing. As mentioned, not filing as required is a factor that the courts might consider if a claimant attempts to pierce the LLC entity veil and reach your personal assets to satisfy a claim.

MULTISTATE TAX ISSUES

One complication to conducting business in the LLC format in several states is that not every state treats an LLC the same for state tax purposes. In most states, LLCs are treated for state tax purposes in the same manner in which they are treated for federal tax purposes. These are called *conformity statutes*. In some states, however, an LLC that is classified as a partnership for federal tax purposes will still be taxed as a corporation for state tax purposes.

This differing tax treatment by several states may cause administrative and accounting difficulties for your LLC. Therefore, before deciding to conduct business in a foreign jurisdiction, you should make a determination that the LLC format will not cause any adverse tax consequences for state tax purposes that might outweigh the benefits of using an LLC.

EXAMPLE: An LLC formed in Florida, Texas, or Pennsylvania, or a foreign LLC doing business in any such state that is subject to that state's income tax, will be taxed as a corporation, rather than as a pass-through entity (i.e., partnership tax treatment), for state tax purposes.

SUMMARY

LLCs face many legal, tax, and other related issues that are complex and can have substantial impact. These laws can differ considerably from state to state. Further, many of the rules are not contained in state statutes, but continue to develop in the cases heard in courts in each state. If your LLC will be transacting business in a foreign jurisdiction, it will create yet another layer of complexity. Advance planning, caution, and adherence to the formalities of properly conducting your LLC are essential.

9 SECURITIES LAWS AND LIMITED LIABILITY COMPANIES

At some point in the life cycle of your LLC, security laws may become an important issue. If you have several passive (i.e., do not participate in management) investors when you organize and form your LLC, you may have to deal with both state and federal securities laws. On an optimistic note, if the operation of your LLC is sufficiently successful, you may want to bring in new investors. Depending on the numbers involved and other factors, it could be essential to address state and/or federal security laws.

Federal and state securities laws applicable to LLCs are always changing. The rules are complex and require the guidance of an attorney specializing in securities law (not a general practitioner). The penalties for noncompliance are significant, and you should not risk violating them.

LLCs AND SECURITIES LAW CONSIDERATIONS

The security laws are enacted by each state as well as the federal government. One of the goals of these laws is to minimize security frauds and schemes that harm investors. They achieve this goal, in part, by requiring anyone issuing securities to file reports that must disclose substantial information in a specified format. Complying with these disclosures, especially when the security may be sold in several states, each with its own reporting requirements, can be expensive.

If a number of passive investors purchase membership interests in your LLC, the membership interests will be classified as securities and the LLC will have to meet the security disclosure and other requirements. The term *security* is defined in the federal securities laws and in the Uniform Securities Act to include an investment contract. The term *investment contract* is defined as a contract, transaction, or scheme whereby a person invests his money in a common enterprise and is led to expect profits solely from the efforts of the promoter or third party. To help deal with the investment contract issue, LLCs should encourage members to retain management responsibilities and thus avoid having the corporate characteristic of centralized management. Investment contracts can occur in an LLC context unless all the members control the major decision making, have the power to remove or employ management, and participate in voting on important business matters.

The key to determining whether an LLC membership interest is a security will be based in part on the allocation of managerial rights. If the LLC is actually managed by the members who collectively make all the important decisions and may act on behalf of the LLC in dealing with third parties, it is likely that the LLC interests would not be considered securities. Even though a manager runs the day-to-day operations of the LLC, the LLC interests are still likely not to be securities if the members retain ultimate control. This could be evidenced by the members having the right in the operating agreement to vote to oust the manager or to participate in important business decisions. If, however, ultimate responsibility for managing is ceded to the manager, with some or all of the members having no real role in business matters (i.e., are treated as if they were limited partners), then the LLC interests are likely to be considered securities. Both the Articles of Organization and operating agreement are critical to the determination of whether an LLC interest is a security. These documents should clearly state that the members retain the power to make important business decisions and—if a manager is engaged—to periodically vote on removal or termination of the manager's contract.

As a final note in this analysis, the number of LLC members may be dispositive of the issue. Interests in an LLC with hundreds of members are assuredly to be considered securities because it is impractical for such large numbers of people to realistically expect to exercise management power.

EXEMPTION FROM REGISTRATION UNDER FEDERAL SECURITIES LAWS

Under the Securities Act of 1933 (the "Securities Act"), the offer and sale of securities must be made pursuant to the registration and prospectus delivery requirements of Section 5 of the Securities Act, or pursuant to an available exemption therefrom. In addition, many state securities laws (**blue sky laws**) require either registration or the availability of an exemption from registration. Failing to register when required may result in civil and criminal penalties. There are some exemptions from the registration requirements of Section 5 of the Securities Act. They include:

1. *The intrastate exemption.* This exemption is for securities offered and sold only to people residing in a single state and where the issuer is also a resident of and doing business in that state.

2. *Regulation D offerings.* Regulation D is a safe harbor promulgated by the Securities and Exchange Commission (SEC) pursuant to Sections 3 and 4 of the Securities Act. Regulation D consists of general rules (Rules 501 through 503, 507, and 508) and three separate offering exemptions (Rules 504, 505, and 506). Compliance with all of the general rules and the provisions of the specific offering exemption rule ensures the availability of an exemption from the registration requirements of the Securities Act.

   a. *Limited offerings under $1 million (Rule 504).* Under this exemption, nonreporting companies (i.e., companies that do not have a class of securities registered under the Securities Exchange Act) may sell up to $1 million of securities in any 12-month period. There are no specific disclosure requirements, and the offering may be sold through general advertising and solicitation.

   b. *Limited offerings under $5 million (Rule 505).* For this exemption to apply, providing that the offer is not made by general soliciting or general advertising, issuers may offer securities totaling less than $5 million in any 12-month period to not more than 35 purchasers and any number of "accredited investors" (generally wealthy individuals or certain types of financial institutions). However, the issuer must provide certain specified disclosure materials if any sales are made to nonaccredited investors.

   c. *Private placement (Rule 506).* Issuers may offer and sell any dollar amount of securities up to 35 purchasers and any number of accredited investors provided that no general solicitation or general advertising is used. Once again, the issuer has to provide certain disclosure materials if any sales are made to any nonaccredited investors. In addition, the issuer must make a determination that each nonaccredited investor has such knowledge and experience in financial and business matters that he is capable of evaluating the merits and risks of the prospective investment.

3. *The accredited investor exemption.* This exemption is similar to Rule 506.

4. *Regulation A.* Regulation A permits issuers to freely sell tradable securities to investors without complying with the registration requirements of the Securities Act. Regulation A's disclosure requirements are simpler than a registration under the Securities Act and permit forms of advertising and solicitation that are not permitted in other

nonregistered offerings. Issuers may provide unaudited financial statements if audited statements are not available. The dollar limit for a Regulation A offering is $5 million. An issuer relying on Regulation A may "test the waters" for potential investor interest prior to incurring the costs of preparing a Regulation A offering statement. Thus, an issuer may publish or deliver to prospective purchasers a written document or make scripted radio or television broadcasts.

Any securities issued in reliance on an exemption from the registration requirements of the Securities Act (except pursuant to Rule 504 or Regulation A) will be restricted securities. As such, they may not be offered or resold without registration under the Securities Act or an available exemption from registration therefrom.

Assuming LLC interests are securities and that an exemption from registration is available at the federal level, the antifraud provisions of the federal securities laws (most significantly Section 10 of the 1934 Act and Rule 10b-5 promulgated thereunder) are applicable to the offer, sale, and purchase of these investments.

STATE SECURITIES LAWS

In addition to complying with the federal securities laws, the offer and sale of securities must also comply with state securities laws (blue sky laws). Various exemptions from state registration are available, including the Uniform Limited Offering Exemption (ULOE), which has been adopted in one form or another by most of the states. The ULOE tracks Rules 505 and 506 and, with certain variations, provides for a state exemption for offerings meeting the requirements of either of these two rules. The ULOE has not, however, been extended to cover Rule 504 offerings.

State securities laws include LLC interests within the definition of *security*. In certain instances, these statutes provide exceptions to the definition when, generally, all of the LLC members are actively engaged in the LLC's management. A number of state statutes also provide that the term security includes an LLC interest "unless the contract requires otherwise." Other states that have not included LLC interests within the statutory definition of a security, have arguably done so by implication in providing for the exemption from registration of LLC interests under certain circumstances (the implication being that registration may be required in other circumstances).

The securities acts of many states include LLCs within the statuary definition of *person* or *entity*, thereby subjecting LLCs to registration requirements for brokers and/or dealers if they wish to offer and sell LLC interests within the state.

The state administrative orders and no-action letters issued have focused primarily on the numbers of investors, their participation in management, the experience of the investors, and whether the purchases were made for investment purposes.

SUMMARY

In addition to reviewing the tax ramifications and other considerations of conducting business in the LLC format, you may also have to consider the possible security law implications. Where your LLC is offering to sell LLC membership interests to more than a few passive investors, always consult with a securities attorney before marketing the interests to be certain that you have properly addressed any applicable state or federal security law.

CAUTION: The consequences of failing to file the required documents and adhere to other security law requirements are severe. You cannot simply rely on the position advocated by some that LLC membership interests are not securities. The conclusion will depend on all of the facts in a particular situation. If there is any issue whatsoever, err on the side of caution and have securities counsel review the matter.

---

10 DISSOLUTION, WINDING UP, AND TERMINATION OF YOUR LIMITED LIABILITY COMPANY

The chapters in this book have followed a natural sequence in the progression of your LLC. First you must decide to form an LLC. Next, you form and then operate the LLC. At some point, the business purpose of the LLC may cease, or some other event may trigger the end of the LLC. This chapter addresses the final stage in the operation of an LLC—its ultimate termination. This is generally a three-step process: (1) dissolution, (2) winding up, and (3) termination, in that order.

Each state's LLC statute provides specific rules relating to the dissolution and ultimate legal termination of an LLC as a legal entity. The following discussion provides an overview of the concepts common to many states' laws.

WHAT CAUSES DISSOLUTION

The first step in ending the legal existence of an LLC is a dissolution of the entity. The events that may cause a dissolution of an LLC may vary from state to state, but generally any of the following six events may trigger a dissolution:

1. The expiration of a fixed duration period set forth in the Articles of Organization. LLCs formed before the check-the-box regulations that made selection of partnership taxation a mere formality may include a fixed date for termination.

2. By written agreement among the members. You and the other owners may agree that the time to move on has arrived.

3. By member disassociation (i.e., the death, retirement, resignation, bankruptcy, or expulsion of any member).

4. The occurrence of a specific event set forth in the Articles of Organization or operating agreement (see the sample operating agreement in Chapter 6). For example, if your LLC was formed to own a specific building, you might provide that the LLC should be dissolved if the building is sold.

5. By judicial action. This could occur if a court determines that a particular LLC should be dissolved, perhaps to pay certain assets to creditors.

6. Loss of license. A professional services LLC may no longer be licensed to render those services. This could occur in a medical practice if the license of a physician in a LLC is revoked.

If the disassociation of a member has triggered dissolution, it can be avoided if all the remaining members, other than the member whose acts resulted in the disassociation, consent to continue the business after that event. Most state default statutes provide that the consent must be unanimous; however, the operating agreement could provide for a level of consent less than unanimous (say three-fourths).

WINDING UP YOUR LLC

Winding up your LLC means paying its obligations and liabilities to creditors, and then making distributions of any remaining funds to the members. To provide the funds necessary to satisfy creditors, the LLC's assets may have to be sold. In some states, a member owning more than 50 percent of the LLC membership interests may choose to wind down the LLC's affairs. The tax consequences of the winding down of your LLC should be reviewed with a tax accountant in advance.

Filing Requirements

The law in many states requires that an LLC seeking dissolution must first file a notice of intent to dissolve, articles of dissolution, or notice of dissolution; then it can file the Certificate of Cancellation or articles of termination.

Distribution of Assets

Generally, on the winding up of an LLC, its assets are to be distributed in the following order:

- To creditors.
- To members in satisfaction of liabilities for distributions.
- To members to return their capital contributions (this includes their initial investments in the LLC).
- To members based on their percentage interests in the LLC. In most simple LLC arrangements, this will be the same percentage by which profits and distributions had been shared in all years. In more complicated arrangements, special allocations and complex adjustments may have to be made to determine how proceeds are to be distributed at this stage.

The winding up of an LLC is completed when all debts, liabilities, and obligations of the LLC have been paid and/or discharged, or adequate provisions have been made for such obligations, and all remaining property and assets of the LLC have been distributed to its members.

Each state's LLC statute must be examined to determine whether an LLC in the process of dissolution and winding up must notify its creditors of the situation. If a particular creditor does not get notice that the LLC is winding up, the claim may survive. However, depending on each particular state's statute, if a creditor is given notice but does not respond within a certain time period, the LLC may be able to disregard the creditor's claim. This can be accomplished by sending a certified letter to all known current and prior vendors.

Practice Tip: What happens to people or companies that the LLC owes money but cannot identify by name, so as to send a notice? For example, someone may have a claim that the LLC was unaware of. These are called *unknown creditors*. The LLC may be able to effect legal notice to these unidentified creditors and cut off their claims if they do not act, by publishing an announcement (notice) of the LLC's dissolution in a local newspaper. Although publishing the notices is an additional expense, the comfort of being able to cut off creditor claims, or at least to have a defense that you have reasonably endeavored to notify claimants, can be well worth the cost.

SUMMARY

After all the business of the LLC has been accomplished or at some sooner time as may be required, the LLC may be legally terminated. Each state's statute provides certain default rules under which an LLC may dissolve, wind up, and terminate unless otherwise provided in the operating agreement. There are various state filing requirements relating to the termination of an LLC and the distribution of assets at such time.

Part Four

TAX PLANNING WITH LIMITED LIABILITY COMPANIES

11 INCOME TAX AND YOUR LIMITED LIABILITY COMPANY

The income tax advantages of LLCs are a major reason for their popularity. As discussed at length in Chapter 1, the LLC can provide you with limited liability and the flow-through tax treatment of a partnership. Understanding this tax treatment in greater detail will help you plan your LLC's activities and minimize your personal income taxes.

For readers brave enough, this chapter describes the basics of LLC taxation. Those readers preferring to avoid the tax maze must consult with an accountant. In all events, however, the complex partnership tax rules should always be reviewed with a professional tax adviser.

HOW IS AN LLC TAXED FOR INCOME TAX PURPOSES?

To determine how your LLC is taxed, you must first identify the characterization of your LLC for income tax purposes (see Chapter 7). Your LLC will generally fall into one of three categories. The first option is to be taxed as a partnership. This is the treatment that the vast majority of LLCs will face, and it is the subject of this chapter. Generally, any LLC with two or more members will be taxed as a partnership. Second, some LLCs with two or more members will choose to be taxed as something other than a partnership for income tax purposes. This is rare and will require professional tax advice, so it is not addressed in this book. Finally, some LLCs will only have one member and will be treated as a disregarded entity for federal income tax purposes. This less common, but important result, is discussed in the following section.

SINGLE-MEMBER LLCs

Most states permit you to form and maintain a single-member LLC. For federal income tax purposes, a sole proprietorship organized as a single-member

LLC will report income as if the LLC did not exist. A closely held business would report income on your Form 1040 Schedule C; and if your LLC owns rental property, it would report income on your Form 1040, Schedule E.

The fact that a single-member LLC is disregarded for income tax purposes can have other ramifications besides avoiding the filing of a partnership income tax return. A single-member disregarded LLC is not treated as separate from its owner for purposes of a like kind or tax-deferred exchange of real estate properties (also called a *1031 exchange*). Thus, you can have real estate owned by a single-member LLC to minimize liability risks and still engage in a like kind exchange by transferring an interest in real property with your single-member LLC for other real property.

LLCs TAXED AS A PARTNERSHIP

Since most LLCs are intended to be taxed as a partnership for federal and state tax purposes, you need to understand the partnership tax rules that will apply to your LLC.

How an LLC and Its Members Are Generally Taxed

LLCs are required to complete and file IRS Form 1065, "U.S. Partnership Return of Income." The income or loss that the LLC realizes is determined at the LLC level, but is reported by the members.

Once an LLC's taxable income (or loss) is determined, it must be allocated among the partners so that each member can report his share on his personal income tax return.

EXAMPLE: Widget, LLC, earns $24,000. There are three equal members. Widget, LLC, files a partnership tax return reporting $24,000 of net income and each member receives an allocable share on Form K-1. Each member uses his Form K-1 at year-end to determine how much income to report on his personal tax return. The members, not the LLC, pay tax.

Partnership taxation, however, is rarely so simple. Many specific types of LLC income and deductions must be reported separately to each member. These include short-term capital gains and losses, long-term capital gains and losses, charitable contributions, alternative minimum tax preference items, and medical expenses. The IRS Form K-1 that LLC members receive will list all of the items that must be separately reported. Each of these is then reported on a different line of the member's personal income tax return. The simple concept of an LLC taxed as a partnership being a tax flow-through (conduit) becomes far from simple in practice.

An LLC's taxable income is generally determined in a manner similar to the taxable income of an individual. However, several specific deductions are not permitted: personal exemption, charitable contribution, net operating loss, capital loss carryover, foreign taxes, and itemized deductions, among others.

Since the LLC is in many respects independent of its members, many tax decisions (called elections), including those concerning the research credit and **depreciation,** are made at the LLC level. These issues may affect different members in very different ways so it can be important to negotiate in the operating agreement what these decisions will be, or at least who will make them.

Members Realize Tax Consequences

An LLC does not pay any federal income tax. Each member is required to report on his federal income tax return his distributive share of all items of income, gain, loss, deduction, credit, and tax preference of the LLC for any taxable year of the LLC ending within or with his taxable year. This is a conduit tax system, with each member reporting a pro rata share of the LLC's income on his tax return, regardless of the actual cash distribution. The result could be a member having to report income without a commensurate cash distribution with which to pay the tax. Consideration should be given to this possibility in negotiating and drafting the terms of the operating agreement. Language can be added to an operating agreement to require minimum distributions to meet tax costs. Because of the different tax status of various members, states, and so on, the calculation for distributions cannot be exact. If a formula is used, or a specified percentage, be certain that it is reasonable for you. The objective in many instances is to assure some reasonable level of distribution to meet expected tax costs. Guidelines could be added for distributions of an estimated amount equal to federal maximum tax rate multiplied by taxable income to assure members have adequate cash flow to pay federal tax. You could suggest, for example, an increase in the federal marginal tax rate by say a flat 5 percent to give some consideration to state income taxes. Because of so many states and variations in tax rates, a more exact approach may be impossible.

PLANNING TIP: Although almost every member will be unhappy about the prospect of phantom income, use of the preceding approach could effectively defeat the asset protection benefits of the LLC. If cash must be distributed, a creditor seizing your LLC membership interest will have a much easier time collecting. You have to weigh the importance of these competing goals for your LLC to properly review and negotiate provisions in the operating agreement.

Tax Considerations on Forming Your LLC

You must consider many tax issues when forming an LLC. The first relates to debt on assets contributed to your LLC. The general tax rule is that no gain or loss is recognized for income tax purposes when members contribute assets to an LLC in exchange for membership interests.

EXAMPLE: Ed and Ron form an LLC called EdRon. Ed contributes oil and gas properties worth $100,000, and Ron contributes accounting textbooks worth $200,000. Ed owns one third of EdRon and Ron owns two thirds. No gain or loss is recognized for tax purposes.

When forming an LLC, however, you must take care to address the possible triggering of gain as a result of the partnership liability allocation rules. If these rules shift liabilities to someone other than the partner/member transferring assets, this could be treated as a deemed cash distribution resulting in gain.

A second tax trap that affects some LLCs on formation has to do with the unexpected triggering of gain on the transfer of appreciated securities to the LLC. Although LLCs are a commonly used estate-planning technique, most people remain unaware of the investment company rule that can inadvertently cause taxation on the formation of a securities LLC.

EXAMPLE: John and Jane Smith form a family LLC to gain greater control over family assets and to facilitate estate planning. John contributes $100,000 of IBM that he bought for $10,000, and $100,000 of GM that he bought for $12,000. Jane contributes $80,000 of 3M that she bought for $25,000, and $200,000 of UPS that she bought for $20,000. Their son Frank contributes $70,000 of Microsoft that he bought for $1,000. Their daughter Cindy contributes $65,000 of ABC REIT she bought for $5,000. While the formation of an LLC is generally tax free, each of the Smiths contributed a nondiversified stock holding and the end result is arguably a more diversified stock portfolio. If the effect of forming the LLC is to diversify each member's previously undiversified stock position, the economic effect is no different than had each person sold the stock and invested in a new securities portfolio. In such cases, the tax laws seek to extract a capital gains tax to achieve that result.

The rules that may trigger this gain are referred to as *investment company rules.* The investment company exception to the tax-free organization of an LLC taxed as a partnership, presents a significant trap for the unwary. Several tiers of requirements must be met to trigger this tax cost. First, the entity must be classified as an investment company by virtue of having more than 80 percent of its assets in the form of marketable securities. Tax will be triggered only if the securities transferred to the LLC are not already diversified portfolios and the transaction must result in significant diversification. If these hurdles are met, all appreciation will be taxed. This will be all the gain to the extent that the fair market value of the LLC interest received in exchange exceeds the tax basis of the assets transferred.

The LLC's Method of Accounting

Once the LLC is formed, you will have to determine the income tax consequences to each LLC member from LLC operations. To do this, you must first understand how the LLC will calculate its taxable income. Generally, the cash or the accrual method of accounting is permitted for an LLC. **Cash basis** is the simplest and is used by many smaller LLCs. You calculate your income for tax purposes under the cash method of accounting, in general terms, by treating money your LLC has actually collected as income, and expenses you have actually paid as deductions.

Some LLCs Must Use a More Complex Method of Accounting

Some LLCs must use an accounting method that endeavors to better match income and expenses with the years to which they relate. This complex method is called the *accrual method* and must be used by any LLC classified by the tax laws as a *tax shelter*. A tax shelter is any enterprise if interests are offered in a registered offering, or a syndicate. A syndicate is anything, other than a C corporation, that allocates greater than 35 percent of its losses to limited partners or *limited entrepreneurs*. A limited entrepreneur is a person who is not a limited partner and does not actively participate in the management of the LLC. LLCs can get around these rulings by taking the position that they do not apply until the business takes losses. For professional practices, this is a viable solution because they rarely incur losses. Another possible solution is that because of a member's active role in management, he is neither a limited partner nor an entrepreneur. The IRS has ruled that LLCs can use the cash method for accounting purposes.

Tax Elections

The LLC will make certain tax elections instead of the individual members making the elections. For example, the method of accounting will be elected at the LLC level. The operating agreement may specify the use of a particular tax election. Alternatively, it may direct that the manager or members will determine the tax elections.

Tax Year

Usually, the tax year for an LLC will be a calendar year. This is because LLCs are required to adopt the tax-reporting period consistent with the tax-reporting period of the members who hold a majority of the LLC's profits and capital interests. This is the identical rule for partnerships.

Allocations of LLC Income, Deductions, and Losses

Once the LLC's income is determined using its method of accounting, the income (or loss) must be allocated to the individual members. The simplest approach is to allocate income, deductions, credits, and so on to each member in the same proportion as that member's interest in the LLC.

EXAMPLE: A 12 percent member would be allocated 12 percent of all LLC items: 12 percent of cash flow; 12 percent of net income or loss; 12 percent of any tax credits (e.g., research and experimentation, low-income housing, or rehabilitation tax credits), and so on.

Allocations, however, do not have to be made in the exact proportions as each member's interest in the LLC if the LLC agreement calls for a different method. This flexibility is one of the principal advantages of the LLC (and partnership) form of organization and sets it apart from all the other forms of conducting business. For example, some members may be given a priority distribution of cash flow. One member may receive 80 percent of the gain ultimately realized on the sale of certain property (such as land and a building that the member contributed to the LLC). Another active member may receive 25 percent of the remaining profits on the eventual sale and liquidation of the LLC, although he only had a 1 percent interest in the LLC's profits and capital (this could be offered as an incentive fee to the active member to encourage his performance). When allocations differ from the plain vanilla approach of each member getting a share based on his membership interests, they are called *special allocations*. This freedom to allocate provides an opportunity to devise a distribution and compensation structure to best achieve the LLC's business goals.

A member's share of income, gain, loss, deductions, and credits are determined by the operating agreement, as long as it conforms with tax law requirements. This is yet another reason a comprehensive and well-planned operating agreement is essential.

These special allocations cannot be made with total freedom. The special allocation must have what is called *substantial economic effect.*

Defining this term has spawned some of the most complicated tax rules. In simple terms, this phrase means that the special allocations must be made for more than mere tax reasons. They should have some meaningful economic and nontax impact on the members making them. Substantial economic effect requires that there be an economic effect (it hits you in the pocket) and that such effect be substantial (not just lip service). The member who receives the special allocation must feel its economic benefit or burden. This requires:

- Members' capital accounts (ledgers reflecting all investments, income, and losses of each member) must be maintained as required under the tax laws. This means, for example, that member capital accounts must be increased by certain items (money you contribute to the LLC, tax-exempt income allocated to each member, allocations of income and gain, etc.). Capital accounts must be decreased by certain items (money distributed, loss, deductions, and certain expenditures, etc.). Your operating agreement should have details requiring all of this.

- On the LLC's liquidation, distributions of LLC property must be made with consideration to each member's capital account.

- Following this final distribution, members with negative capital accounts are required to restore (contribute) these amounts, or meet certain other complex requirements (we mean complex; Einstein would get a headache just contemplating them). You could have a negative capital account if you were distributed more than your capital account balance when the LLC ended.

If the principal purpose of the formula in the operating agreement for allocating the LLC's income or loss, and gain or loss on a sale or other disposition of LLC property, is the avoidance or evasion of taxes, then such allocation would not be binding on the IRS. The IRS would then reallocate net income and losses among the members based on their interests in the LLC.

Payments to Members

Fixed or guaranteed payments to a member for services that the member supplies to the LLC, or for the use of capital, are often treated as if the payments were made to an independent person who is not a member.

EXAMPLE: Jack is a member in the Jack and Jill LLC. Jack provides accounting services to the LLC (he tallies the pails going up and down) and receives a regular monthly payment for these services. These payments are treated as if the Jack and Jill LLC had paid an independent accountant to do the work, and are therefore deductible by the LLC. The LLC thus obtains the equivalent of a tax deduction for this guaranteed payment. The member, Jack, would report the payment as ordinary income. This is accomplished by treating the guaranteed payment to Jack as part of Jack's share of the LLC's ordinary income.

Payroll (Self-Employment) Taxes and Your LLC

The self-employment income of every individual is taxed under the Self-Employment Contributions Act. This tax involves a 12.40 percent tax for old-age, survivor, and disability insurance (which is capped by the contribution and benefit base for an employee's wages) and a 2.90 percent tax for hospital insurance (which is uncapped), totaling a tax of 15.30 percent. There is a deduction, however, for one-half (½) of the self-employment taxes paid. The determination of the benefits a self-employed individual may have in a qualified retirement plan depend on the self-employment income attributable to such individual.

Self-employment income includes a partner's distributive share of net income and loss from a partnership engaged in a trade or business. The term *partnership* for this purpose should include any entity that is classified as a partnership for federal tax purposes, such as an LLC. A limited partner in a limited partnership, however, does not include his distributive share of partnership income or loss in net income from self-employment, other than specific guaranteed payments to a limited partner. This is because limited partners cannot actively participate in partnership management. General partners can.

It is unclear how to apply these rules to LLCs because members can participate in management, but depending on the circumstances and operating agreement, may be prevented from doing so. So the general/limited partner distinction that worked in the partnership context does not quite fit the LLC context. The question remains, how to apply self-employment income taxes to LLCs: Should members be treated more like general partners or limited partners? One approach was to state that if the member actively participated in LLC activities for 500 or more hours, was personally liable on LLC debt, or could contract in the name of the LLC, that person would be treated like a general partner and his LLC earnings would be subject to self-employment taxes.

Until the law becomes clearer, you should review this issue with your tax adviser and take steps to corroborate whatever position you decide to take.

Passive Loss Rules Limit Your Deduction of LLC Losses

Overview of the Passive Loss Rules and How They Affect Investors

The passive loss rules arose out of concern that many wealthy taxpayers were sheltering too much of their income from taxation through investments in real estate and other tax shelters. The general approach is to segregate the perceived culprits—tax shelter and rental real estate investments—and to then limit your use of the tax losses from such investments to offset the tax on your other income. The income or loss from these suspect investments is labeled passive. The other major categories are active (e.g., wages) and portfolio (e.g., dividends and interest). More specifically, passive investments (activities) are those that (1) involve the active conduct of a trade or business in which you do not materially participate, or (2) are rental activities (and in which you are not an active professional real estate participant).

Material Participation

Material participation requires you to be involved on a regular, continuous, and substantial basis in the particular activity. Some of the rules for determining whether you materially participate are based on the hours you work in a particular activity.

Use of Losses

Generally, losses from passive activities can only be used to offset income from passive activities. Losses that are not used currently are suspended until the earlier of (1) your realizing passive income to offset such losses, or (2) your selling your entire interest in the activity. When you sell your entire interest, suspended losses from that activity can be used without limitation.

What Happens to Tax Losses That Cannot Be Deducted Currently

If the passive loss limitation applies so that tax losses you have incurred from your LLC cannot be deducted, these losses are generally deferred until a later tax year when they can be used to offset passive income. If you have income or gains in the passive income category in the next tax year, you can apply your unused passive loss carry forwards from loss years or certain income tax credits earned in prior tax years to obtain a tax savings.

To the extent that you have not been able to use up your passive loss carry forwards from prior years before you sell your investment, you can use these losses to offset the gain you would otherwise have to recognize on the sale.

EXAMPLE: An investor owns 50 percent of an LLC. The LLC investment was made in 2002. As a result of depreciation and other deductions exceeding income in the early years of the venture, the investor realizes losses each year of $25,000. Since this is the investor's only passive investment, there is no other passive income that they could offset. Thus the losses are suspended and remain unused. By 2006, the investor has accumulated unused (suspended) losses of $125,000 at the rate of $25,000 per year for five years. At the end of 2006, the investor sells his LLC interest for $200,000. This profit is reduced by the $125,000 in losses not yet used. Thus, the gain that should be taxed is only $75,000.

What Types of Taxpayers Are Subject to the Passive Loss Limitation Rules

The passive loss rules apply to all individual taxpayers, estates, and trusts. These limitations apply to certain corporations as well. The objective of applying the limitations so widely is to prevent taxpayers from avoiding the limitations by structuring activities or investments in a different form (e.g., holding a passive real estate rental property that generates tax losses in a corporation) to circumvent the rules. Generally, C corporations are not subject to the passive loss limitation rules, but a special rule subjects certain closely held C corporations to those rules. C corporations are regular corporations (not S corporations), which are subject to the corporate level tax.

Partnerships, LLCs, and S corporations are flow-through or conduit entities. Most tax consequences—income, gain, loss, and deductions—flow through to the individual partners, members, or shareholders and are reported on their tax returns. Thus, the passive loss rules are generally applied at the partner or shareholder level. Each partner or shareholder must evaluate his work efforts to determine whether the business is an active business endeavor for him.

What Is an Activity?

The overview of the passive loss rules makes it clear that the definition of the term *activity* is critical to applying and planning for the passive loss rules. The scope of an activity delineates an active business from rental activities. For a business or investment endeavor to be considered nonpassive (the losses deductible without limitation) you must materially participate. The broader the term activity is defined, the easier it will be for you to meet one of the threshold tests for material participation.

The definition of activity is important to determine the type and nature of accounting records that you must keep. Several factors may be considered in determining whether various investment or business endeavors constitute one or more activities: (1) the economic interrelationship and interdependence of the various endeavors (similar customers, common employees, etc.); (2) the extent of common control; (3) the degree of organizational interrelationship between the various undertakings; (4) physical location (separate locations are more likely to constitute separate activities); and (5) similarities and differences in the activities being compared. The groupings used should reflect an appropriate and reasonable economic unit and should not be for the purpose of avoiding the passive loss rules. Generally a real estate rental activity cannot be grouped with a non-real-estate rental activity.

You must apply the groupings that you use consistently. Where the economic activities are conducted by a partnership or S corporation, the grouping decision will have to be made largely at the entity level. A partner, member, or shareholder may then further combine the activities of various partnerships, LLCs, and S corporations.

How to Categorize Income, Losses, and Business Activities into the Appropriate Categories

An important matter for taxpayers subject to the passive loss limitation rules is the definition of the different income types and the income, gain, loss, and deductions that are included in each category. The definitions are critical since a tax loss that is classified as passive on a particular activity may be subject to limitations on when it can be deducted. By planning your activities appropriately, you might be able to spend enough time with that particular business or investment to convert it into an active business and avoid having passive loss limitations restrict your deduction of the loss. Alternatively, should your real estate losses be sufficiently large, you might find it worthwhile to spend sufficient time in managing and operating your real estate investments to qualify as an active real estate professional. Thus you would avoid the passive loss limitation rules being applied to you (not the particular investment). To engage in this potentially valuable tax planning, you must understand the definitions of the different types of investments and income.

Passive Income/Loss

A business or investment activity will generate passive income if you do not materially participate in its operations or management. Material participation requires that you be involved in the activity on a regular, continuous, and substantial basis. In addition, this material participation must occur throughout the year. The test as to whether you meet this standard is applied each year. Thus, it will generally not suffice to work for a small portion of a year, or for one year but not in other years, to render a business an active endeavor when, in reality, your participation is negligible. Also, if your partner in a business venture materially participates, it does not mean that you automatically are a material participant. Your involvement is tested separately.

Owning an interest as a limited partner will generally not be treated as being a material participant. Partnership agreements for limited partnerships usually restrict the potential involvement of limited partners in the management of partnership matters. Most importantly, under the state laws that govern partnerships, limited partners are not allowed to actively participate in the management and operations of the partnership. If they do, they could risk losing their limited liability. Limited liability means that if the partnership defaults on a loan, the limited partners will generally only be liable up to the amount of their capital contributions or investments. There is an exception. Where you are both a limited and general partner, participate in the partnership's activities for more than 500 hours during the year, and have materially participated in the activity during any 5 of the preceding 10 years (or the activity is a personal service activity), you will be considered to materially participate.

Another way to grasp the meaning of a passive activity is to define what is not a passive activity. Portfolio investments and active business endeavors do not generate passive income. These two categories are described in detail later in this chapter.

As initially enacted, interests in real estate rental activities were generally categorized as passive whether or not there was material participation. An important exception permits active real estate professionals to offset passive income against active income in certain instances. This is described later in the chapter. There are also several other exceptions to the general rule that a rental real estate activity produces only passive income or loss. These are discussed later in the listing of exceptions.

Fish or Fowl—Is an LLC Member Analogous to a GP or LP?

A key question in determining the application of the passive loss rules to LLCs is how to compare the efforts and character of a member of an LLC with those of either a general partner or limited partner in a partnership. The actual treatment is unclear because the rules were originally conceived for partnerships but did not address LLCs. Within the context of a limited partnership, general partners can and do participate in management, whereas limited partners are prohibited by state law, and usually by the limited partnership agreement, from participating in management. The regulations presume, therefore, that an LP does not materially participate in the limited partnership activities unless the presumption can be overcome. This presumption can be overcome if the LP can demonstrate that he has spent more than 500 hours per year in the activity of the limited partnership's business, or other bright-line tests.

In contrast to the limited partnership, an S corporation shareholder faces no presumption as to material participation under the regulations. If the S corporation shareholder can demonstrate under the facts and circumstances that he is a material participant in the corporation's activities (or meets any of the other seven tests provided for in the regulations), he can be deemed a material participant and is not subject to the passive loss limitation rules.

LLC members do not fit into either the FLP or S corporation categories. The result is uncertainty in applying the material participation rules to LLCs. The test similar to an S corporation shareholder should be applied to determine if a member of an LLC materially participated in the LLC activities.

Basis (Investment) in Your LLC Membership Interest

Your investment in your LLC is referred to in tax jargon as your *basis*. This important concept can affect the tax consequences of many transactions.

A member may deduct his proportionate share of net losses incurred by the LLC from his other taxable income, if any. It is limited, however, to his tax basis (investment) of his interest in the LLC. If a member's share of LLC losses exceeds his tax basis for his interest at the end of any taxable year, such excess loss may be carried over indefinitely. It can be deducted at the end of any succeeding year, to the extent of his tax basis of his interest in the LLC.

Generally, each member's tax basis for his LLC membership interest is equal to the price paid for the interest, plus his pro rata share (measured by his share of LLC profits) of those liabilities of the LLC to which purchased and constructed property is subject and to which none of the members have personal liability (known as nonrecourse liabilities). The rules for determining how much and which LLC debts get added to your investment for making various tax calculations are extremely complex. The following brief introduction should encourage you to seek professional guidance.

Such a debt also cannot be in excess of the fair market value of the property burdened by such liabilities. All members are allocated a portion of such a nonrecourse liability in the same proportion as the members share in LLC profits. Each member's tax basis is increased by his pro rata share of LLC taxable income and is reduced (but not below zero) by his share of the LLC's taxable loss. It is also reduced by the amount of any distributions (including any reduction in his share of LLC nonrecourse liabilities such as the LLC's amortization of such liabilities) during the tax year. If the tax basis of a member's interest should be reduced to zero, any distributions (including any reduction in LLC nonrecourse liabilities in excess of his share of the LLC's taxable income) for any tax year will be treated as gain from the sale of his LLC membership interest.

In addition to these complex rules, many other limitations may restrict your ability to deduct your share of LLC tax losses. These include the at-risk rules, passive loss rules, and other limitations.

Transferability—Possible Termination of LLC for Tax Purposes

Once you have mastered the income tax rules affecting the taxation of your LLC while it is operating, you might think you are done. Not even close. A host of complex rules affect the income tax consequences of distributions of property from your LLC, the death of a member, and the sale or purchase of a membership interest.

If 50 percent or more of the capital and profit interests in an LLC are sold or exchanged within a single 12-month period, the LLC will terminate for tax purposes. The fact that the LLC continues to exist under state law does not change this income tax result. Termination of a partnership can raise multiple issues and problems. Investment tax credits can be recaptured; The partnership may have to switch from its calendar year to a fiscal year resulting in a bunching of income in one year; partnership tax elections are terminated; and depreciation is affected. In such an event, members could recognize gain to the extent their pro rata shares of any cash received plus their pro rata share of the LLC's debt exceeded the tax basis for their interest in the LLC. To avoid this problem, the members could be precluded from making transfers sufficient to trigger such a termination by the provisions of the operating agreement.

These rules can be important considerations if your LLC merges with another entity. If two or more LLCs and/or partnerships merge or consolidate into one LLC, the resulting LLC will be considered a continuation of the merging or consolidating partnerships and/or LLCs, the members of which own an interest of more than 50 percent in the capital and profits of the resulting partnership. Thus, an LLC can be considered to be a continuation of a predecessor entity and a termination will not occur for tax purposes.

How LLC Distributions and Liquidations Are Taxed

One of the first steps in determining the tax consequences of a family business owner's interest in an LLC being sold or liquidated is to determine the investment (tax basis) in the membership interest. The sale of a family membership interest is generally treated as the sale of a capital asset. The capital gain (or loss) is the difference between the proceeds (called the **amount realized**) and the member's adjusted tax basis in his LLC interest.

Usually the first item included in the calculation of a member's tax basis is the cash and tax basis of property the member contributed to the LLC in exchange for receiving membership interest. No gain or loss is generally recognized on this type of contribution transaction.

A member's tax basis (investment) in the LLC is increased by his share of LLC taxable income, which is allocated to him and reported on his individual tax return. Basis is also increased by the member's share of tax-exempt income. When a distribution is made to a member, his tax basis is decreased by the amount of the distribution.

A member's tax basis may also include LLC debts. If none of the members have any personal liability for a nonrecourse LLC liability (a debt that the lender cannot sue the members individually to recover on), then the tax laws provide that all of the members can include a portion of such liability in their tax basis (i.e., their investment in the LLC). The proportion that each member would share in such liability is the ratio in which they share in LLC profits.

A member does not recognize gain on an LLC distribution, except to the extent that any money received exceeds the member's adjusted basis in his membership interest before the distribution. Under the general rule, a member does not recognize gain on a distribution of property, but instead takes a basis in the distributed property equal to (1) the basis of that property in the LLC's hands if the distribution is a nonliquidating distribution (i.e., an interim distribution), or (2) the member's basis in his membership interest if the distribution is a liquidating distribution.

Any increase in the member's share of liabilities is considered to be a contribution of money by the member to the LLC and thus would increase his basis in the LLC. Any decrease in the member's share of liabilities is considered by the IRS as a distribution of money by the LLC to the member and thus would decrease his basis in the membership. If this decrease in the member's share of liabilities is greater than the basis in his membership interest, the member will recognize gain.

A member receiving a distribution of marketable securities generally will have to recognize taxable gain equal to the excess, if any, of the fair market value of the securities over the partner's basis in the partnership interest. There are, however, several exceptions.

There is an important exception to the preceding rule that the sale of a membership interest is treated as the sale of a capital asset. Where a portion of the sale proceeds relate to two special types of assets, a member may have to report part of his gain on the sale as ordinary income. These two special assets are **unrealized receivables** and substantially appreciated inventory. They are referred to as *hot assets*. Unrealized receivables are the right to income that has not been reported under the method of accounting used by the LLC.

EXAMPLE: Medical Associates is an LLC of physicians. It reports income on a cash basis. This means income is only reported when patients pay their bills, not when the medical services are provided. If the LLC is sold, the accounts receivable due from patients who have received services but have not yet paid would be unrealized receivables.

Unrealized receivables also include certain depreciation recapture and other technical adjustments. Defining the second category of special assets, substantially appreciated inventory, is much more complicated. It includes inventory-type items (the term is much broader than what is generally considered to be inventory). When you sell your membership interest in an LLC, it will be more difficult to avoid ordinary income treatment on your share of the LLC's substantially appreciated inventory. These are highly technical, and potentially costly, issues that you must address with tax professionals.

Adjusting the Tax Basis in LLC Assets

You buy 50 percent of an LLC that owns a $1 million building for $500,000. The LLC purchased the building years ago and has fully written it off (depreciated it) so no deductions remain. This creates a tremendous inequity for you. You just paid for the LLC that owns the building, but you do not get any depreciation deductions to shelter your share of rental income. LLCs can take advantage of a special tax election to address this problem. Although the election is complicated, you should at least be aware of it.

When a member sells a membership interest, or dies, an LLC may make a special tax election to address the problem highlighted in the preceding paragraph. The concept of tax basis was introduced earlier. You must understand two types of basis to plan with this special election. The *inside basis* of an asset is the basis that the LLC has in the asset (e.g., the building in the preceding example). The *outside basis* is your basis in your LLC membership interest. This special election, called a *Code Section 754 Election* after the tax law containing it, permits the inheriting or purchasing member's share of LLC assets to be increased or decreased to equal the outside basis of that member's membership interest.

EXAMPLE: Sam is a new member in an LLC. Sam pays $400,000 for a 20 percent interest in an LLC whose sole asset is a building that has appreciated substantially since the LLC purchased it many years ago. The building is on the LLC's books at $500,000, so that Sam's share of it (the "inside basis") is $100,000. The LLC is depreciating the building over 39 years. Sam has a problem. He has in effect paid $400,000 for a partial interest in the building but is only getting depreciation based on the LLC's original purchase price of the building, which is much lower. Also, if the building were sold for $2 million (Sam's share being 20 percent, or the $400,000 he paid), the LLC would realize a $1.5 million gain ($2 million less $500,000 basis), Sam's share being $300,000. This is not a reasonable result since Sam's interest in the building only sold for the price he just paid for it. If the LLC's only asset were sold, it would probably liquidate and Sam would get an offsetting capital loss. Unfortunately, some LLCs have multiple assets so liquidation is not guaranteed. The capital loss limitations could also create problems.

If the LLC makes a special Section 754 tax election, Sam can get an adjustment to prevent being taxed on the $300,000 he really did not earn if the building is sold. He also can get a depreciation deduction that more closely reflects his actual investment in the building. The adjustment equals the difference between the $400,000 Sam paid and his $100,000 share of the LLC's basis in the building (the tax regulations use the selling member's basis in his LLC interest as allocated to the building instead). Since we have assumed the building is the only LLC asset, Sam would then depreciate this amount over 39 years for an additional depreciation deduction on his personal tax return. This would be in addition to his share of the LLC's depreciation deduction (which is included in the calculation of the new member's share of the LLC's income reported to him on Form K-1).

EXAMPLE: John and Mary are equal members in an LLC that holds real property with a fair market value of $1,000 and a basis of $600 (real property value remains constant for the purposes of this example). John dies and leaves his membership interest to his wife, Susan. Since under Section 1014 of the Internal Revenue Code, a person acquiring property from a decedent takes a basis in the property based on the fair market value of the property at the time of the decedent's death, Susan's basis in the LLC is $500, or half of the value of the LLC's assets. If a Section 754 election is in effect, Susan can step up her inside basis from $300 to $500. If later the LLC sells its real property for $1,000, Susan realizes no gain. Her share of the amount realized is $500, and her share of the inside basis is $500. Estate tax repeal will change this.

Under a Section 754 election, a step-down basis can also occur. If the fair market value in the preceding example was $600 and the basis was $1,000, Susan's basis would have decreased from $500 to $300. Once an election is made, it can only be revoked with permission from the IRS.

STATE TAX CONSIDERATIONS

There is no consistency among the states that have LLC legislation for the treatment of LLCs for state tax purposes. Some states, like Florida and Pennsylvania, tax LLCs at the entity level, and other states, like Texas, tax LLCs with an earned surplus tax. The classification of LLCs in those states that do not have LLC legislation is not uniform.

SUMMARY

Most LLCs are taxed as partnerships so that the LLC will pay no entity-level tax, and all of its income, losses, and credits will flow through to the individual member's tax return. Many partnership tax rules that apply to an LLC affect the allocation of income and losses, deductibility of losses, taxation of the sale or exchange of a member's interest, and basis of the assets in an LLC on the sale or exchange of a member's interest. You should review these complex rules with a tax specialist.

For Your Notebook

CONSENT TO CONSULTING AGREEMENT

NOTE: Use the following documents if the LLC wants to retain a key person under a consulting agreement. Be sure to discuss with your accountant whether the person your LLC is hiring is really a consultant or should more properly be classified as an employee for tax purposes. This is an important decision because the tax consequences of a mistake can be costly. There are also legal implications to classifying a person as an employee or consultant (independent contractor).

LLCNAME
Action Taken by Unanimous Written Consent
of the
Board of Managers and Members
To Authorize Consulting Agreement

The undersigned, being all of the Managers and Members of the LLC, hereby take the following actions:

RESOLVED, The LLC retains CONSULTANT-NAME as a consultant to the LLC on the terms and conditions set forth in the Consulting Agreement attached.

RESOLVED, The LLC enter into a Consulting Agreement substantially in the form attached.

RESOLVED, The Managers of the LLC are hereby authorized to take any and all actions to effect the above.

Dated: SIGNDATE

_____
MEMBER-1NAME, Member and Manager

_____
MEMBER-2NAME, Member

_____
MEMBER-3NAME, Member and Manager

_____
MANAGER-1NAME, Manager

[Attach a signed consulting agreement to this page]

CONSULTING AGREEMENT

AGREEMENT dated DAY MONTH, YEAR, between CONSULTANT-NAME, an individual who resides at CONSULTANT-ADDRESS (the "Consultant"), and LLCNAME, a New Jersey LLC doing business at LLC-ADDRESS, (the "LLC").

WHEREAS, the LLC operates a DESCRIBE-BUSINESS business (the "Business").

WHEREAS, the LLC wishes to retain the Consultant as an independent contractor, and the Consultant wishes to be retained in such capacity and perform certain services for the LLC, to promote the interests of the Business.

THEREFORE, the parties hereto agree as follows:

1. *Consulting.*

a. LLC hereby retains Consultant and Consultant hereby accepts such engagement, for the term and under the conditions and requirements specified herein, as a consultant to the LLC, with such duties and responsibilities as may reasonably be assigned to pursuant to this Agreement. The Consultant's compensation shall be that specified below.

b. Consultant's principal duties shall include DESCRIBE-DUTIES. However, Consultant shall have no authority to accept, reject, or modify any contract entered into by the LLC's Managers, or to negotiate the sale of any significant portion of the Business without the express written consent of the LLC.

c. Consultant shall receive an annual salary to be determined in the reasonable discretion of the Managers, which shall be based on going market rates for each of the various services consultant performs (including but not limited to leasing, managing, etc.), payable (the "Compensation"). Consultant shall bill LLC for all **ordinary and necessary business expenses** and the LLC shall pay such amounts.

d. The Consultant shall devote Consultant's best efforts, at the times and places she reasonably deems appropriate to her duties hereunder. However, it is expressly agreed that Consultant may serve as a consultant, manager, investor, or employee to other persons, without limitation.

e. The principal place of business of the Consultant shall be at such places as Consultant, in Consultant's reasonable discretion, may choose from time to time. Consultant shall provide the LLC not less than Twenty (20) days advance Notice of any change in the principal place of business.

f. The Consultant shall be responsible to DETAIL ADDITIONAL ITEMS.

2. *Status.*

The Consultant shall be treated in all respects as an independent contractor and the LLC shall not withhold any taxes on account of services rendered to it by Consultant. Consultant represents to LLC that Consultant regularly holds itself out as a consultant to others, maintains its own office, has business cards other than for the services provided to LLC, and assumes all risk of Consultant's classification as an independent contractor and not an employee.

3. *Term of Retainer.*

The term for which Consultant shall be retained hereunder shall commence on the date hereof and shall terminate upon the earlier of: (i) the cessation of the Business of the LLC; (ii) the death, or substantial disability of Consultant; or (iii) the last day of the 24th month following the date of this Agreement, unless this Agreement is not canceled by the parties in which event it shall be renewed for One (1) additional year pursuant to this Agreement.

4. *Extension and Termination.*

a. If Consultant shall be terminated by LLC, Consultant shall be entitled to any amounts due and owing as compensation under their Agreement to the extent earned, as defined herein, on a pro rata basis, plus reimbursement for costs.

b. This Agreement can be terminated by either party on One Hundred Twenty (120) days written notice provided in accordance with the terms hereof.

c. If neither party hereto terminates this Agreement as provided herein, then the term of this Agreement shall be renewed for the following calendar month subject to all the terms and conditions hereof. However, notwithstanding anything herein to the contrary, this Agreement shall terminate on December 31, 2010.

5. *Disability or Death.*

The Consultant shall be deemed substantially disabled if (i) the Consultant and the LLC agree that the Consultant is substantially disabled; or (ii) for a period of Sixty (60) consecutive days, the Consultant is unable, as a result of any physical, mental or emotional illness, ailment, or accident to effectively discharge Consultant's duties hereunder. If the Consultant shall be substantially disabled as defined herein, the LLC may then immediately upon Notice to the Consultant terminate this Agreement and the LLC's obligation to pay the Consultant the Compensation hereunder.

6. *Expenses.*

LLC shall be responsible for any and all expenses which Consultant reasonably incurs in performing the duties assigned hereunder. The Consultant shall be responsible to provide reasonable corroboration to the LLC of any such expenses.

7. *Notices.*

All notices and other communications hereunder shall be in writing and shall be deemed given if delivered personally or mailed, by either registered mail or certified mail return receipt requested, to the parties hereto at the addresses listed herein, or at such other address for a party as shall be specified by notice given pursuant hereto ("Notice").

8. *Waiver.*

The failure of Consultant or LLC to seek redress for violation of, or to insist upon the strict performance of any covenant or condition of this Agreement shall not prevent a subsequent act which would have originally constituted a violation from having all the force and effect of an original violation.

9. *Miscellaneous.*

This Agreement constitutes the entire agreement between the parties hereto, supersedes all existing agreements between them and cannot be changed or terminated except by a written agreement signed by the parties and may not be assigned by either party. This Agreement shall be construed in accordance with the substantive law of STATENAME.

LLCNAME

By _____
     MANAGER-NAME, Manager

CONSULTANT

_____
CONSULTANT-NAME

12 ESTATE TAX PLANNING AND YOUR LIMITED LIABILITY COMPANY

LLCs can provide a tremendous opportunity for anyone engaged in estate planning. The flexibility and unique characteristics of the LLC make it an ideal entity to use in many estate-planning transactions. You do not have to be a Rockefeller to benefit from an LLC. Even if your estate is under the $1,000,000 (2002, increasing to $1,500,000 in 2004, with further increases scheduled thereafter) estate tax deduction (called the "applicable exclusion"), an LLC can still minimize **probate** problems and costs, make it easier and cheaper to give gifts to your children or other heirs and assure greater control.

LLCs can provide numerous estate-planning benefits:

- An LLC provides its members with limited liability to protect personal assets from LLC claims. The LLC itself can protect LLC assets from non-LLC claims.

- From a tax perspective, the LLC provides tremendous flexibility because it will generally be treated as a partnership for federal income tax purposes if properly structured. As a partnership, the LLC can take advantage of special allocations, basis adjustments, and other favorable income tax planning issues addressed in Chapter 11.

- The operating agreement, the naming of successor managers, and the restricting of the transfer of LLC membership interests can assure control and succession of the assets or business owned by the LLC.

This chapter illustrates many of the benefits of using an LLC for estate planning.

USES IN ESTATE PLANNING

The combined advantages of all the benefits described previously make an LLC ideal for achieving specific estate-planning steps.

Ownership and Gift Program for Small Real Estate Investment Property

A common estate-planning strategy is to make gifts of noncontrolling minority interests in a small rental real property. In the past, a typical approach would have been to transfer the property to a general partnership or limited partnership and thereafter gift interests in the partnership to your children or other desired **donees.** The partnership technique was used to achieve divisibility of the otherwise indivisible real estate holdings. This avoided the necessity of having to prepare numerous deeds each year to make the necessary transfers.

An LLC offers a substantial advantage over a partnership in that, unlike a partnership, no member has to be personally liable in an LLC. The LLC statutes allow for the appointment of a manager to manage the property as contrasted with a general partnership where every partner will have the right to participate in the management and affairs of the partnership. This is a substantial advantage where a parent is giving minority interests over a period of time and wants to retain some measure of control over the property. This can also be useful even following the parent's complete gift of all interest in the property. A particular child or family member can be designated as the manager, and in some states a manager does not have to be a member. Thus, a parent can gift his entire membership interest in the LLC and still remain as the LLC's manager. This can avoid potential problems of deciding who should determine whether the property should be sold, refinanced, improved, and so forth. The control over management that an LLC allows is a critical benefit.

PLANNIING OPPORTUNITY: If Pa and Ma have a limited liability company in which each of them are 50 percent members, they could set up two classes of membership. Class A would be voting membership interests and represent 1 percent of the total equity of the LLC. Class B would be nonvoting membership interests which would represent 99 percent of the equity of the entity. Pa and Ma could then gift the 99 percent Class B interest to their children and/or trusts for their primary benefit. Pa and Ma would continue to control the entire entity as the sole owners of the 1 percent Class A voting membership interest. In this way, they could determine the salaries and bonuses they would be entitled to, whether the property should be sold, whether distributions should be made, and all other partnership decisions. They would effectively transfer their entire equity interest in the LLC to their children and/or trusts for their benefit while still retaining full control over the entity. Pa and Ma would also be entitled to reduce the value of the gifts due to lack of control and marketability discounts.

Membership interests could be assigned each year in amounts designed to effect gifts of $11,000, or $22,000 where joint gifts were used (these are 2002 figures which will be increased in the future for inflation), so there would be no gift tax because of the annual gift tax exclusion. The IRS has challenged these common transactions so careful planning is essential.

Ownership of More Significant Real Estate Used in a Family Business

A common planning technique is to separate business real estate from the family operating business. The taxpayer transfers the real estate to an entity, such as a family LLC, independent of the operating company, and then makes gifts of membership interests in that real estate to younger generations. These gifts are often made to trusts, including special trusts that can leverage the gifts for gift tax valuation purposes. A lease of the real estate to the family business typically follows these transactions. The rental payments received by the LLC from the family business can then be used to fund educational payments and other needs of the younger family members. This planning can provide substantial income tax savings as well as estate tax savings when the children are in a lower tax bracket than the parents making the gifts.

If there are multiple real estate properties, or other significant passive assets, the best planning is to have a separate LLC for each parcel of real estate or significant asset. For example, if two warehouses are used in the business, a separate LLC should own each of the warehouse premises. Each LLC would then lease the premises owned by it to the entity operating the business. Thus, if there is a lawsuit, claim, or other problem with one real estate property (examples are tort liabilities and environmental hazards), the liabilities of that real estate will not negatively impact the other real estate. Although having multiple entities will add complexity to the business structure, it will enhance the liability protection of the business owners.

Another alternative is to form a single investment LLC and have that LLC form a separate wholly owned (subsidiary) LLC for each property. This will provide liability protection similar to that of multiple independent

LLCs, but minimize the administrative work and tax filings (only the primary LLC would have to file).

A common technique in these transactions has always been to argue for the most substantial minority interests discount and/or **lack of marketability discount** possible on the real estate interests transferred by gift to the children and/or other donees. Care must be taken to assure that the manager's powers in an LLC are not so broad as to prevent the technical completion of the gift, or to otherwise pull the asset transferred back into the parent's/**donor's** estate. The fiduciary duties that the manager owes the members under state law should not be compromised. Preferably, the parent/donor should not serve as manager.

Closely Held Operating Businesses

LLCs are a simpler and more flexible technique than most other forms of business ownership, especially in light of common estate-planning strategies. Most closely held businesses are organized as S corporations. When someone who owns S corporation stock wants to transfer by gift shares to a trust for a child's benefit as part of an estate plan, the Qualified Subchapter S Trust (QSST) or costly Electing Small Business Trust (ESBT) rules have to be addressed. These rules present substantial complications and costs when trusts are to hold stock in an S corporation without jeopardizing the S corporation tax status. In addition to these estate-planning complications, there are numerous operating difficulties in the S corporation context. For example, different classes of stock (other than classes that differ only with respect to voting rights) cannot be issued. Thus, the traditional recapitalization or different tiers of ownership with different rights that many estate-planning techniques favor cannot be used with S corporations. In addition, if these were gifts of stock to children and the donor wanted to make distributions of income to himself, the corporation would have to make a proportionate distribution of income to the children. This would be necessary to avoid running afoul of the prohibition against two classes of stock in an S corporation.

The LLC provides a useful alternative to the preceding scenario where more than one owner is involved in the entity. An LLC can provide the same limited liability and the flow-through tax treatment that the S corporation provides. Yet, the many restrictions applicable to S corporations, such as the limited number of shareholders, the limited types of trusts that could own the stock, and the one class of stock requirements are not applicable. Therefore, the LLC presents a substantial advantage over the S corporation, particularly where the value of the donor's estate will grow to a substantial size and complex estate planning techniques are necessary to reduce estate taxes.

NOTE: Many business owners are reluctant to make outright transfers of ownership interests to a child or other family member. They fear that the recipient may get divorced, die, or not be mature enough to manage the asset, resulting in creditor problems, tax liens, and/or bankruptcy. Therefore, they generally opt to transfer the ownership interest into a trust. With an S corporation, this trust must be carefully tailored to meet stringent IRS requirements. The trust can only be set up for the benefit of one beneficiary and must provide for mandatory distributions of income. There is limited flexibility in structuring the trust to avoid many of the problems mentioned earlier. With a limited liability company, the trust can be drawn with a wide variety of provisions to deal with various scenarios.

Using LLCs to Make Gifts to Children

Few adults are comfortable giving a child valuable assets outright (i.e., with no controls, such as a trust). The LLC provides an excellent tool for controlling gifts to a child. The parent can gift the assets to the LLC, name the parent as manager, and then gift interests in the LLC to the children. The parent would retain a measure of control, perhaps even more than could be retained in a trust since the parent/donor who sets up a trust (the *grantor*) cannot be a trustee (manage the trust).

In pursuing this planning, care must be taken to address the family partnership rules. These tax rules permit a child to receive a gift of an LLC membership interest, and for this to be respected for tax purposes, as long as certain requirements are met. The child must truly own the interest in the LLC and capital must be a material income-producing factor for the LLC. In a real estate LLC, the property (capital) will be the only income-producing factor unless the parent is providing substantial services. This rule also requires that the parent be paid reasonable compensation for any services such parent provides to the LLC. Where services will be provided, the operating agreement should try to assure payment of a fair compensation for such services.

SAMPLE CLAUSE: For example, consider the following language: "Notwithstanding anything in this Operating Agreement to the contrary, should any provision of this Operating Agreement, or any act of the Parties, result in a violation of the family partnership provisions of Internal Revenue Code Section 704(e) and the regulations and cases thereunder, the manager may amend this Agreement, or take any other actions reasonably necessary to prevent such violation, or to correct such violation."

Operating Agreement—Buy-Sell Agreements

A truly important component of a gift of a membership interest in an LLC to a child or any other relative is to have properly structured buy-sell provisions in the operating agreement. At the very least, this agreement should cover such issues as the ability of the donee to transfer his interest, the death of the member, sales in violation of the agreement, and involuntary transfers of the member's interest such as incident to a divorce or bankruptcy.

The following buy-sell provisions can be used as a structure when there is a gift of a membership interest to a child.

Voluntary Transfers

The child would not be permitted to transfer his membership interest without the consent of a majority of the remaining members. This has the important benefit of limiting the child's ability to transfer his interest. The provision could further state that if the child receives a bona fide offer, he is to offer the membership interest back to the LLC first and the remaining members second. The LLC and then the remaining members would have an option to buy the child's membership interest at the lessor of the bona fide offer price or 50 percent of an agreed on value (or formula value). The rationale behind this provision is to give the LLC or the remaining members the option to buy the membership interest at the lower of these two prices.

The terms of the buyout by the LLC or the remaining members would be either the terms of the bona fide offer or a 10-year note providing for the lowest rate of interest to avoid the imputation of interest by the IRS, whichever the purchaser party (i.e., the LLC or the remaining members) desires.

EXAMPLE: For example, assume the agreed on value of the member's interest is $100,000 and the child receives an offer for $200,000 payable in the form of a 5-year note calling for 10 percent interest. The LLC then would have the option to buy the child's interest at $50,000 (i.e., 50 percent of the $100,000 agreed on value). It could do so either over a term of 5 years with 10 percent interest or over 10 years with the lowest rate of interest to avoid imputation of interest by the IRS, whichever the LLC or remaining members desire.

Involuntary Transfer or Sale in Violation of the Agreement

If the member's interest falls into the hands of a creditor or judgment holder or the child sells in violation of the agreement, then the LLC first and the remaining members second could have first and second options to buy the child's interest at the lower of what is actually paid for the member's interest or 50 percent of the agreed on value. The terms can be whatever the terms of the purchase are (if any) or the 10-year note with the lowest rate of interest to avoid imputation of interest by the IRS. Even if the LLC or the remaining members do not exercise their options to purchase the child's membership interest, the transferee of the child's membership interest will not be permitted to participate in the management of the LLC.

Death of the Child

If the child were to die, then the LLC first and the remaining members second could have first and second options to buy the child's membership interest at the agreed on value (or formula price). This purchase can be funded with life insurance. If it is funded with life insurance, then the agreement can provide that to the extent of the life insurance funding, all the proceeds would be used to buy the child's membership interest. To the extent of any shortfall, then the remaining purchase price would be paid over 10 years with the lowest rate of interest to avoid imputation of interest by the IRS.

Comparison of LLCs with Trusts

One of the most commonly used estate-planning tools is the transfer by the donor of an asset or business to a trust formed during the donor's life (an inter vivos trust). By using an LLC, all of the members receive an allocation of income as long as the LLC complies with the family partnership rules, discussed earlier. If the trust is not a grantor trust, the income of the trust will be taxed to the trust and thus subject to the applicable tax rates for trusts. It may be desirable to have the income realized by the trust to be taxed at individual rates and not at the trust rates. To achieve this, the trustee will be required to distribute the income to the beneficiaries. This causes the income to be taxed to the beneficiaries at their respective tax rates. However, you may not want your children to receive a distribution of income. LLCs avoid these difficulties since the income recognized by the LLC is passed through to its members, causing the income to be taxed at the members' individual rates without having to distribute the income to all or certain members.

LLCs Are More Flexible than Irrevocable Trusts

A popular estate-planning tool is the irrevocable trust. This trust, once formed, cannot be changed. An irrevocable trust may be essential to achieving your estate-planning objective of removing any future appreciation in the assets in the trust from your estate. Although this popular tool has many benefits, there is one major and important restriction. This type of trust cannot be amended to deal with the changing environment (i.e., change in relationships). An LLC can deal with a changing business environment better than a trustee who has strict fiduciary restrictions. Another advantage of an LLC over an irrevocable trust is that the donor may retain managerial control over transferred assets. To change an LLC, all you have to do is amend the operating agreement by signing a new one. Thus, LLCs can offer a flexible tool in lieu of a typical irrevocable trust.

LLCs can even cure problems with existing trusts. Assume you set up trusts for your children; your eldest is about to reach age 21 and the trust is to end. If you have the trustee invest all trust assets in the family LLC when the child's trust ends, instead of receiving cash, your child receives membership interests in the family LLC. These are nonliquid assets, and you as parent can control most LLC functions by serving as its manager.

LLCs Are Useful to Avoid Ancillary Probate

An interest in an LLC is deemed to be intangible personal property. This can be important for a nonresident, since the ownership of intangible personal property should not subject the estate of a nonresident decedent to ancillary probate proceedings to effect the transfer of an LLC interest. This will also affect the manner of transferring an LLC interest as a gift (or for other purposes).

VALUATION OF TRANSFERRED LIMITED LIABILITY COMPANY INTERESTS

When valuing an asset for estate or gift tax purposes, the value is the asset's fair market value at the time of the gift or the time that the item can be included in the decedent's estate. The fair market value is the value at which a purchaser would pay for the interest to a seller, neither being under any compulsion to buy or sell, and each with reasonable knowledge of the relevant facts. The valuation of gifts or **bequests** of LLC interests is a complex task that involves many issues. The following discussion highlights a few of them.

A significant incentive for using an LLC in an estate-planning context is the significant leveraging that valuation discounts make possible. The two primary types of discounts are lack of control discounts and lack of marketability discounts. These discounts range from 10 percent to 50 percent.

The IRS is concerned about parents or other donors making transfers of ownership interests in businesses while retaining certain rights. These retained rights, and hence the interests given, become difficult to value, and historically many taxpayers tried to take advantage of these difficulties. To minimize abuses, the tax laws provide that if a donor transfers an asset to an LLC while retaining distribution or liquidation rights that would decrease the value of a gift (e.g., to the donor's child), it will be valued for gift tax purposes as if these retained rights did not exist unless the gift meets strict requirements. The result is that unless you follow the "cookbook" rules established by the IRS, the value of the LLC interest given will not be reduced by the value of the rights you keep. This tax rule provides that when a donor transfers an equity interest in an LLC to a member of the donor's family, the gift would have a greater value for gift and estate tax purposes than it would otherwise have had. This depresses the value of the donor's retained interest in the same enterprise. To accomplish this goal, the subtraction method of valuation in determining the value of the gift is used. An exception to this Code section is found where the interest retained by the donor is of the same class as the gifted interest.

GRANTOR RETAINED ANNUITY TRUSTS (GRATs) AND LLCs

A common estate planning technique for the wealthy is to use techniques to make large gifts at discounted rates. The GRAT, or Grantor Retained Annuity Trust, is one such technique. GRATs can be used with gifts of securities, interests in family businesses, and even other assets. A GRAT can be illustrated as follows. Parent has a substantial estate and wishes to reduce it through a large gift to child. Parent makes a gift of $1 million of securities into a special trust called a GRAT. If the gift had been made outright to the child, it would have been valued at the $1 million fair value of the securities and the parent could have had to pay a substantial gift tax. If the gift is instead made to a GRAT, the parent could reserve the right to receive the income from the GRAT for a period of years, say 3, 5, 10, or even more years. The more years for which the parent reserves the right to receive the income from the gift, the longer the child will have to wait to receive the benefit of the assets, and hence the lower the value of the gift for gift tax purposes. If the parent reserved a right to income for a sufficient number of years, the value of the gift could be reduced to $1 million (2002) or less. This could enable the parent not to exceed the $1 million gift exclusion and not pay any current gift tax cost.

When planning for GRATs, gifts of LLC membership interests could be used in the planning. Membership interests in the LLC can be given to the

GRAT. The income that the LLC's assets produce would fund the payment of the income stream to the parent. At the end of the term of the GRAT, the LLC membership interests could then be distributed to the child.

NOTE: For a more detailed analysis of GRATs, see Shenkman, *The Complete Book of Trusts,* 3rd ed. (New York: John Wiley & Sons, 2002).

SUMMARY

The LLC entity is an estate-planning vehicle as well as a form of business entity. If senior family members desire to gift a portion of investment real estate, they could gift membership interest in an LLC that owns the real property instead of gifting a direct interest in the property. The donor would be able to take discounts on the gifted interest for minority interests and lack of marketability and would not be required to execute a new deed when making each gift. In addition, the LLC provides substantial benefits relating to the gifting of ownership interests over the gifting of ownership interests in an S corporation. If a donor wishes to make a transfer to a trust for the donee's benefit, there are specific restrictions on the types of trusts that can be used if the gifted interest is S corporation stock. These restrictions do not exist in the context of LLCs. Finally, a donor of an LLC membership interest who desires to retain control over the company can accomplish that objective more easily with an LLC than with other business entities.

Part Five

SPECIFIC BUSINESSES AND FINANCIAL GOALS AND YOUR LIMITED LIABILITY COMPANY

13 HOME-BASED BUSINESSES AND LIMITED LIABILITY COMPANIES

Tens of millions of Americans operate home-based businesses. These range from small part-time endeavors that supplement spending money to substantial consulting, marketing, and other enterprises. Too often, the "home" part of the home-based business leads to informality that regular businesses would not tolerate. There is no reason for this. You can run a home-based business in as formal and professional a manner as any other business. A critical area of informality for most home businesses is their legal organization—there is none. This is a big mistake. You should carefully evaluate forming a one-member LLC to operate your home-based business. This formality can protect you from liability and safeguard most of your personal assets if a suit or claim is ever filed against your business. Using an LLC will also make your business sound and appear more professional. An LLC after a business name gives it a formal and serious image and image counts.

LEGAL DOCUMENTS

The legal documentation for a home-based business LLC can be relatively simple. You will need:

- Certificates to form and maintain the legal status of your business.
- A one-member operating agreement, which is illustrated in the "For Your Notebook" section at the end of this chapter. You can use this agreement to create a succession plan to help your business through periods of your illness, disability, or absence. Without the formality of the LLC and the operating agreement, these serious issues are unlikely to be addressed.

- A lease between the LLC and yourself so that the LLC can use the home office.

- Other agreements used by any business or LLC in regular operations.

- New insurance polices. You may require new insurance, or an addendum (called a *rider*) to your existing homeowners insurance to reflect that your business is now organized as an LLC.

- New bank accounts in the name of the LLC. The bank will likely ask you for your LLC seal (a metal clamp that embosses the name of the LLC on paper) and a copy of your operating agreement (which is another reason to prepare one). Since the LLC is a separate legal entity from you, new bank accounts are essential.

- Cancellation of your DBA. Many owners of home businesses take the appropriate legal step of filing a DBA (Doing Business As) document (certificate) with the local county clerk or other appropriate government agency when they operate a home business under a name different from their own. If you have done this, you may wish to cancel that DBA by filing an appropriate certificate once your LLC is formed. You can contact the county clerk where you filed the original to find out what form is needed.

LIABILITY PROTECTION

To assure that forming an LLC will provide liability protection for your home-based business, you must operate your LLC using the same formalities as any other business. If you have a franchise or other contractual arrangement that permits you to sell or work with the business or products you have, you must assign or transfer these contractual rights from your name personally to the name of your LLC. First, verify with the companies you work with that the contract rights can be assigned to an LLC. They might require a personal guarantee from you, a change in the original documents, or other matters. Once you have taken care of that obligation, have your attorney help you transfer the contract rights to the LLC.

INCOME TAX REPORTING

As mentioned in prior chapters, a one-member LLC is a disregarded entity for federal income tax purposes; there are no reporting requirements. Before you transferred your home-based business to the LLC, you reported your income or loss for the home-based business on your personal Form

1040, Schedule C. You will continue to do so. The only changes will be that the name listed on Schedule C for your business will have "LLC" at the end.

If you formerly reported under your Social Security number, file Form SS-4 with the IRS to obtain a tax identification number for your LLC.

SUMMARY

Home-based businesses are burgeoning. Using an LLC will give you important legal protections and the improved image of a serious business. This chapter addressed some of the key points to consider in restructuring your home-based business as an LLC.

NOTE: For further information about legal, tax, and other issues of operating a business in your home, see Shenkman, *Homeowners Legal Bible* (New York: John Wiley & Sons, 2002).

For Your Notebook

ONE-MEMBER LLC OPERATING AGREEMENT FOR HOME BUSINESS

OPERATING AGREEMENT
FOR
LLCNAME LLC
A STATENAME Single Member Limited Liability Company

THIS OPERATING AGREEMENT is made and entered into as of MONTH DAY, YEAR by and among LLCNAME, LLC, a STATENAME Limited Liability Company (the "Company") and the one person executing this Operating Agreement as the sole member of the Company ("Member") and hereby states as follows:

WITNESSETH:

a. Whereas, the Member desires to enter into this operating agreement ("Operating Agreement" or "Agreement") for the purposes of governing the Company, to and for the purpose of DESCRIBE HOME-BUSINESS ("Business").

b. Whereas, the Member had operated the Business heretofore as a sole proprietorship and intends through this Operating Agreement and the Exhibits attached to transfer all assets of such predecessor sole proprietorship to the Company.

NOW, THEREFORE, in consideration of the mutual premises below, and other good and valuable consideration receipt and sufficiency of which is hereby acknowledged, it is agreed as follows:

1. *Organization.*

a. *Formation.*

The Company has been organized as a STATENAME Limited Liability Company under and pursuant to the STATENAME Limited Liability Company Act (the "Act") by the filing of Articles of Organization ("Articles") with the Department of the State of STATENAME as required by the Act.

b. *Name.*

CAUTION: If you have other names you are operating under, and they are names of your business (not a supplier, franchiser, etc.) consult with an intellectual property attorney to determine what steps you need to take to protect the name. Merely setting up an LLC will not assure this.

The name of the Company shall be the "LLCNAME, LLC." The Company may also conduct its business under one or more assumed names.

c. *Duration.*

The Company shall continue in existence perpetually.

d. *Registered Office and Resident Agent.*

NOTE: Naming successor agents here will facilitate the continued operation of your business in the event of your illness or death.

The Registered Office and Resident Agent of the Company shall be as designated in the initial Articles or any amendment thereof AGENTNAME, c/o AGENTADDRESS. The Registered Office and/or Resident Agent may be changed from time to time. Any such change shall be made in accordance with the Act, or the terms of this Agreement if different. If the Resident Agent shall ever resign, the Company shall promptly appoint SUCCESSOR-1AGENT, who resides at SUCCESSOR-1AGENTADDRESS, who shall serve as the successor Agent. If SUCCESSOR-1AGENT, is unable or unwilling to so serve, then the Company shall promptly appoint SUCCESSOR-2AGENT, who resides at SUCCESSOR-2AGENTADDRESS, who shall serve as the successor Agent. If he or she is unable or unwilling to serve as Agent, then the Managers by majority vote shall designate a successor Agent by giving written notice to the Members.

e. *Tax Status for Company.*

The Company shall be taxed as a sole proprietorship for tax purposes unless and until at least one additional Member is added in which event the Company shall thereafter be treated as a partnership for tax purposes.

2. *Books, Records, and Accounting.*

PLANNING TIP: Maintaining good books and records for your LLC, separate from your personal records, is essential to maintain the independent legal status, and hence liability limitation, of your LLC.

a. *Books and Records.*

The Company shall maintain complete and accurate books and records of the Company's business and affairs as required by the Act and such books and records shall be kept at the Company's Registered Office and shall in all respects be independent of the books, records, and transactions of the sole Member.

b. *Fiscal Year; Accounting.*

The Company's fiscal year shall be the calendar year.

c. *Member's Capital Accounts.*

A Capital Account for the sole use of each Member shall be maintained by the Company. The Member's Capital Account shall reflect the Member's capital contributions and increases for any net income or gain of the Company. The Member's Capital Account shall also reflect decreases for distributions made to the Member and the Member's share of any losses and deductions of the Company.

3. *Capital Contributions.*

By the execution of this Operating Agreement, the initial Member hereby agrees to make a Capital Contribution of [Describe dollars and assets contributed] for the capital interests of the Company. Future Capital Contributions may be made in the sole discretion of the sole Member.

4. *General Powers of Sole Member.*

NOTE: Consider modifications to restrict or expand the powers based on the business involved. Consider the provision to authorize an additional signatory on a bank account. It may be advisable for a one-member LLC to have a second authorized signer in the event of the illness, disability, or absence of the sole member.

The sole Member has authority to:

a. Conduct the ordinary and usual decisions concerning the business and affairs of the Company.

b. To do all things necessary or convenient to carry out the business and affairs of the Company.

c. Purchase, lease, or otherwise acquire any real, personal, tangible, or intangible property.

d. Sell, convey, mortgage, grant a security interest in, pledge, lease, license, exchange, or otherwise dispose of or encumber any real, personal, tangible, or intangible property.

e. Open one or more depository accounts and make deposits into and checks and withdrawals against such accounts and to designate and authorize any additional signatory on such accounts.

f. Borrow money, incur liabilities, and other obligations, establish lines of credit, mortgages, and other credit and financing facilities relating to the Business.

g. Obtain insurance covering the Business and affairs of the Company and its property.

h. Commence, prosecute, or defend any proceeding in the Company's name or relating to the Business.

i. Enter into any arrangements or agreements, and execute any contracts, documents, and instruments relating to the Business.

j. Engage consultants and agents, define their respective duties, and establish their compensation or remuneration. This right shall include the right to designate a person to operate the Company and conduct the Business in the event of the illness, disability, or death of the sole Member. If such person is appointed, such person shall be referred to as the "Manager" and shall have any rights, powers, and obligations granted or created herein to the sole Member except as the sole Member shall otherwise restrict or limit in a document appointing said Manager.

NOTE: Consider restrictions. For example, a one-member LLC to hold passive investment real estate may wish to confirm this intent to minimize the likelihood of dealer classification for income tax purposes.

As an express limitation on the nature of the Business and the powers granted to the Manager herein, the Company is intended to hold real estate for investment purposes only, and no activities inconsistent with such limited purposes shall be undertaken.

5. *Death, Disability, Dissolution.*

a. *Death of Sole Member.*

NOTE: Consider addressing how the interests should be divided. For an elderly owner, it may be advisable to admit another member (or a trust as a second member) and address succession planning issues in a more detailed multimember operating agreement. Consider the need to address specific powers, modification of the Prudent Investment Act, and so on, in the will of the sole Member.

Upon the death of the sole Member, if the Member has not theretofore appointed a Manager who is then willing to act, then the personal representative of the estate of the sole Member may act as Manager hereunder or appoint a person to so serve as Manager until the Member's Interests and Capital Account of the deceased sole Member have been transferred or distributed.

b. *Disability of Sole Member.*

Upon the disability of the sole Member, if the Member has not theretofore appointed a Manager who is then willing to act, then the guardian, committee, or conservator of the disabled sole Member may act as Manager hereunder or appoint a person to so serve until the Member's Interests and Capital Account of the disabled sole Member have been transferred or distributed.

c. *Dissolution.*

The Company shall dissolve and its affairs shall be wound up on the first to occur of:

(1) At a time, or on the occurrence of an event, specified in the Certificate of Formation or this Operating Agreement.

NOTE: What is impact on third parties?

(2) By the written consent of the sole Member.

6. *Miscellaneous Provisions.*

a. *Terms.*

Nouns and pronouns will be deemed to refer to the masculine, feminine, neuter, singular, and plural, as the identity of the person or persons, firm, or corporation may in the context require. The term "Code" shall refer to the Internal Revenue Code of 1986, as amended.

b. *Article Headings.*

The Article headings and numbers contained in this Operating Agreement have been inserted only as a matter of convenience and for reference, and in no way shall be construed to define, limit, or describe the scope or intent of any provision of this Operating Agreement.

c. *Entire Agreement.*

This Operating Agreement constitutes the entire agreement among the sole Member and the Company and contains all of the agreements among said parties with respect to the subject matter hereof. This Operating Agreement supersedes any and all other agreements, either oral or written, between said parties with respect to the subject matter hereof.

d. *Severability.*

The invalidity or unenforceability of any particular provision of this Operating Agreement shall not affect the other provisions hereof, and this Operating Agreement shall be construed in all respects as if such invalid or unenforceable provisions were omitted.

e. *Binding Effect.*

Subject to the provisions of this Operating Agreement relating to transferability, this Operating Agreement will be binding upon and shall inure to the benefit of the parties, and their respective distributees, heirs, successors, and assigns.

f. *Governing Law.*

This Operating Agreement is being executed and delivered in the State of STATENAME and shall be governed by, construed, and enforced in accordance with the laws of the State of STATENAME.

IN WITNESS WHEREOF, the parties hereto make and execute this Operating Agreement on the dates set below their names, to be effective on the date first above written.

IN WITNESS WHEREOF, the sole Member has hereunto set such Member's hand and seal as of the day and year first above written.

Dated: DAY   MONTH,   YEAR   COMPANY SEAL:

LLCNAME

By: _____
    MANAGER-NAME, Manager

_____   MONTH   DAY,   YEAR
MEMBER-1 NAME

14 REAL ESTATE INVESTMENTS AND LIMITED LIABILITY COMPANIES

An LLC may carry on any lawful business, purpose, or activity. However, an LLC offers an especially beneficial structure for owning real estate investments. Too many investors have structured real estate ownership in their individual names, or in the general partnership format. These approaches may offer simplicity from a legal perspective and favorable tax treatment, but they do not limit the personal liability of the owners. Although many lenders require personal guarantees of the principals regardless of the ownership structure, it is still prudent to use an entity that provides limited liability to its owners for other potential claims, such as for environmental infractions (although there are exceptions), personal injury claims, and ordinary trade creditors.

NOTE: The reaction of some real estate owners is "that's why I carry insurance." Insurance, however, is not foolproof. Premium payments can be missed causing policies to lapse. Insurance can cancel coverage or refuse to renew coverage. Every policy has exclusions so that a particular liability may not be covered. Further, the liability could exceed the amount of the insurance coverage. You may fail to adhere to conditions in a policy. Using an LLC should not be a reason to lessen insurance coverage. However, having insurance coverage should not be a reason to overlook the importance of the limited liability that an LLC can provide.

LLCs generally are the best form for ownership of commercial real estate. The operating agreement provides flexibility in control, management, and sale decisions. A single LLC can be formed that in turn can form multiple wholly owned (subsidiary) LLCs, each owning a single property. This is an administratively convenient and cost-effective method of operating while preserving maximum insulation from claims. An LLC can easily provide a mechanism to divide the ownership of a single real estate property among many heirs.

LLCs ARE SUPERIOR TO OTHER ENTITIES FOR HOLDING REAL ESTATE

CAUTION: The ownership of real estate as a sole proprietor, tenant in common, joint tenancy, or general partnership is potentially very dangerous from a liability standpoint. A recent situation that exemplifies the danger involved two brothers who owned a residential rental apartment complex. One day they received an urgent phone call to come to the complex. When they arrived there, fire trucks were at the scene and all the tenants had been evacuated. Ultimately, the fire department determined that gas was coming up from the ground and spreading throughout the building. The brothers have now been subject to a class action lawsuit by the tenants and all of their assets are vulnerable to a potential judgment against them.

CAUTION: Another problem with sole proprietorships is that if the real estate is in a state other than where you reside, your heirs will have to incur the costs and time delays of probate in that state as well. In addition, this may subject the estate to additional estate and/or inheritance taxation. Using a partnership, corporation, or LLC to own the property may obviate the need for ancillary probate and reduce and/or eliminate potential taxes.

The LLC can provide a cost-effective and simple approach for ownership for real estate investments.

Disadvantages When Using S Corporations for Real Estate Investments

An S corporation is rarely an appropriate ownership vehicle for real estate investments. This is because the entity level debt of an S corporation cannot be included in the tax basis of its shareholders even if the stockholders personally guarantee the debt. Also, special allocations, common to many real estate ventures, cannot be structured within the scope of the S corporation's one-class-of-stock requirement.

EXAMPLE: Assume that stockholders X and Y own an S corporation, with X and Y making no capital contributions to the corporation. The corporation acquires the building and real estate for $1 million. The corporation obtains the funds necessary to buy the building and real estate by borrowing $1 million, which X and Y personally guarantee. Assume further that there is a $25,000 net loss in the first year of business primarily resulting from depreciation deductions. Neither X nor Y is entitled to use any of the loss on their individual tax returns because they have no basis—the liability cannot be included in their tax basis and therefore their tax basis is zero.

Alternatively, if this entity is structured either as a partnership or an LLC, X and Y will get full benefit for the $1 million of debt even if neither of them personally guarantees the debt. Therefore, each of them will be able to take a deduction on his tax return for $12,500 subject to the passive loss rules.

General Partnership versus Limited Partnership versus LLC to Own Real Estate Investments

As a result of the problems attendant to using an S corporation for real estate, many owners have elected either to use a general partnership or a limited partnership. With a general partnership, the partners expose themselves to unlimited liability. Either a limited partnership with a corporate general partner or an LLC would be a more prudent entity for limiting this liability.

When comparing a limited partnership with an LLC, both entities can limit the liability of their owners. In a limited partnership, however, the general partner will still have unlimited liability. Setting up a corporation as a general partner can alleviate this problem, but it creates an additional tax return and administrative responsibilities (see Chapter 3). By comparison, the LLC provides limited liability for all owners and avoids the need for two entities (the corporation as a general partner and the limited partnership). Thus, LLCs cost less to start up and involve fewer annual tax returns and complications.

Although the LLC can protect the members from outside creditors, the operating agreement requires additional capital from members for reasons common in real estate investments. These include construction overruns, debt service deficiencies, and working capital needs resulting from expiration of leases such as broker's commissions and tenant fit-up costs. The LLC operating agreement can provide that capital will be called for such needs and can further provide remedies for failure to contribute, such as dilution of percentage of total membership interests in the LLC. Nonetheless, the agreement can also provide that no member is personally liable to the LLC, its members, or any third party for failure to so contribute.

Thus, for real estate investors in particular, the choice often was between a limited or general partnership. The LLC offers an excellent option for ownership of real estate.

LLCs Compared with Limited Partnership Syndications

Real estate syndications (almost invariably structured as limited partnerships) were the rage prior to the Tax Reform Act of 1986, which attacked the tax shelter industry and severely wounded the real estate industry in the process. As a result of the abusive tax-oriented real estate syndications of the 1980s, many wealthy investors seeking to diversify their portfolios into passive real estate investments view anything called a real estate syndication (or real estate limited partnership) as a four-letter word. The LLC offers an important advantage over the limited partnership because a negative association does not taint its name, even if that advantage is primarily a psychological edge.

Real Estate Investments Trusts and LLCs

A real estate investment trust (REIT) is a trust or corporation organized to hold real estate assets. Typically, a large number of shareholders own it. Although a REIT may be classified as a corporation, if it meets the many strict REIT tax requirements, it can qualify to avoid tax on most of its income, which it then passes through to its shareholders. The requirements are complex. When there can be a more limited ownership, the LLC sometimes can offer a possible alternative to a REIT. An LLC can have a significant number of investors, own real estate, and provide many of the benefits of the REIT for real estate investing. Most importantly for real estate investors, this can all be accomplished with far less complexity and administrative cost.

LLCs ARE NOT ALWAYS THE IDEAL CHOICE

Sometimes it is inappropriate to use an LLC for real estate planning. These situations primarily concern a principal residence or a vacation home for personal use. Generally, you should not transfer any personal use property into an LLC because it may undermine the business nature of the LLC and neither the courts nor the IRS will respect it. If you do transfer a personal use property into the LLC, you should then set up an arm's-length lease and pay rent as if you were an unrelated person.

If you are endeavoring to remove real estate from your taxable estate, the LLC is a tremendous tool. However, it is not the appropriate tool for a personal residence. Instead, a special trust specifically designed for personal residences, called a qualified personal residence trust (QPRT) may be a better approach.

NOTE: See Shenkman, *The Complete Book of Trusts*, 3rd ed. (New York: John Wiley & Sons, 2002).

TAX CONSIDERATIONS OF REAL ESTATE AND LLCs

The income tax issues affecting LLCs were described in detail in Chapter 11. Many of the income tax advantages of LLCs are uniquely suited to real estate investments held in the LLC format. Some of the key benefits to real estate investors using LLCs include:

- For real estate investments, especially if depreciation and other deductions generate a tax loss, the passive loss limitations rules are an important tax-planning consideration. The passive loss rules generally limit a real estate investor's ability to deduct losses from real estate and other passive investments to the income from passive investments. In some cases, therefore, it can be advantageous to have a loss from a real estate rental treated instead as active income.

- The LLC provides an opportunity for real estate owners to characterize income and losses derived from the entity as potentially active income or losses. In a limited partnership, a limited partner's allocable share of income and losses derived from the partnership will generally be treated as passive. Depending on the activity of a member, his participation may be deemed active and hence the income and losses flowing from the LLC may be active.

- Real estate transactions have historically relied more heavily on special allocations of income, gain, and loss from an investment than has any other type of business or investment transaction. The LLC offers more flexibility than any type of corporate entity to allocate tax benefits.

- In a limited partnership (heretofore the entity of choice for real estate investments), mortgage debt for which the lender had recourse to the general partner could not be allocated to the limited partners, thus adversely affecting the limited partners' ability to claim deductions. An LLC is not subject to this restriction. All investors obtain limited liability (the goal that limited partners seek under the traditional real estate limited partnership), and they can also have recourse liabilities allocated to them. This contrasts favorably with the limited partnership, where limited partners were only allocated nonrecourse liabilities.

OTHER REAL ESTATE ISSUES AFFECTING THE USE OF LLCs

When drafting an operating agreement for a real estate transaction, specify in detail the person or persons necessary to authorize a particular action. Who can approve a new mortgage or sign a deed (e.g., one manager, all managers, a majority of members, two-thirds of the members)? The greater the detail as to key operating actions, the easier it will be for the LLC to engage in significant transactions such as the purchase, financing, or sale of real estate.

Where you want to convert an existing property owned by you outright, or in a general partnership, into an LLC, be certain to investigate the necessity of obtaining new casualty insurance as well as the effect on the validity of your title insurance policy.

SUMMARY

Using an LLC for real estate investments offers substantial benefits over using a corporation or partnership for such purposes. Anyone involved in real estate activities, whether a local rental property, or a substantial commercial project, should consider forming an LLC.

15 PROFESSIONAL PRACTICES AND LIMITED LIABILITY COMPANIES

A common form of ownership of a professional practice (e.g., accounting and law firms) has been the partnership. The problem that this creates is vicarious liability of one partner for the acts of another partner. This means that each partner in a professional partnership is personally liable for all the debts of the partnership in addition to being potentially liable for the negligent or wrongful acts of his partners. This is the classic *weak link* scenario: One partner who fails to perform at the appropriate professional level practiced by the balance of the firm becomes the weak link. Every partner in the firm can be personally liable (to the extent of losing his home) for the acts of the single partner.

Because of the unlimited liability of all of the partners in a professional partnership, many professionals have opted to use a professional corporation or association as the business structure for their practice. Generally, the professional corporation or association provides limited liability to each of the stockholders. There is an important exception to this limited liability. Under this exception, a stockholder remains personally liable for any acts of malpractice that he may commit as well as those of anyone under his supervision. The other stockholders remain insulated from such liabilities.

The liability protection afforded to a professional through an LLC will be similar to that afforded a professional corporation or a professional association. Therefore, an LLC member will only be liable for his personal malpractice and those under his supervision. He will not be liable for the malpractice committed by other members nor for contractual liabilities of the LLC.

TIP: Before any professional invests any time analyzing which entity to choose, he should investigate which entities are needed or can be used by persons in his licensed profession. Some states do not permit legal professionals to be active in an LLC.

TAX CONSIDERATIONS OF THE LLC AND THE PROFESSIONAL CORPORATION

Professional corporations are classified as personal service corporations, which require significant monitoring at year-end to avoid double taxation. This generally requires the payment of bonuses to stockholders resulting in cash flow problems and is difficult to monitor.

If an S corporation is used, ownership restrictions, botched S elections, and corporate taxation on liquidation become potential problems. Furthermore, an S corporation requires proportionate distributions of income to its stockholders, which is not a requirement for a professional corporation or a professional LLC.

A professional LLC will generally be preferable for accountants, lawyers, and other licensed professionals. Such an entity provides greater flexibility in membership and income distribution. It also permits clear avoidance of double taxation both during operation and on liquidation.

PROFESSIONAL SERVICE LLC

Licensed professionals who want to practice within the limited liability structure offered by the LLC can organize themselves as professional service LLCs.

Where a professional firm, such as an accounting or legal firm, operates in several states, the LLP can facilitate interstate operations while maintaining the limited liability characteristic of a professional corporation.

CAUTION: The LLP may seem at first to provide limited liability that is equivalent to that of a professional corporation (or professional association), but this is not always true. Although some state statutes grant the LLC liability protection similar to that afforded to the professional corporation, many LLP statutes do not. Instead, they have no limitation on liability with respect to leases, bank loans, and so on. For many professional practice firms, these contractual liabilities (e.g., member guarantees on a lease) are some of the largest liabilities of the entity.

LIMITED LIABILITY PARTNERSHIP

Another entity that may be used only by professionals is the limited liability partnership (LLP). The LLP is a partnership that provides limited liability to its partners for liability arising from the malpractice of other partners. Similar to an LLC and a professional corporation, it does not protect the malpracticing partner from liabilities arising from his own malpractice and from those under his supervision. Furthermore, it generally does not provide protection to a partner for business and tort liabilities of the LLP. Therefore, each partner remains jointly and severally liable for all commercial debts such as leases, sexual harassment claims, and accounts payable of the LLP. Many professional service entities have opted to use an LLP instead of an LLC because LLCs in certain states are subject to corporate level taxes.

In some states, professional LLCs are permitted and have become prevalent. In other states, there is still uncertainty whether professionals may use LLCs. Furthermore, the appropriate licensing authorities generally need to authorize the use of LLCs.

EXAMPLE: Assume there are three partners in a general partnership, M, N, and O, who practice accounting. N commits malpractice giving rise to a $3 million judgment. Each of M, N, and O are liable for the entire $3 million liability.

If the entity were a professional corporation, an LLC, or an LLP, then only the entity and N would be liable for the $3 million liability. M and O would have no personal liability.

Where an LLP is used, a professional may escape liability for malpractice where he was not involved. Instead, the member who supervised the person committing the malpractice would be held accountable. This situation can create a practical dilemma. Why should any member want to be the managing partner (member) of a firm, or the head of a department that addresses risky legal issues? Members requested to serve in these capacities may only be willing to do so where they have a commitment from other firm members to make a contribution in the event of a lawsuit. Thus, an agreement for all members to contribute may be inevitable. When creating an LLP, it is essential to take care in analyzing and drafting the provisions in the operating agreement. If it requires a partner to contribute where the LLP's assets are exhausted, this could compromise the limited liability benefits of the LLP. This risk can be addressed by stating that no third parties are to be beneficiaries of the provision requiring contributions. Further, the contribution provision could be made inapplicable in the case of fraud, willful misconduct, and other acts where contribution by other partners is inappropriate. The reality, however, is that where a claimant is aware that the operating agreement includes a contribution provision, claims may be made for greater amounts, lessening the prospect of settlement.

EVALUATING THE CHOICE OF ENTITY TO PROVIDE PROFESSIONAL SERVICES

When evaluating the organizational form of your professional service entity, you must consider several factors.

Protection from Personal Liability

Liability exposure is a concern for all professional service providers. Many types of potential liability may arise from the membership in a professional practice. The preferred form of organization depends on the likely kinds of liability that may arise.

In most states, the professional corporation and LLC forms provide protection for owners of professional practices from malpractice liability of another owner if there is no agreement among the owners to share in the liability. However, malpractice liability is not the only liability that professional practices fear. Contracts are another major source of personal liability. These include long-term office leases, equipment leases, accounts payable, and staff salaries. Tort liabilities, liability for sexual harassment, and discrimination also are concerns.

Availability of the Entities under State Law

In choosing a business format, you must first verify whether an LLC can be used in the particular profession. Is an LLC permitted by its particular licensing authority?

Securities Law Aspects

In certain instances, interests in a professional firm may either constitute securities, or be exempt from status as a security. Characterization of ownership interests as securities may affect a firm's ability to use the cash method of accounting, which could cause a firm to recognize income sooner than it otherwise would have been required.

Costs and Burdens of Converting an Existing Entity to a New Entity

The cost of changing a partnership to an LLC needs to be carefully determined. Generally, this conversion is free of income tax. In some jurisdictions, this will require a formal assignment of the partnership assets to the LLC. Other states permit a merger of the partnership into an LLC, which is a much more streamlined transition.

The transition from a professional corporation to an LLC is a potentially costly conversion. If the professional corporation is a regular corporation, the transfer results in the liquidation of the professional corporation. This could give rise to double income taxation. If the professional corporation is an S corporation, it will still be a liquidation, which will give rise to at least one level of taxation (under certain circumstances it will result in double taxation). Some professionals will run parallel entities: the new LLC and the old C corporation while it collects accounts receivable and winds down.

Impact on Firm Culture

Conversion of a professional practice to an LLC raises sensitive issues and causes a reexamination of the practice's business relationships. Some owners may not want to have centralized management (e.g., a manager-managed LLC), because they prefer the general partnership characteristic of each partner having significant voting rights. Cultural aspects must be considered in terms of each firm's unique relationship with and among its owners and its history.

A major concept that the owners of a professional practice must wrestle with is whether an owner should be liable for the malpractice liability of another owner. In a partnership, all of the partners remain liable for the malpracticing partner's liability. If the owners use an LLC (or an LLP and a professional corporation), then the remaining members are not liable for the liability arising from this malpractice. The owners must decide what their ultimate objectives are under this scenario.

LLCs AND LLPs AND PROFESSIONAL MALPRACTICE INSURANCE

The use of an LLC or LLP should not in any manner induce you to reduce your malpractice coverage. The LLC structure is not infallible so insurance coverage is essential. The professional firm itself probably has significant assets that require protection. Likewise, do not let your malpractice insurance lull you into believing that you do not need to limit liability with an entity such as an LLC or LLP.

NOTE: Some state LLC statutes permit the members to select other members who agree to be liable for specific debts, but not for others.

LIABILITIES OF OWNERS AND PARTICULAR ENTITIES

Type of Liability	General Partnership	Professional Corporation or Association	LLC	LLP
Liability for one's own malpractice	Yes	Yes	Yes	Yes
Liability for malpractice of others	Yes	No	No	No
Liability for the malpractice of others under one's supervision	Yes	Yes	Yes	Yes
General commercial and tort liability	Yes	No	No	Yes

SUMMARY

Professional practices, such as accounting and law firms, have typically been formed as partnerships. Professional corporations have been used as an alternate form for transacting professional practice businesses. Certain states, but not all, allow for the practice of professionals in the LLC format. Even if the professional practitioner forms as an LLC, he will not be protected against personal liability for professional malpractice or the malpractice of individuals under his direct supervision. Some courts have found partners vicariously liable for acts of others even where the others were not within their direct supervision. Thus, for professionals, the LLP or LLC, depending on the laws applicable in your state, can be an excellent vehicle to minimize, although by no means eliminate, the risk of professional malpractice.

16 HIGH-TECHNOLOGY ENTERPRISES AND LIMITED LIABILITY COMPANIES

The LLC should be carefully evaluated when considering entities to form and operate a high-technology enterprise. New high-tech companies typically present serious risks for investors in these enterprises. The bursting Internet bubble and the stock market meltdown during 2001 and 2002 demonstrated this danger. Three LLC characteristics are advantageous for such start-ups: liability protection, tax attributes, and control.

LLCs PROVIDE LIABILITY PROTECTION

It is attractive, if not imperative, to limit your personal liability when facing the significant risks of high-tech investments. Investors must be able to limit personal liability because these ventures are often highly leveraged with borrowed funds. In addition to not being required to furnish personal guarantees for any such borrowed funds, investors seek protection from personal liability if the LLC is unable to repay any such loans.

TAX CHARACTERISTICS OF LLCs ARE WELL SUITED TO TECHNOLOGY START-UP COMPANIES

Tax attributes of LLCs also make them ideal. Highly risky investments often use special allocations to compensate investors for their different levels of risk. Some investors who contribute more capital may want to be entitled to preferred distributions from the company, which would not be permitted in an S corporation.

LLCs CAN PROVIDE INVESTORS WITH CONTROL

Some investors in high-tech, high-risk start-ups want to have more control and input than a limited partner would have in a limited partnership. A limited partner with too much control risks losing the personal liability shield that is so important to investors. By contrast, an investor in an LLC can participate in the entity's management and control without risking personal liability. Thus, limited liability, participation in management, and flexible allocations make an LLC an ideal structure for new high-technology companies.

SUMMARY

High-tech start-up enterprises will continue to surface, with some succeeding, and others not. The unique risks and the tax and control issues of the high-tech start-up lend themselves to organization as an LLC.

17 FOREIGN INVESTORS AND LIMITED LIABILITY COMPANIES

LLCs resemble entities that have long been used in other countries. In fact, the concept originated in European law. This circumstance makes LLCs familiar to many foreign investors who may have less acquaintance with other entities used in the United States, such as limited partnerships. An LLC, with its pass-through tax treatment and limited liability protection, may be an ideal vehicle for international investors.

FOREIGN INVESTORS IN LLCs

Nonresident aliens may find that an LLC is an attractive structure for U.S. investment and business transactions because there are no restrictions on what type of person can own membership interests in an LLC. This LLC flexibility contrasts favorably with S corporations, which prohibit nonresident aliens as shareholders.

EXAMPLE: Ten individuals want to organize a business venture that will actively involve all of the individuals. One individual, J, is a Japanese citizen and is not a resident of the United States. All of the entrepreneurs consider limited liability and pass-through taxation to be essential. The entrepreneurs can attain all of their goals only with an LLC. The business could not be formed as an S corporation because J is a nonresident alien and a business is ineligible to be an S corporation if it has a nonresident alien shareholder. The entrepreneurs could not accomplish both their goals of maintaining joint control over the business and achieving limited liability with a limited partnership since limited partners may not participate in management without risking loss of limited liability. There would be unlimited liability if they were a general partnership. Finally, there would not be pass-through taxation if the entity were a C corporation.

An LLC that is treated as a partnership for federal tax purposes should also be subject to the same rules relating to partnership withholding requirements for foreign partners. Accordingly, an LLC will be required to pay a withholding tax with respect to each foreign member's distributive share of the LLC's income from a United States business (in tax parlance, income that is *effectively connected* with a trade or business in the United States). The withholding tax for a foreign member currently would be 35 percent (the highest corporate tax rate); for a foreign corporate member and 39.6 percent (the highest individual tax rate); for a foreign noncorporate member, multiplied by the partnership's effectively connected income, which is allocable to each member.

An LLC will also be required to pay a withholding tax for each foreign member's distributive share of the LLC's income that is not "effectively connected" with a trade or business in the United States. A flat 30 percent tax is levied on the gross amount of noneffectively connected "fixed or determinable annual or periodical gains, profits, and income," such as rents, dividends, and interest.

TAX TREATIES SHOULD BE CONSIDERED

The United States has entered into comprehensive bilateral trade and tax treaties with scores of countries. Before planning any transaction with foreign investors, give careful consideration to the contents of any applicable treaty. You must consult the treaty to determine whether the U.S. tax laws or the laws of the foreign country, or some combination, will be applied. The LLCs may be familiar, and the ideal vehicle in many circumstances, but you should not make the final decision without first reviewing any applicable treaty provisions.

The tax rates previously discussed may be subject to modification by specific tax treaties between the United States and foreign countries.

SUMMARY

An LLC is an ideal vehicle for nonresident aliens to conduct business in the United States and maintain their limited liability since nonresident aliens are permitted to be members in an LLC. Such entity would receive the pass-through tax treatment of partnerships with the limited liability protection typically associated with corporations. If an LLC is structured so that it will be taxed as a partnership, the IRS will likely treat the LLC as a partnership and require the entity to withhold taxes attributable to the distributive share of a foreign member in the LLC.

18 DIVORCE AND LIMITED LIABILITY COMPANIES

LLCs are becoming a more and more popular form for organizing business and investment activities. This partnership/S corporation hybrid offers tax and legal advantages that may make it the vehicle of choice for new transactions. If you are getting divorced, you and your advisers must understand some of the nuances of LLCs that may affect how you negotiate various financial and legal aspects of your divorce settlement. LLCs are important to understand in determining a spouse's earnings for alimony and child support calculations; for valuing a spouse's assets for determining equitable distribution; and in valuing a spouse's assets for negotiating a prenuptial agreement. Similarly, the terminology of LLCs is essential to understand in proceeding with discovery requests. (This is where your lawyer formally asks for financial information from your spouse to help you and your financial advisers determine an appropriate settlement.) The terminology is also used in depositions (where your spouse is formally questioned in front of a court reporter concerning various aspects of the marriage, financial matters, etc.) in the context of divorce litigation.

UNIQUE FEATURES OF LLCs

LLCs differ in many important ways from the more traditional business forms. These differences can have important implications on the matrimonial process.

Salaries and Closely Held Business Calculations Affect Child Support and Alimony Payments

The following example illustrates some of the issues that must be considered in evaluating business entities in a divorce.

EXAMPLE: Abe owns 100 percent of the stock of B Corporation. This asset was acquired during the marriage and is subject to equitable distribution. Abe has drawn an annual salary of $300,000 for the three years preceding the divorce action and the corporation shows no profit on which a corporate level tax will be paid. Abe pays ordinary income tax on the $300,000; he loans to the corporation $50,000 of after-tax money to cover capital repayment in corporate debt. Will the court or the adversary representing Abe's spouse in the divorce action recognize this corporate need or seek to demonstrate that the loan by Abe to B Corporation is purely voluntary, not a beneficial tax device, and the full salary of $300,000 is available for alimony and child support? Since in many jurisdictions, child support is controlled by guidelines that stipulate a fixed percentage of income as reported on the federal tax return, can or will the court adjust the information on the tax return?

An LLC taxed as a partnership could deflate or ignore salary payments since distributions can be made with no entity level tax, but the pass-through of an LLC's profits appears to be synonymous with earnings of an S corporation. This difference in tax treatment may cloud the issue relevant to the determination of alimony and child support (i.e., what is the true cash flow available for these purposes).

EXAMPLE: Donna is currently in the midst of a divorce and owns 99 percent of an LLC that is taxed as a partnership. She has chosen for the past three years to draw $50,000 as salary and show a profit of $200,000 since she contemplates selling the business when the divorce ends. In calculating her share of child support as mandated by child support guidelines, is the $50,000 reported as salary the controlling number, or is the $200,000 profit also to be included? Edward, the husband, works for AT&T. He earns $250,000. Is child support 50/50 or one-sixth/five-sixths? This was a long marriage. Does Edward pay alimony to Donna because of the disparate earnings?

Imputation of Income Tax

Many cases addressing the implication of a hypothetical tax have found the event triggering the tax too uncertain to justify an imputation of tax liability. Many LLC statutes require that the LLC be terminated no later than a specified number of years after formation. Will this date change the view of the courts as to the imputation of a tax? Even where no tax is imputed, will this statutory cutoff date provide a termination date for calculating future values of a business? If the statutory cutoff date is only five years away, can an appraiser assume the business will be reformed? Since the value for matrimonial purposes generally considers the five years preceding the filing of the complaint, what impact does the five-year termination have on the valuation?

How Do Various Classes of LLC Members Affect the Divorce Negotiation Process?

An LLC may have different classes and groups of membership interests, each with different voting and distribution rights. Where these different classes and groups are present, the valuation process will become complex. What is a voting right worth? Were voting rights avoided solely to argue for a reduced value in the matrimonial action? It may be necessary to make projections of distributions under different scenarios to value the potentially complex variations in distribution rights. Although this might appear similar to the issues faced in valuing different classes of stock in a C corporation, it can be more complex since special allocations used in sophisticated investment transactions of limited partnerships can be present.

Does a Divorcing Spouse's Serving as an LLC Manager Affect Settlement Negotiations?

Where a spouse is the LLC's manager, the compensation as manager, as well as the possible right to control compensation and distributions, must be addressed. Some states even permit the operating agreement to include penalties to charge a manager for certain improper acts. Should these penalties reduce the value of the manager's interests?

SUMMARY

LLCs have become one of the most favored and common vehicles for investments and businesses. Thus, for more people undergoing divorce, and their advisers, it has become essential to address the analysis, valuation, and interpretation of LLCs, LLC legal documentation, LLC operations, and so forth. This affects discovery, trial, valuation, and many other matters as well as the determination of child support.

In the context of matrimonial law, the in's and out's of LLCs are important for determining the value of a membership interest. In authorizing child support and alimony, this value helps establish an equitable distribution between divorcing spouses and the wages of a particular spouse who may or may not be an LLC's manager

19 FAMILY BUSINESSES AND LIMITED LIABILITY COMPANIES

Safeguarding and planning for the succession of a family business is as sacred as mom and apple pie. When properly used in the planning arsenal, LLCs are an effective tool to achieve the following goals of family businesses:

- Protection of their assets from claims. Using separate LLCs to own key assets such as a building can protect these assets. Risky assets, such as a fleet of delivery trucks, can be segregated from the rest of the business assets in an equipment-leasing or delivery LLC.

- Restriction of transferability of ownership to assure that the business remains in the family. The terms of the LLC operating agreement can be crafted to eliminate the risk of transfer.

- Estate planning to assure that the estate tax will not destroy the business. In many situations, LLCs are an ideal entity to minimize estate taxes by qualifying the assets they hold for discounts, converting real estate into an intangible asset to avoid ancillary probate and estate taxation in other states (a legal proceeding following death in a state other than the state in which you live), and so on.

LLCs, S corporations, and limited partnerships may all be good choices for certain family businesses. An S corporation provides easy transferability of ownership interests (i.e., stock) and the option of deductible estate planning through stock bonuses to family employees. By paying compensation to the family members for bona fide services, the corporation receives a deduction for the payment and the parent does not have to pay a gift tax since the money transferred is a wage and not a gift. The amount paid for compensation must be within reason compared with what unrelated people would be paid. Otherwise, the IRS could challenge the transaction and recharacterize a portion of the salary as a dividend distribution to the parent followed by a gift to the child.

Only certain trusts, however, can be a shareholder in an S corporation, which significantly limits estate-planning opportunities. This serious issue is overlooked in many estate plans until a problem arises. LLCs can be owned by all types of estate-planning vehicles (i.e., any trusts).

NOTE: For a detailed discussion of S corporations and trusts, see Shenkman, *The Complete Book of Trusts*, 3rd ed. (New York: John Wiley & Sons, 2002).

CHARACTERISTICS OF A FAMILY LLC

The LLC has significant estate-planning advantages over an S corporation, which until the LLC laws become so widespread, had been the entity of choice for a family business. The LLC is beneficial to the family business owner because it provides the tax benefits of a partnership (only one level of taxation and tremendous flexibility in allocating income to the various owners). Although an S corporations provides for only one level of tax on income, it is a more complex and cumbersome conduit than an LLC, and there are some important exceptions to the single level of tax rule. LLCs can prevent the transfer of voting rights to individuals outside the family through restrictions in the operating agreement. Senior members of family businesses desire to maintain control of their business within the family. Because LLCs allow for different classes of members and managers, ownership interests can be transferred to younger family members while older family members retain management control. There is a great flexibility to structure decision making and profit distributions that meet myriad family situations.

The LLC provides limited liability to family members who ultimately become members in the LLC.

Compared with an S corporation, an LLC will permit distributions to some members (presumably the senior members) and not to other members (the junior members such as children and grandchildren).

EXAMPLE: Assume that Pa and Ma are each 50 percent members of an LLC that is run by managers. Pa and Ma could gift membership interests in the LLC and have such gifted interests placed in trust for the benefit of their children. The trust would be a nonvoting member and would not be a manager in the LLC. Ma and Pa would continue to control the LLC as managers. In addition, Ma and Pa would be able to take a distribution of their share of the profits of the LLC and not be required to make corresponding distributions to the trusts for their children. If Ma and Pa had formed an S corporation, there would need to be pro rata distributions of income to the trust as well as to Ma and Pa.

FAMILY PARTNERSHIP (LLC) RULES

When forming a family LLC, it is important to be familiar with a special tax restriction called the *family partnership rules*. These rules were enacted to prevent the income tax planning abuse of a parent "giving" ownership of an LLC (partnership) to a child as a device to transfer income to the child to be taxed at a lower income tax bracket.

EXAMPLE: Dad formed an LLC through which he operates a computer consulting business. Dad sells clients computers and then sets up the computers to achieve the tasks his clients need. Dad's computer LLC earns about 10 percent of its profit from markups on computer equipment, and 90 percent of its profits from Dad's consulting. Dad is paying tax at a maximum 40 percent state and federal rate so he gifts his son 50 percent of the LLC so that the son, who pays tax at a 20 percent rate, can report half of the income.

The preceding example is really a scheme to minimize tax. There cannot be much economic substance since what Dad has effectively done is simply reported income he earned from rendering consulting services on son's income tax return at a lower rate. The family partnership rules seek to prevent this abuse. For a child (donee) to be treated as the real owner of the LLC interests he received as a gift, the child must really own a capital interest in the LLC. In this example, the LLC had no assets, just Dad's expertise. Capital must also be a material income-producing factor. If these tests are not met and the donee is a member of the donor's family, the IRS will reallocate the income of the LLC unless two requirements are met. The parent/donor must be paid reasonable compensation for the services he provides (Dad's consulting in the example). Reasonable compensation is generally measured by what an unrelated person would earn for the same services. If a parent and co-owner of the LLC works 65 hours per week as a skilled manager in a family manufacturing business, but only draws a salary of $100 a week, the IRS will challenge the arrangement. The low salary would result in the transfer of more earnings to the children who received gifts of membership interests in the LLC from the parent. This would occur because the parent's low salary reduces the LLC's deductions, hence increasing the profits to be distributed to all members.

PLANNING TIP: If you believe that any family member's salary could be challenged, take steps to document and support it. Save copies of industry or trade organization salary and compensation services, use a time clock, or maintain time records to prove the actual hours worked, and so on.

The second requirement for the family LLC to be respected by the IRS is that the child (donee) should receive income in proportion to his ownership of the LLC.

EXAMPLE: Parent gives child 10 percent of the membership interests in an LLC. Profits, after reasonable salaries for the year, are $50,000. Child must receive a $5,000 distribution and parent $45,000. If parent gives child no distribution, the IRS may disallow the transaction claiming that parent never really gave a gift of the membership interest to child.

DISCOUNTS ON VALUING LLC MEMBERSHIP INTERESTS FOR GIFTS AND ESTATE TAX

Valuation Discounts

LLCs are a popular estate-planning tool, in part because if you give a child or other heir a small percentage of an LLC, say 10 percent, the value for gift and eventually for estate tax purposes is less than 10 percent of the value of the entire LLC. This reduction in value, as explained later, is a key part of estate planning with LLCs.

A significant incentive for using an LLC is the leveraging the LLC entity makes possible through valuation discounts. The gift tax value of transfer of property is its fair market value as of the date of the gift (how much are the LLC membership interests worth), and the property transferred in the LLC is the membership interest, not the underlying LLC assets (the building the LLC owns). The result is that gifts of LLC membership interests are often subject to significant inherent limitations. Therefore, your tax adviser can justify transfer-tax-saving valuation discounts.

Lack of Control Discount

A gift (transfer) of a noncontrolling (minority) membership interest in an LLC does not convey any power to control the LLC's management. A buyer will pay less for a noncontrolling interest in an entity (40 percent of an LLC membership), than he would pay for an outright ownership and control of the underlying assets (40 percent ownership of a $1 million building). Therefore, the gift tax value of the LLC interest should be reduced accordingly.

Lack of Marketability

A partial interest in a family-controlled entity can be extremely difficult, if not impossible, to liquidate. This lack of marketability should be factored in when determining a gift tax value of a transferred LLC interest. The lack of marketability discount has two components. The first is the absence of a ready market for selling the LLC interest to a third-party buyer. An LLC member's inability to withdraw from the LLC creates a *lock-in* discount. Both state law and LLC operating agreements often restrict a member's ability to sell, transfer, withdraw, or "put" the membership interest to the LLC. Such restrictions would reduce the purchase price of an LLC interest sold in an arm's-length transaction.

In a family-controlled LLC, special rules apply that may minimize, or even eliminate, these discounts. Some of these rules require that certain restrictions on transferring LLC membership interests included in the operating agreement must be disregarded for gift or estate tax valuation purposes unless they are no more restrictive than those that would otherwise apply under state law.

PLANNING TIP: Your LLC can be formed in a state with favorable LLC laws. If the limitations in an operating agreement on the ability of a member to withdraw are not more restrictive than the restrictions contained in state law, this tax restriction would not apply and your LLC would qualify for a larger valuation discount.

Range of Discounts

Because valuing interests in closely held entities is very subjective, it is difficult to precisely determine the discount in any given situation. Nevertheless, it should be substantial for any membership interest. The tax court typically approves valuation discounts in the range of 20 percent to 50 percent. Generally, a written analysis and calculation should support discounts.

ANNUAL EXCLUSION GIFTING WITH FAMILY LLCs

The current federal tax law allows every person to make annual gifts of up to $11,000 to any other person each year without incurring a gift tax. Husband and wife can elect to have one spouse's $11,000 annual exclusion (figure to be inflation adjusted in future years) applied to the other spouse's gift. Thus, if a husband makes a $22,000 gift to a child, the wife can elect to use her $11,000 annual exclusion so that the entire $22,000 gift is covered by both spouses' annual exclusions. For a gift to qualify for the $11,000 annual gift tax exclusion, the gift must be of a **present interest.** A present interest is defined to be "an unrestricted right to the immediate use, possession, or enjoyment of property or the income of property." The gift of an LLC interest may be a present interest for purposes of the annual exclusion even though a donee may not receive management rights or participate in the determination of when to make distributions from the LLC to its owners.

PLANNING TIP: Peter and Emily own a $2 million piece of real estate, and they want to gift LLC membership interests to their three children. The annual exclusion and spousal gift splitting would permit an annual gift of $22,000 to each child, or an aggregate of $66,000 of membership interests each year without gift tax consequences. Peter and Emily could contribute the $2 million piece of real estate to an LLC and gift membership interests in the LLC to the children.

If a valuation discount of one-third can be justified for the gifted LLC membership interest, a 1.5 percent membership interest could be given to each child each year. Effectively, an interest allocable to $33,000 of LLC assets (i.e., 1.5 percent of $2 million) would have a $22,000 gift tax value. A slightly higher percentage would have the full $22,000 value. Thus, gifts of membership interests allocable to $99,000 of LLC assets (rather than $66,000) could be transferred to the three children, fully covered by the gift tax annual exclusions:

1.5 percent interest (before discounts) = $33,000
less: ⅓ discount = (11,000)
Value of gift = $22,000

APPLICABLE EXCLUSION (UNIFIED CREDIT)

The applicable exclusion (amount you can gift or bequeath tax free) is $1 million. This figure will increase in future years for estate tax purposes (i.e., bequests at death), but the gift tax exclusion will remain at $1 million. Generally, this permits you to bequeath up to $1 million of assets to any person or persons without paying federal estate taxes on this amount. As an alternative, you may use this exclusion to offset gift taxes during your lifetime (but for gift tax purposes, the $1 million exclusion will not be increased). To the extent you exhaust this credit during your lifetime to avoid gift taxes, it is not available to avoid estate taxes.

You can use the exclusion effectively to transfer substantial assets out of your estate. The leveraging effect of an LLC is even more dramatic when you use the $1 million exclusion in addition to the annual gift tax exclusion.

PLANNING TIP: If, in the preceding example, Peter and Emily were to transfer a $4 million piece of real estate to an LLC, they could each transfer a 35 percent membership interest to their three children. The value of this transfer before discounts would be $1,400,000 each. Again, assuming a one-third discount could be justified, the value of the gift would be decreased to $933,338 and would be fully covered by each spouse's $1 million applicable exclusion:

$$
\begin{aligned}
\text{35 percent interest (before discounts)} &= \$1,400,000 \\
\text{less: } \tfrac{1}{3} \text{ discount} &= \underline{(466,662)} \\
\text{Value of gift} &= \$933,338
\end{aligned}
$$

Effectively, Emily and Peter would have transferred $2,800,000 of assets in the aggregate, but because of their combined $2 million exclusion and LLC discounts, they would not pay gift taxes.

LLCs COMPARE FAVORABLY TO TRUSTS

Trusts are one of the most common entities used in family estate and business planning. Where interests in a family business are going to be given to a child (even one of adult age), parents frequently make the gifts to a trust. When parents use this approach, they can remove the value of the family business interest from the estate while still assuring that someone other than the child has control over the asset. This person is the trustee who manages the trust and controls the distributions of income and principal to the child, depending on the provisions in the trust agreement (the legal document that your lawyer drafts stating what the trust should do). Trusts are used not only to control a child's access to money, but also to help protect the child's assets against divorce and even from creditors.

An LLC can offer similar benefits when properly used. But an LLC has one very substantial advantage over the use of trusts in family estate and business planning. To realize the benefits of the trust as described, it must be irrevocable. This generally means that you will have no right to change the trust in the future if circumstances warrant. An LLC is far more flexible since, subject to the tax restrictions discussed in this chapter, you and the other members can vote to change the LLC operating agreement at any time, and as often as you wish.

An LLC can substitute in some instances for the benefits obtainable through a trust because the managers of the LLCs, subject to the family partnership rules discussed earlier, can control the distributions to members. An LLC can protect membership interests from creditors and an ex-spouse by preventing these outsiders from becoming substitute members.

Using an LLC instead of a trust for holding interests in a family business may also provide an income tax advantage. Trust income is taxed very quickly at the highest marginal tax brackets. Broader, and hence more favorable, tax brackets apply to individuals who own LLC membership interests in the family business.

SUMMARY

The LLC may be the ideal entity to form a family business. The LLC provides the tax benefits of a partnership, the limited liability of a corporation, and flexibility of control, which is important to the senior members of the family. Membership interest in an LLC may be an ideal vehicle for gift giving because the donor may be entitled to take minority and lack of marketability discounts on the gifted membership interests. This would enable him to gift more than the true value of the gifted interest. This can be a terrific way to leverage the use of the donor's gift tax annual exclusions and lifetime applicable exclusion in estate planning.

20 ASSET PROTECTION AND LIMITED LIABILITY COMPANIES

Malpractice risks, large jury awards, divorce, and so on. The risks of our litigious society are considerable, and no one with significant net worth can be assured of immunity from suits. In addition to securing appropriate insurance coverage, you should take steps to protect your assets. LLCs provide an excellent and flexible structure for asset protection planning.

ASSET PROTECTION IN GENERAL

Fraudulent Conveyances

Like so many good things, the more you want asset protection, the less likely it is that you are going to get it. Asset protection techniques have less, if any, value where creditor problems have already occurred. Where lawsuits are already pending, the courts could ignore family transfers to LLCs or otherwise as merely your attempt to cheat claimants (fraudulent conveyances). The moral of the story is that you should do your planning before you truly need it. Asset protection planning in advance of receiving creditors' claims merely to avoid the risks of possible future creditors, as opposed to likely future creditors, should not be problematic or treated as fraudulent.

EXAMPLE: Mr. A knows that a judgment of $1 million has been obtained against him personally for a loan that is in default for nonpayment. Mr. A then transfers all of his assets to an LLC owned by both Mr. A and Mrs. A hoping that the creditor will not be able to take possession of the assets transferred to the LLC. Mr. A hopes that the creditor will only be allowed to take his interest in the LLC, but not as a member, merely as an assignee, with no management rights. The transfer by Mr. A to the LLC could be disregarded as a fraudulent conveyance because Mr. A already had notice of the judgment against him. If Mr. A transferred his assets to the LLC merely because he was paranoid of the possibility that he might have a creditor in the future, but did not know of any such creditors at the time of the transfer, the transfer should not be disregarded.

More than Asset Protection

Any steps that you take to protect assets should also serve other purposes. To lend the most credibility to asset protection planning, the actions should be consistent with your overall personal financial and estate planning goals, the diversification of assets, and so forth. If you can associate a business motive or other nonasset protection motive with asset protection, it will give the transactions more credibility as not having been done merely to impede creditors. Transfers are more likely to be respected if they are made pursuant to an overall estate and personal financial plan and employ commonly used techniques that are not motivated by asset protection.

EXAMPLE: Father transfers real estate to a family limited liability company and retains control over the only voting membership interest, thus retaining control over the LLC. The children and father are the nonvoting members. By transferring the property to an LLC, it is not in his individual name to be claimed by creditors. The LLC structure permits control by the voting member over the management of the real estate, which is essential to prevent squabbles between the numerous owners. Children, as nonvoting members, cannot participate in management decisions so that the operations remain controlled by father, who is the senior person with the most substantial real estate expertise. As the children nonvoting members prove their competence, a particular child may obtain voting rights, facilitating participation in active management. Thus, the family LLC can provide a mechanism for transferring ownership interests to the next generation. All of these nonasset protection goals are legitimate and can provide important corroboration that the transactions were intended as structured, and should be respected.

Don't Put All Your Eggs in One Basket

The greater the number of entities involved in the ownership of an asset, the more components into which various interests and rights in that particular asset have to be divided. Having numerous entities and contractual relationships makes it more difficult for a creditor to get to that asset. Consider transferring each material asset to its own separate limited partnership, LLC, or other entity to insulate each asset, investment, or business from the liabilities of the others, as well as from your personal assets. Where a single LLC owns several assets, all of the assets can be attacked if one asset becomes subject to a liability or claim. If, instead, you form several LLCs, each owning one particular asset, a liability may attach to one asset, but the assets owned by the other LLCs should be insulated from such liability.

EXAMPLE: If LLC A owns real properties X, Y, and Z, and a liability resulting from the LLC's ownership of property X comes into existence, all three properties (as well as any other assets of the LLC) may be available to the creditor, not just property X. However, if LLCs B, C, and D are created to hold real properties X, Y, and Z, respectively, and a liability resulting from LLC C's ownership of real property Y comes into existence, only the assets of LLC C may be available to the creditor, and real properties X and Z should be safely insulated.

If an existing LLC owns several assets and the members decide to divide the single LLC into several separate and distinct LLCs, the issue arises whether the division of the existing LLC will be a termination of the LLC for tax purposes, which can have potentially adverse tax consequences. For example, the LLC tax year will end, which can result in a bunching of taxable income into one year. Where the LLC distributes cash on its termination and the amount of such cash exceeds the member's tax basis in the LLC, the member will recognize gain. These, as well as several other adverse tax consequences, can occur.

The LLC will not be deemed to have terminated where the successor LLCs are considered to be a continuation of the prior LLC. This will occur where the members of the successor LLC had interests of more than 50 percent in the capital and profits of the prior LLC. Since in most cases, no significant change in ownership will accompany the restructure, this requirement should usually be satisfied and the LLC should not be deemed to have terminated as a result of the division.

EXAMPLE: A father owns a building and widget manufacturing business. He wants to restructure the business to facilitate a gift program for estate tax purposes, assure management of the property in a centralized and professional manner, and provide protection from future unknown creditors or claimants. The building is transferred to an LLC whose interests are to be owned by the family members. The children's interests in the LLC can be owned by trusts for their benefit, instead of by the children directly. One LLC can own the building, and a second LLC can own the business. A prospective claimant would have to challenge all of the entities involved in the various structures to reach all assets. In addition, the other limitations and restrictions on a creditor's ability to attach membership interests in an LLC as discussed later in this chapter, would hinder the creditor in collecting any judgment.

Asset Protection and the Importance of Following Up on Details

The best-laid plan is useless if you fail to adhere to the formalities and details. It is important to run your LLC with the proper business and legal formalities recommended throughout this book. If you don't respect your LLC as a legitimate independent entity, don't expect the courts to do so either.

EXAMPLE: If after creating an LLC, the owners essentially disregard and ignore the identity of the LLC, it will be less likely to withstand a claimant creditor's challenge than an LLC whose owners have carefully respected the formalities of separate entity status.

The Requirement of Good-Faith Effort

When contemplating asset protection steps, you must make a good-faith effort to estimate all outstanding claims and reserve in the family business owner/transferor's name adequate assets to reasonably meet those claims and any expected costs.

PLANNING TIP: As part of your planning, have your accountant prepare a personal financial statement to demonstrate solvency before and after any transfers. Make a good-faith listing of all liabilities and claims. Order credit reports from all major credit reporting agencies. Save copies of credit reports for both you and your business interests at the time the planning steps are to be implemented. Have a title search done on real estate you own. Have your lawyer order a lien and judgment search on your assets. This can help demonstrate that at the time of the planning you were solvent and not making any transfers to impede creditors.

Solvency alone may be an insufficient test to meet. Where assets are so depleted that the transaction itself is characterized as constructively fraudulent, the transfer may be set aside. No transfer should be made with the intent to defraud creditors. No statements should be made, or actions taken, indicating such an intent to defraud.

Asset Protection and Arm's-Length Transactions

Extra care must be taken so that all transactions are handled as if between unrelated people (on an arm's-length basis). Where the rights and interests in an asset are divided, each component of the transaction should stand independently and be consummated on terms that can be demonstrated to be arm's length.

EXAMPLE: Real estate is transferred by gift to various trusts for minor children. The trustees retain and pay a qualified local real estate broker for a written appraisal of a fair rental price and use that information to set the rent that the business will pay to the trusts. It might be preferable to have the fair rent determined by a certified appraiser, such as a MAI appraiser, who would be an arguably more objective party. Further, the trustees of the trust should save the real estate sections from several local real estate and general circulation newspapers to demonstrate the state of the market at the time the transaction was consummated.

The Importance of Proper Documentation

The documentation relating to any transaction that is intended to protect assets from future unknown creditors, or between related parties, must be thorough and complete.

EXAMPLE: Where a family member is retained as a consultant by the family LLC, an independent consulting agreement with arm's-length terms should be negotiated and signed. It should be a full-fledged document with all of the provisions that an agreement between unrelated parties would include. It should not be a one-page "quickie." Likewise, loans between related parties should be documented with written loan agreements (promissory notes) prepared just as they would be for independent parties. This means with all of the protections and provisions that an unrelated party would require (e.g., only reasonable grace periods, acceleration clause, reasonable interest rate and payment schedule, default provisions). If the collateral for a loan is real estate, a mortgage should be recorded. If the collateral is personal property, the Uniform Commercial Code Financing Statement, Form UCC-1, should be filed where appropriate.

ASSET PROTECTION AND LLCs

The numerous benefits of a LLC make it an ideal tool for asset protection. If properly structured, an LLC will provide limited liability protection to its owners while providing pass-through partnership tax treatment. Moreover, an LLC may generally conduct any lawful business. Therefore, an LLC may be lawfully used for just about any purpose that is acceptable for a limited partnership. An LLC, however, unlike a limited partnership, does not have to have any partner personally liable for the entity's debts (e.g., a general partner).

Since many foreign jurisdictions are familiar with the LLC concept, a structure comprising an LLC and foreign trust may even be easier to implement than a family limited partnership and a foreign trust.

State law and the operating agreement can prevent a creditor from becoming a full (substituted) member of the LLC without consent of the other members and/or manager, or unless that creditor meets specified requirements. As a mere assignee of a membership interest under a charging order, the creditor cannot have any control over the operations or distributions made by the LLC. Because a partnership interest is personal property, a partner has no direct interest in the underlying assets of the partnership so that a creditor cannot obtain rights to the LLC assets.

Where a creditor forces the sale of an LLC membership interest, the result will be that the purchaser, if a sale were permitted, would at best be a mere assignee of the limited partnership interest. A creditor may not even have the right to force such a sale.

SAMPLE CLAUSE: General Requirements of Transfer: No transfer of any nature shall be made of any interest in this LLC, unless the provisions of this Article are complied with. No Member, or estate of a deceased Member, or guardian or custodian for a disabled Member shall, without the prior written consent of the Manager, which may be withheld for any reason in the absolute discretion of the Manager, mortgage, pledge, sell, assign, hypothecate, or otherwise encumber, transfer, or permit to be transferred in any manner or by any means whatever, whether voluntarily or by operation of law, all or any part of their interests in this LLC.

The assignee of an LLC membership interest is generally entitled to receive the profit (or loss) allocated by the LLC to the assigned membership interest. This is the same interest that the assignor would have been entitled to receive. The manager, in a manager-managed LLC, could thus limit distributions to an amount less than the income earned. The result could be that the member could receive phantom income reportable for tax purposes but without any commensurate cash distribution to pay the tax. As a mere assignee, rather than a substituted member, a creditor should not have any right to examine partnership books and records.

SUMMARY

As individuals work throughout their lifetimes and accumulate substantial assets, it makes sense that they want to take all steps possible to protect their assets. Accordingly, many successful individuals do asset protection planning. This generally involves removing assets from the individual's name and placing ownership in an entity that may be owned and/or controlled by such individual and/or family members. Having the assets owned by a separate and distinct entity such as an LLC, instead of by the individual himself helps create a layer of protection for the assets from the claims of creditors. The LLC is an excellent vehicle for asset protection planning. An investor in real property or a business owner who also owns real property on which the business operates could transfer the property out of his individual name into an LLC. The transferor and family members, who would have small membership interests, could own the LLC. The transferor could retain control over it by being the manager. No member of the LLC, however, would be personally liable for any of its debts and obligations arising after the transfer to the LLC.

21 LOAN TRANSACTIONS AND LIMITED LIABILITY COMPANIES

With the increasing use of LLCs in business and investment transactions, banks and other lenders will make more and more loans to LLCs. What are the special consequences of having loan transactions with LLCs?

WHAT LENDERS SHOULD REQUIRE FROM LLCs BORROWING MONEY

Any lender that makes a loan to an LLC must take various steps to help assure repayment:

- The loan documents should include statements (called *representations and warranties*) by the LLC that it is properly organized and validly existing under applicable state laws.

- The business purpose of the LLC as set forth in the LLC's Certificate of Formation must be broad enough to permit the LLC to borrow funds and to use them for the intended purpose.

- The operating agreement should not contain restrictions preventing the loan. Also, any requirements for the approval of the loan in the operating agreement must be followed. In addition to the lender requesting representations as to this, the lender should insist on copies of the relevant document for review by the lender's lawyer. For example, the operating agreement could have special approval or voting standards for a loan transaction. The lender needs to be sure that these have been met before releasing any funds.

- Many operating agreements specify the capital contribution that each member will make to the LLC. If the lender is relying on the existence of these funds (or other assets contributed), it should be verified that they have in fact been contributed and that the loan documents specify this reliance.

- Since no member or manager is personally liable for loans or debts of the LLC, unless the LLC's collateral is sufficient, the lender may insist on a personal guarantee from one or all members.

- An asset protection benefit to members in using the LLC entity is that a creditor can only receive an assignment of a member's interest, not become a substitute member, without approval of the manager or all other members (depending on what the operating agreement states). Where a creditor receives only an assignment of a membership interest, the creditor must report its allocable share of LLC income for tax purposes. If the LLC does not make any distribution to that member, the member has phantom income that creates a real out-of-pocket cost, but no cash. No lender wants to find itself in this position. Therefore, a lender who wants a security interest in a membership interest in an LLC to secure repayment of its loan must be certain that right is carefully limited to receiving actual distributions only, and not to becoming an assignee of a membership interest.

- Where a lender loans money to a corporation, it can physically take possession of a shareholder's stock certificate and a stock power signed in blank (a document permitting the lender to transfer the stock if there is a loan default). If the LLC has membership certificates (some do, many do not), then a similar procedure should be followed to protect the lender's interests.

HOW LOANS AFFECT LLC MEMBERS

From the members' perspective, there is an important tax benefit to the members of an LLC, as discussed in prior chapters. In an S corporation, debts of the corporation cannot be allocated to the shareholders's basis in their corporate stock. In a limited partnership, recourse financing can only be allocated to the general partner's basis in their partnership interests. An LLC offers important borrowing advantages over both of these entities. Unlike S corporations, LLC debts can be included in the tax basis of the members' membership interest. Unlike limited partnerships, all members of an LLC are allocated recourse financing (unless a particular member personally guaranteed the financing).

SUMMARY

Since LLCs are still relatively new, many types of common commercial transactions will have to adapt to these nuances. Lending funds to LLCs will become more common. Lenders must protect their interests relative to the characteristics of an LLC, and not simply continue to use past practices that were designed for corporate borrowers.

APPENDIX A

Limited Liability Company Statutes in the United States

The following tables present a summary of the LLC laws in each state. LLCs are, relative to other types of legal entities, quite new. As a result changes should be expected to occur. As the tax and legal rules mature, even some of the basic rules summarized in this Appendix could change. Therefore, it is essential that you consult with an attorney in your state before organizing an LLC.

TIP: If your LLC may operate in a state other than where you reside, be certain the lawyer you hire is qualified to assist you with that other state. Ask your lawyer whether an attorney in the other state should also be retained.

Alabama

State Statute. The Alabama LLC Act, Ala. Code §§ 10-12-1 through 10-12-61, became effective October 1, 1993.

Formation. Articles of Organization must contain the following information: name; duration, if less than perpetual; purpose; registered agent and office; names and mailing addresses of the initial Members; reservation of right to admit new Members; right to continue following act of dissociation or dissolution; whether there will be a Manager(s); and any additional matters.

Minimum Number of Members. One.

Default Rules. The following are examples of default rules provided by the Alabama LLC Act. Unless otherwise provided in the Articles of Organization or Operating Agreement:

- Members will manage the LLC.
- The LLC's profits and losses will be apportioned on the basis of the pro rata value of the contributions of each Member.
- A Member on 30 days' notice can withdraw from the LLC.
- Unanimous consent of the Membership is required for a person who wants to become a Member.
- A Membership interest is assignable.
- An assignment does not dissolve the LLC.
- The unanimous vote of the Members is required for an assignee to become a Member.
- An assignor is not released from his or her obligations to the LLC.
- The full assignment of a Member's interest is an act of dissociation.

State Classification. An LLC will be classified in the same manner as it is classified for federal income tax purposes.

State Entity Level Tax. None.

Alaska

State Statute. The Alaska Limited Liability Company Act, Alaska Stat. §§ 10.50.010 through 10.50.995, became effective July 1, 1995.

Formation. Articles of Organization must contain the following information: name; purpose; whether there will be a Manager(s); registered agent and office; and any additional matters.

Minimum Number of Members. One.

Default Rules. The following are examples of default rules provided by the Alaska LLC Act. Unless otherwise provided in the Articles of Organization or Operating Agreement:

- Members will manage the LLC.
- Members share equally in allocations and distributions.
- Action requires the unanimous consent of the Members.
- A Member is able to assign his or her interest without restriction.

State Classification. An LLC will be classified in the same manner as it is classified for federal income tax purposes.

State Entity Level Tax. None.

Arizona

State Statute. The Arizona Limited Liability Company Act, Ariz. Rev. Stat. Ann. §§ 29-601 through 29-857, became effective September 30, 1992.

Formation. Articles of Organization must contain the following information: name; the latest date on which the LLC is to dissolve; registered agent and office; and whether management is by Members or Managers, and the name and address of those who are to participate in management.

Minimum Number of Members. Two.

Default Rules. The following are examples of default rules provided by the Arizona LLC Act. Unless otherwise provided in the Articles of Organization or Operating Agreement:

- Members will manage the LLC.
- The LLC's profits and losses will be apportioned among its Members and classes of Members according to the relative capital contributions that they have made or promised to make in the future.
- A majority vote of the Managers or Members is required to (a) make decisions, (b) authorize distributions, (c) repurchase a Member's interest, (d) file notices of winding up, and (e) authorize nonmandatory amendment of the LLC's Articles of Organization.
- The Members' unanimous vote is required to (a) authorize activities outside the company purpose, (b) issue an interest in the LLC, (c) approve a plan of merger or consolidation, and (d) change the form of management the Articles of Organization authorizes.

State Classification.   For all state and local taxes, except state income tax, an LLC is treated as a limited partnership. For state income tax purposes, an LLC will be classified in the same manner as for federal income tax purposes.

State Entity Level Tax.   None.

Arkansas

State Statute.   The Arkansas Small Business Entity Tax Pass Through Act of 1993, Ark. Code Ann. §§ 4-32-101 through 4-32-1401, became effective April 12, 1993.

Formation.   Articles of Organization must contain the following information: name; registered agent and office; and whether there will be a Manager(s).

Minimum Number of Members.   One.

Default Rules.   The following are examples of default rules provided by the Arkansas LLC Act. Unless otherwise provided in the Articles of Organization or Operating Agreement:

- The right to manage the affairs of the LLC rests with the Managers.

- Members must fulfill their contribution promises even when unable to do so.

- Compromising an obligation to contribute to the LLC requires an unanimous vote of the Members.

- Unanimous consent of the Membership is required for new Members to be admitted.

State Classification.   LLCs are taxed as partnerships.

State Entity Level Tax.   None.

California

State Statute.   The California Limited Liability Company Act, Cal. Corp. Code §§ 17000 through 17655, became effective September 30, 1994.

Purposes.   California is the only state that does not permit an LLC to be formed for a limited purpose. A California LLC may engage in any lawful business activity except banking, insurance or trust.

Formation.   Articles of Organization must contain the following information: name; purpose (which may not be a limited purpose); registered agent and office; whether the LLC is to be managed by Managers and not by all its Members if the LLC is to be managed by Managers; and any other matters.

Minimum Number of Members.   One.

Default Rules.   The following are examples of default rules provided by the California LLC Act. Unless otherwise provided in the Articles of Organization or Operating Agreement:

- Members will manage the LLC.

- Allocations and distributions are made in proportion to the contributions by the Members.

- If a Member has no power to withdraw from the company by voluntary act, the Member may withdraw at any time by giving written notice to the other Members.

- A Member's interest is assignable upon the consent of a majority of the Members not transferring their interests.

State Classification.   An LLC will be classified in the same manner as it is classified for federal income tax purposes.

State Entity Level Tax.   There is an annual $800 minimum franchise tax.

Colorado

State Statute.   The Colorado Limited Liability Company Act, Colo. Rev. Stat. §§ 7-80-101 to 7-80-1101, became effective April 18, 1990.

Formation.   Articles of Organization must contain the following information: name; registered agent and office; a statement as to whether the LLC will be managed by Members or Managers; and the names and addresses of initial Manager(s) or Member(s) (if it is managed by Members).

Minimum Number of Members.   One.

Default Rules.   The following are examples of default rules provided by the Colorado LLC Act. Unless otherwise provided in the Articles of Organization or Operating Agreement:

- Managers and Members can conduct business and lend money with the LLC.
- Only a Manager can incur debt or liability.
- Distributions will be made on the basis of the value of the contributions made by each Member to the LLC.
- A Member is only entitled to receive cash distributions.

State Classification.   An LLC will be classified in the same manner as it is classified for federal income tax purposes.

State Entity Level Tax.   None.

Connecticut

State Statute.   The Connecticut Limited Liability Company Act, General Statutes of Conn §§ 34-100 to 34-242, became effective October 1, 1993.

Formation.   Articles of Organization must contain the following information: name; whether there will be a Manager(s); the purpose of the LLC; and the address of the principal; and the name of the registered agent.

Minimum Number of Members.   One.

Default Rules.   The following are examples of default rules provided by the Connecticut LLC Act. Unless otherwise provided in the Articles of Organization or Operating Agreement:

- Profits and losses and distributions will be apportioned according to a Member's basis of value as shown on the LLC's books.
- The LLC can only distribute cash and a Member only has the right to receive cash as a distribution.
- A Member who allows a lien to be filed, or gives a security interest or pledges his or her interest, does not surrender Membership rights.
- A Member can withdraw from the LLC on 30 days' notice.
- New Members can be admitted by a majority in interest.

State Classification.   An LLC will be classified in the same manner as it is classified for federal income tax purposes.

State Entity Level Tax.   None.

Delaware

State Statute.   The Delaware Limited Liability Company Act, Del. Code Ann. §§ 18-101 through 18.1109, became effective October 1, 1992.

Formation.   The Certificate of Formation must set forth the following information: name; registered agent and office; and a specific date of dissolution, if desired.

Minimum Number of Members.   One.

Default Rules.   The following are examples of default rules provided by the Delaware LLC Act. Unless otherwise provided in the Articles of Organization or Operating Agreement:

- The Manager or Member may conduct numerous forms of business dealings with the LLC.

- Specific factors causing a Member to lose his or her Membership in the LLC will apply by default. These Membership-terminating factors include filing of bankruptcy; assignment for the benefit of creditors; and debtor protection court pleading.

- Members are obligated to perform their promises to contribute property or cash or to perform services even if they are unable to perform because of death, disability, or other reason.

- Members, in proportion to their capital interests, will share in the profits and losses of an LLC.

- On withdrawal from the LLC or when receiving distributions, a Member will receive the fair value of his or her interests in a reasonable time. Payment will be made in cash. The Member has the same status against the LLC as a creditor.

- Membership interests are assignable in whole or part.

- An assignee is not liable for the liabilities of the assignor Member unless or until he is authorized by the Company Agreement or he becomes a Member.

State Classification.   An LLC will be classified in the same manner as it is classified for federal income tax purposes.

State Entity Level Tax.   There is a $100 tax on domestic and foreign LLCs.

District of Columbia

State Statute.   The District of Columbia Limited Liability Company Act, D.C. Code Ann. §§ 29-1001 through 29-1075, became effective July 23, 1994.

Formation.   Articles of Organization must contain the following information: name; the latest date on which the LLC is to dissolve; and registered agent and office.

Minimum Number of Members.   One.

Default Rules.   The following are examples of default rules provided by the District of Columbia LLC Act. Unless otherwise provided in the Articles of Organization or Operating Agreement:

- No Manager, Member, employee, or other agent of an LLC shall have any personal obligation for any debt, obligations, or liabilities of an LLC, whether such debts, obligations, or liabilities arise in contract, tort, or other act of an agent, Manager, Member, or employee of the LLC.

- Members shall manage the LLC.

- The Members of an LLC shall vote in proportion to their respective interests in the profits of the LLC.

- Decisions concerning the affairs of the LLC shall require the consent of those Members with voting rights holding at least a majority of the interests and profits of the LLC.

- A Member is obligated to the LLC to perform any enforceable promises to contribute property or cash or to perform services. If a Member dies and does not make the required contribution of property or services, at the option of the LLC, such Member is obligated to contribute cash equal to that portion of the value of the stated contribution that has not been made.

- If a Member is unable to perform any enforceable promise to perform services because of disability or death, such Member or such Member's successor or assign shall have the option of either:

    Contributing cash equal to that portion of the value of a stated contribution that the Member had promised to make in services but had failed to make.

    Forfeiting the Member's interest in the LLC.

- Profits and losses shall be allocated on the basis of value, as stated in the LLC records, of the contributions made by each Member to the extent they have been received by the LLC and have not been returned.

- A Member, regardless of the nature of such Member's contribution, has a right to demand and receive a distribution from an LLC in cash only.

- A Member shall not be required to accept (in lieu of the Member's share of a pro rata cash distribution) a distribution of any asset in-kind from an LLC to the extent that the percentage of the asset that would otherwise be distributed to such Member would exceed the percentage that such Member's membership interest bears to all Membership interests in the LLC.

- A Member may resign from an LLC on not less than six months' prior written notice to the LLC or to each member at such Member's address on the books of the LLC.

- Except as provided in the statute, a Member's financial rights associated with his or her interest in the LLC is assignable in whole or part.

State Classification. An LLC will be classified in the same manner as it is classified for federal income tax purposes.

State Entity Level Tax. There is a 10 percent tax on D.C. source income earned by unincorporated businesses.

Florida

State Statute. The Florida Limited Liability Company Act, Fla. Stat. §§ 608.401 through 608.705, became effective in 1982. The Act was substantially rewritten by the 1993 Legislature. The new Act became effective in October 1993.

Formation. Articles of Organization must contain the following information: name; mailing address of the principal office of the company; name and address of the LLC's registered agent; and any additional matters.

Minimum Number of Members. One.

Default Rules. The following are examples of default rules provided by the Florida LLC Act. Unless otherwise provided in the Articles of Organization or Operating Agreement:

- All capital contribution commitments must be performed by a Member.
- Management of an LLC rests with the members in relative proportion to their capital accounts.
- When the LLC is managed by Managers, only Managers can obligate the LLC; when the LLC is managed by Members, only Members can contract LLC debts.
- A Member, before withdrawing from the LLC, must give six months' written notice.
- A Member cannot assign his or her LLC interest, in whole or part, without the approval of a majority of the nonassigning Members.

State Classification. An LLC will be classified in the same manner as it is classified for federal income tax purposes.

State Entity Level Tax. None.

Georgia

State Statute.   The Georgia Limited Liability Company Act became effective March 1, 1994.

Formation.   Articles of Organization must contain the following information: name.

Minimum Number of Members.   One.

Default Rules.   The following are examples of default rules provided by the Georgia LLC Act. Unless otherwise provided in the Articles of Organization or Operating Agreement:

- The unanimous consent of the Members is required for the admission of additional Members.
- A person who ceases to be a Member has no management rights in the LLC.
- All LLCs are Member-managed.
- A Member is not entitled to receive an in-kind distribution.
- Members' interests are assignable in whole or part.
- The unanimous vote of the Members is required for an assignee to become a Member.
- A Member, on six months' written notice to the LLC, can withdraw.

State Classification.   An LLC will be classified in the same manner as it is classified for federal income tax purposes.

State Entity Level Tax.   The LLC pays 5 percent withholding tax on behalf of nonresident Members' distributive shares of LLC income.

Hawaii

State Statute.   The Hawaii Limited Liability Company Act became effective in 1995.

Formation.   Articles of Organization must contain the following information: name; address of initial designated office; registered agent and office; name and address of each organizer; duration; whether the LLC is to be Manager-managed, and, if so, the name and address of each initial Manager; and whether the Members of the LLC are to be liable for its debts and obligations.

Minimum Number of Members.   One.

Default Rules.   The following are examples of default rules provided by the Hawaii LLC Act. Unless otherwise provided in the Articles of Organization or Operating Agreement:

- In a Member-managed LLC, each Member has equal rights in management.
- In a Manager-managed LLC, the manager or managers have the exclusive authority to manage and conduct the company's business.
- Distributions shall be made in egual shares.

State Classification.   An LLC will be classified in the same manner as it is classified for federal income tax purposes.

State Entity Level Tax.   None.

Idaho

State Statute.   The Idaho Limited Liability Company Act, Idaho Code §§ 53-601 through 53-672, became effective July 1, 1993.

Formation.   Articles of Organization must contain the following information: name; registered agent and office; address of the registered office; whether there will be a Manager(s); the name and address of the Managers (or Members if there are no Managers).

Minimum Number of Members. One.

Default Rules. The following are examples of default rules provided by the Idaho LLC Act. Unless otherwise provided in the Articles of Organization or Operating Agreement:

- Managers make decisions by majority vote.
- A Member is liable for his or her contributions to the LLC and this obligation cannot be compromised without the unanimous consent of the Membership.
- Distributions must be paid in cash to a Member unless an in-kind payment is authorized in the Operating Agreement.
- Assignments of Membership interests are permitted.
- A person who receives a pledge of a Member's Membership interest is not an assignee.
- Assignees can become Members only with the unanimous consent of the Members.
- Assignees have no right to participate in management.
- An assignor is not released from his or her liability to the LLC.
- A Member who assigns his or her entire interest in the LLC loses Membership in the entity.
- Unanimous consent of the Membership is required for a person to become a Member.
- Members, on 30 days' notice may withdraw.

State Classification. An LLC will be classified in the same manner as it is classified for federal income tax purposes.

State Entity Level Tax. None.

Illinois

State Statute. The Illinois Limited Liability Company Act became effective January 1, 1994.

Formation. Articles of Organization must contain the following information: name; purpose; registered agent and office; whether there will be a Manager(s); the name of the Manager(s); the latest date on which the LLC is to dissolve; address of the LLC's principal office; name and address of each organizer; and any additional matters.

Minimum Number of Members. One.

Default Rules. The following are examples of default rules provided by the Illinois LLC Act. Unless otherwise provided in the Articles of Organization or Operating Agreement:

- A Member may transact business and lend money to the LLC.
- New Members must have the unanimous consent of existing Members to be admitted.
- All decisions of Members must be approved by the Members owning a majority vote of the book value of Membership interests.
- Membership interests in the profits are assignable in whole or part.

State Classification. An LLC will be classified in the same manner as it is classified for federal income tax purpose.

State Entity Level Tax. The LLC pays a 1.5 percent tax on partnerships.

Indiana

State Statute. The Indiana Business Flexibility Act, Ind. Code §§ 23-18-1-1 through 23-18-13-1, became effective July 1, 1993.

Formation.   Articles of Organization must contain the following information: name; registered agent and office; the latest date on which the LLC is to dissolve; whether there will be a Manager(s); and any additional matters.

Minimum Number of Members.   One.

Default Rules.   The following are examples of default rules provided by the Indiana LLC Act. Unless otherwise provided in the Articles of Organization or Operating Agreement:

- Members have the power and authority to manage the LLC.
- Governing decisions are by majority vote when there is more than one Manager.
- Absent a unanimous vote of the Membership, the LLC cannot reduce the obligation of a Member to repay a distribution or make a capital contribution.
- A Member cannot be required to receive a distribution in-kind rather than cash.
- A vote of all Members is required for admission of Members.
- Members' interests are assignable.
- The unanimous consent of the Members is required for an assignee to become a Member.
- A Member, on 30 days' notice, may withdraw from the LLC.

State Classification.   An LLC will be classified in the same manner as it is classified for federal income tax purposes.

State Entity Level Tax.   None.

Iowa

State Statute.   The Iowa Limited Liability Company Act, Iowa Code §§ 490A.100 through 490A.1601, became effective September 1, 1992.

Formation.   Articles of Organization must contain the following information: name; duration, which may be perpetual; registered agent and office; address of principal office; and any additional matters.

Minimum Number of Members.   One.

Default Rules.   The following are examples of default rules provided by the Iowa LLC Act. Unless otherwise provided in the Articles of Organization or Operating Agreement:

- Members will manage the LLC.
- Members can withdraw on six months' notice.
- Managers will be elected by majority vote of the Members.
- Managers can be removed by a majority vote of the Members with or without cause.
- Decisions by Managers will be made by majority vote.
- Members vote in proportion to their contributions to the LLC's capital.
- A majority vote is needed to approve: Dissolution and winding up.
- The sale, lease, exchange, mortgage, pledge, or other transfer of all or substantially all of the LLC's assets.
- A unanimous vote is needed to approve an amendment of the Articles of Organization or Operating Agreement.
- Members will share the LLC's profits and losses in proportion to their capital interests.
- Interests of the Membership are assignable in whole or part.

- A Member ceases to be a Member on assignment of his or her entire Membership interest.
- The unanimous consent of the existing Members is required for the assignee to become a Member.

State Classification.   An LLC will be classified as a partnership under federal classification guidelines.

State Entity Level Tax.   None.

Kansas

State Statute.   The Kansas Limited Liability Company Act, Kan. Stat. Ann. §§ 17-7601 through 17-7652, became effective July 1, 1990.

Formation.   Articles of Organization must contain the following information: name; the latest date on which the LLC is to dissolve; purpose; registered agent and office; whether there will be a Manager(s); the name and addresses of the Managers; reservation of right to admit new Members.

Minimum Number of Members.   One.

Default Rules.   The following are examples of default rules provided by the Kansas LLC Act. Unless otherwise provided in the Articles of Organization or Operating Agreement:

- Management of the LLC rests with the members, with each Member having one vote.
- Members can transact business and lend money with the LLC.
- The allocation of gain, income, loss, deduction, or credit will be allocated to Members in proportion to the right to share in distributions to the LLC.

State Classification.   An LLC will be classified in the same manner as it is classified for federal income tax purpose.

State Entity Level Tax.   None.

Kentucky

State Statute.   The Kentucky Limited Liability Company Act, KRS Chapter 275.001 to 275.455, was enacted March 29, 1994.

Formation.   Articles of Organization must contain the following information: name; registered agent and office; address of the principal office; whether there will be a Manager(s); the services to be practiced; specific date of dissolution (if any, otherwise it will be deemed perpetual); and any additional matters.

Minimum Number of Members.   One.

Default Rules.   The following are examples of default rules provided by the Kentucky LLC Act. Unless otherwise provided in the Articles of Organization or Operating Agreement:

- Members manage the company.
- There will be only one class of Members.
- Management action requires a majority of Members on a per capita basis.
- Approval of action requires only a simple majority of the Members on a per capita basis.

- The Members share in all allocations and distributions on the basis of the value of contributions made.
- A Member's interest is assignable without restriction, except that the assignee will not have any right to participate in Management of the company.
- Consent of all Members is required for admission of members, whether they take their interest directly from the company or by assignment.
- If a Member has no power to withdraw from the company by voluntary act, the Member may not withdraw without the consent of all other remaining members.

State Classification.   An LLC will be classified in the same manner as it is classified for federal income tax purposes.
State Entity Level Tax.   None.

Louisiana
State Statute.   The Louisiana Limited Liability Company Act, La. Rev. Stat. Ann. §§ 12:1301 through 12:1369, became effective July 7, 1992.
Formation.   Articles of Organization must contain the following information: name; purpose; and any additional matters.
Minimum Number of Members.   One.
Default Rules.   The following are examples of default rules provided by the Louisiana LLC Act. Unless otherwise provided in the Articles of Organization or Operating Agreement:

- Voting is by plurality vote of the members.
- Silence permits management to be removed with or without cause.
- Silence results in management by the Members.
- When voting requirements of Managers/Members are not established, each Manager has one vote and decisions are made by majority vote.
- If a Member's obligation to pay capital contributions because of death, disability, or other reason is not limited, then the payment must be made.
- The vote to compromise a capital contribution must be unanimous.
- Allocation of profits and losses will be equally among the Members.
- The withdrawing Member is entitled to his or her fair market value share of distributions within a reasonable time. All payments must be in cash and not in kind.
- Failure to control/limit the assignability, pledge, or encumbrance of membership interests in the Articles or the Operating Agreement results in the assignability and pledge or encumbrance of Membership interests. Pledge or encumbrance of a Member's interest does not cause him or her to lose Membership status.
- Unanimous consent of Membership is required for an assignee to become a Member or participate in the management of an LLC.

State Classification.   An LLC will be classified in the same manner as it is classified for federal income tax purposes.
State Entity Level Tax.   None.

Maine
State Statute.   The Maine Limited Liability Company Act, Me. Rev. Stat. Ann. Tit. 31, §§ 601 through 762, became effective January 1, 1995.

Formation. Articles of Organization must contain the following information: name; registered agent and office; whether there will be a manager(s); the names and addresses of the managers and the minimum and maximum number of managers permitted; and any additional matters.

Minimum Number of Members. One.

Default Rules. The following are examples of default rules provided by the Maine LLC Act. Unless otherwise provided in the Articles of Organization or Operating Agreement:

- Members manage the LLC.
- There will be only one class of Members.
- Management action requires a majority of Members on a per capita basis.
- Unless otherwise provided for in the statute, approval of action requires only a simple majority of the Members on a per capita basis.
- The company is not obligated to indemnify an employee or agent.
- A Member's successor is obligated to the company to pay his or her obligation for contributions.
- Members share equally in allocations and distributions.
- A withdrawing Member is not entitled to receive any distributions, now or later.
- A Member's interest is assignable without restriction, except the assignee will not have any right to participate in management of the company.
- Consent of all Members is required for admission of Members, whether they take their interest directly from the company or by assignment.
- If a Member has no power to withdraw from the company by voluntary act, the Member may do so at any time by giving 30 days' written notice.

State Classification. An LLC will be classified in the same manner as it is classified for federal income tax purposes.

State Entity Level Tax. None.

Maryland

State Statute. The Maryland Limited Liability Company Act, Md. Code Ann. §§ 4A-101 through 4A-1103, became effective October 1, 1992.

Formation. Articles of Organization must contain the following information: name; the latest date on which the LLC is to dissolve; principal agent and office; purpose; and any additional matters.

Minimum Number of Members. One.

Default Rules. The following are examples of default rules provided by the Maryland LLC Act. Unless otherwise provided in the Articles of Organization or Operating Agreement:

- Each Member is an agent of the LLC.
- Oral Operating Agreements are permitted.
- All Members will vote in proportion to their interests in the profits of the LLC and management decisions will be made by majority vote.
- Members can do business with the LLC.
- Members must make promised capital contributions to the LLC. Required contributions can be compromised only with the unanimous consent of the Members or pursuant to terms of the Operating Agreement.
- The interests of the LLC are assignable.

- A Member has the right to withdraw on six months' written notice.
- Merger is permitted.
- An LLC dissolves upon the unanimous consent of the Members or at the time of the entry of a decree of judicial dissolution, except as provided by the unanimous consent of the Members.
- The remaining Members may wind up an LLC.

State Classification.   All LLCs will be classified in the same manner as it is classified for federal income tax purposes.

State Entity Level Tax.   The LLC pays 5 percent withholding tax on behalf of nonresident Members' distributive shares of LLC income.

Massachusetts

State Statute.   The Massachusetts Limited Liability Company Act, The Acts and Resolve of 1995, Chapter 281, was enacted January 1, 1996.

Formation.   Articles of Organization must contain the following information: name and address; latest date on which the LLC is to dissolve; principal agent and office; name and address of the managers, if any; name of any other person authorized to execute documents; general character of business; purpose; and any additional matters.

Minimum Number of Members.   Two.

Default Rules.   The following are examples of default rules provided by the Massachusetts LLC Act. Unless otherwise provided in the Certificate of Incorporation or Operating Agreement:

- The decision of Members who own more than fifty percent of the unreturned contributions shall be controlling.
- Management shall be vested in the Members.
- A Member is obligated to perform any promise to contribute cash or property or to perform services to the LLC.
- A Member has no right to demand and receive any distribution from an LLC in any form other than cash.
- An LLC interest is assignable, in whole or in part.
- An assignment entitles the assignee to share in profits and losses.
- Until an assignee becomes a Member, the assignee shall have no liability as a Member.

State Classification.   An LLC will be classified in the same manner as it is classified for federal income tax purposes.

State Entity Level Tax.   None.

Michigan

State Statute.   The Michigan Limited Liability Company Act became effective June 1, 1993.

Formation.   Articles of Organization must contain the following information: name; purpose; registered agent and office; whether there will be a Manager(s); and duration.

Minimum Number of Members.   One.

Default Rules.   The following are examples of default rules provided by the Michigan LLC Act. Unless otherwise provided in the Articles of Organization or Operating Agreement:

- All Members must comply with promises to contribute to the LLC.
- Unanimous consent of the Membership is required for Members to be excused from performing contributions promised to the entity.
- A Manager or Member entitled to participate in a decision to make a distribution is presumed to have assented to a distribution once he or she files a written dissent with the company.
- Members manage the LLC. However, management rights can be enlarged or restricted in the Operating Agreement.
- A majority vote of the Members elect managers.
- Managers can be terminated without cause.

State Classification.   An LLC will be classified in the same manner as it is classified for federal income tax purposes.
State Entity Level Tax.   None.

Minnesota
State Statute.   The Minnesota Limited Liability Company Act became effective January 1, 1993.
Formation: Articles of Organization must contain the following information: name; registered agent and office; name and address of each organizer; and duration of the LLC.
Minimum Number of Members.   One.
Default Rules.   The Minnesota LLC Act lists 22 statutory provisions that may be modified in the Articles of Organization.

- Members vote in proportion to their contributions to the capital of the LLC.
- The profits and losses of an LLC will be shared by the Members in proportion to their value of their capital interests.

State Classification.   An LLC will be classified in the same manner as it is classified for federal income tax purposes.
State Entity Level Tax.   There is no entity level tax, but there is an annual flat fee for farming partnerships.

Mississippi
State Statute.   The Mississippi Limited Liability Company Act became effective July 1, 1994.
Formation.   The Certificate of Formation must contain the following information: name; duration, if less than perpetual; registered agent and office; whether there will be a Manager(s); and any additional matters.
Minimum Number of Members.   One.
Default Rules.   The following are examples of default rules provided by the Mississippi LLC Act. Unless otherwise provided in the Articles of Organization or Operating Agreement:

- A Member may transact other business and lend money to the LLC and, subject to other applicable law, has the same rights and obligations with respect thereto as a person who is not a Member or Manager.
- An LLC shall indemnify a Manager, Member, or other person who is wholly successful, on the permits or otherwise, in the defense of any proceeding to which he

or she was a party because he or she is or was a Manager, Member, or agent of the LLC against reasonable expenses incurred by him or her in connection with the proceeding.

- One or more LLCs may merge with or into one or more domestic or foreign LLCs with such LLC or foreign LLC being the surviving organization.
- Written consent of all Members is required for a person acquiring an LLC interest directly from the LLC.
- Members manage the LLC.
- Each Member of an LLC shall be entitled to one vote on any matter entitled to be voted on by the Members.
- Unless otherwise provided in the statute, any action required or permitted to be taken by the Members of an LLC must be by a majority vote of the Members.
- Subject to the consent of all Members at the time, a person ceases to be a Member on his or her death or the entry of an order by a court of competent jurisdiction adjudicating the person incompetent to manage his or her person or estate.
- If a Member has no power to withdraw by voluntary act from an LLC, the Member may do so at any time on giving 30 days' written notice.
- A withdrawal by a Member before the expiration of that term is a breach of the Certificate of Formation in situations where the LLC is for a definite term or particular undertaking.
- Members elect the Manager.
- Any action required or permitted to be taken by the Managers of an LLC may be taken on a majority vote of the Managers.
- Profits and losses must be apportioned on the basis of the value, as stated in the LLC records, of the contributions made by each Member to the extent that they have been received by the LLC and have not been returned.
- Distributions must be made on the basis of the value of the contributions made by each Member to the extent that they have been received by the LLC and have not been returned.
- Regardless of the nature of his or her contribution, a Member has no right to demand and receive any distribution from an LLC in any form other than cash.
- An interest of the LLC is assignable in whole or in part.
- On assignment of the Member's entire LLC interest, a Member ceases to be a Member.
- The Manager, or if management of the LLC is not vested in a Manager, and the Members who have not wrongfully dissolved an LLC, may wind up the LLC's affairs.

State Classification.   An LLC is presumed to be a partnership unless classified otherwise for federal income tax purposes.

State Entity Level Tax.   None.

Missouri

State Statute.   The Missouri Limited Liability Company Act, Mo. Rev. Stat. §§ 347.010 through 347.735, became effective December 1, 1993.

Formation.   Articles of Organization must contain the following information: name; purpose; registered agent address; whether there will be a Manager(s); the latest date on which the LLC is to dissolve; the right to continue following a Member's withdrawal; and name and address of each organizer.

Minimum Number of Members.   One.

Default Rules.   The following are examples of default rules provided by the Missouri LLC Act. Unless otherwise provided in the Articles of Organization or Operating Agreement:

- Managers need not be Members of the LLC.
- The unanimous vote of the Membership is required to:

  Issue an interest in an LLC or to admit a new Member.

  Approve a merger or consolidation.

  Change management from Member-managed to Manager-operated or vice versa.

  Authorize activity outside the scope of the purpose of the LLC.

  Affect a Member's contribution to the LLC.

- Decisions on any matter connected with the business or affairs of the LLC requires a majority vote of the membership.
- All Managers and Members can do business with and lend money to the LLC.
- Distributions to the Members are controlled by a majority vote.
- Assignments of Membership interests can be made in whole or part.
- If an assignee becomes a Member, the assignor is still liable for his or her obligations to the LLC.

State Classification.   An LLC will be classified in the same manner as it is classified for federal income tax purposes.

State Entity Level Tax.   None.

Montana

State Statute.   The Montana Limited Liability Company Act became effective October 1, 1993.

Formation.   Articles of Organization must contain the following information: name; the latest date the LLC is to dissolve; address of the principal place of business; registered agent and office; a statement as to whether the company will be managed by Members or Managers; whether there will be a Manager(s); if a professional LLC, a statement of the services it will render; and any additional matters.

Minimum Number of Members.   One.

Default Rules.   The following are examples of default rules provided by the Montana LLC Act. Unless otherwise provided in the Articles of Organization or Operating Agreement:

- To compromise an obligation to contribute to the LLC requires the unanimous vote of the Members.
- Each Member must be repaid his or her capital contributions and then each Member shares equally in distributions.
- The unanimous consent of the Membership is required to admit new Members.

State Classification.   An LLC will be classified in the same manner as it is classified for federal income tax purposes.

State Entity Level Tax.   None.

Nebraska

State Statute.   The Nebraska Limited Liability Company Act became effective September 9, 1993.

Formation.   Articles of Organization must contain the following information: name; purpose; address of the principal office; registered agent; total amount of cash or property contributed; the right to admit new Members; whether there will be a Manager(s); and any additional matters.

Minimum Number of Members.   One.

Default Rules.   The following are examples of default rules provided by the Nebraska LLC Act. Unless otherwise provided in the Articles of Organization or Operating Agreement:

- Management of the company rests with the Members in proportion to their capital contributions.
- A majority of the Membership must approve a Member withdrawing property.
- The assets of the LLC are shared by Members in relation to the capital account.

State Classification.   An LLC will be classified in the same manner as it is classified for federal income tax purposes.

State Entity Level Tax.   None.

Nevada

State Statute.   The Nevada Limited Liability Company Act, Nev. Rev. Stat. §§ 86.010 through 86.590, became effective October 1, 1991.

Formation.   Articles of Organization must contain the following information: name; registered agent and office; name and address of organizers; provision discussing the management of the company; and any additional matters.

Minimum Number of Members.   One.

Default Rules.   The Nevada LLC Act contains the following default rule. Unless otherwise provided in the Articles of Organization or Operating Agreement:

- Members, when they retain management rights, can incur obligations and bind the company for debt.
- Members vote in proportion to their contributions to the capital of the LLC.

State Classification.   Nevada does not have an income tax for partnerships or corporations. However, LLCs are subject to franchise taxes, must obtain a business license and pay an annual fee of $85 to the Secretary of State.

State Entity Level Tax.   None.

New Hampshire

State Statute.   The New Hampshire Business Flexibility Act, N.H. Rev. Stat. Ann. §§ 304-C:1 through 304-C:85, became effective July 1, 1993.

Formation.   Articles of Organization must contain the following information: name; purpose; registered agent and office; latest date on which the LLC will dissolve; and whether there will be a Manager(s); and any additional matters.

Minimum Number of Members.   One.

Default Rules.   The following are examples of default rules provided by the New Hampshire LLC Act. Unless otherwise provided in the Articles of Organization or Operating Agreement:

- Except the Act, an LLC can indemnify its Managers and Members.
- A majority of Managers and Members decide business matters.
- Management is reserved to the Members.

- Members who are Managers have the rights and powers of both positions.
- A Member is responsible for his or her capital contributions to the LLC; this obligation can be compromised only by the unanimous vote of the Membership.
- Except as provided in other documents, an assignee has no liability as a Member solely as a result of the assignment.
- A vote of all the Members is required for admission of Members.
- The unanimous consent of the Members is required for an assignee to become a Member.

State Classification. An LLC will be classified in the same manner as it is classified for federal income tax purposes.

State Entity Level Tax. The LLC pays a tax on dividends, interests and business profits.

New Jersey

State Statute. The New Jersey Limited Liability Company Act became effective January 26, 1994.

Formation. Articles of Organization must contain the following information: name; registered agent and office; a statement that the LLC to have perpetual duration; and any other matters.

Minimum Number of Members. One.

Default Rules. The following are examples of default rules provided by the New Jersey LLC Act. Unless otherwise provided in the Articles of Organization or Operating Agreement:

- The LLC is managed by Members.
- Members are liable to perform their capital obligations to the company even when performance is impossible.
- Members can forgive the failure to perform member obligations to the LLC only with the unanimous consent of the Members.
- Distributions will be made in proportion to the agreed value of contributions to the extent they have not been returned.
- A Member is entitled to receive distributions prior to winding up of the LLC or his retirement.
- A Member may resign on six months' written notice.
- A Member has no liability after three years for improper distributions.

State Classification. An LLC will be classified in the same manner as it is classified for federal income tax purposes.

State Entity Level Tax. None.

New Mexico

State Statute. The New Mexico Limited Liability Company Act became effective June 17, 1993.

Formation. Articles of Organization must contain the following information: name; registered agent and office; the latest date on which the LLC is to dissolve; and a provision on the management by nonmember Managers; and if it is a single member LLC.

Minimum Number of Members. One.

Default Rules. The following are examples of default rules provided by the New Mexico LLC Act. Unless otherwise provided in the Articles of Organization or Operating Agreement:

- Silence with respect to use of Managers results in Members managing the LLC.
- To remove a Member, the vote or consent of all Members is necessary.
- Unless approved by all Members, no Member has the right to withdraw any part of his or her contribution to capital.
- The unanimous vote of the membership is required for an assignee to become a Member.
- An individual must have the written consent of all Members to obtain a Membership interest from the entity.
- A Member can withdraw on 30 days' written notice when the LLC has perpetual existence.

State Classification.   An LLC will be classified in the same manner as it is classified for federal income tax purposes.

State Entity Level Tax.   None.

New York

State Statute.   The New York Limited Liability Company Law became effective October 24, 1994.

Formation.   Articles of Organization must contain the following information: name; county; latest date of dissolution, if any; office and agent for service of process; a designation of the secretary of state as agent of the LLC; a statement whether management of the LLC is vested in a Manager; any limit on the grant of limited liability; and any additional matters.

Minimum Number of Members.   One.

Default Rules.   The following are examples of default rules provided by the New York LLC Act. Unless otherwise provided in the Articles of Organization or Operating Agreement:

- Members manage the LLC.
- There will be only one class of Members.
- Management action requires a vote of a majority of the Members' profits interest.
- Any or all Managers may be removed by a majority in interest vote.
- After an event that terminates the continued Membership of a Member, a vote to continue the company requires the consent of a majority in interest of all other remaining Members.

State Classification.   An LLC will be classified in the same manner as it is classified for federal income tax purposes.

State Entity Level Tax.   The LLC pays $50 per Member annually, with a minimum fee of $325 and a maximum fee of $10,000.

North Carolina

State Statute.   The North Carolina Limited Liability Company Act, N.C. Gen. Stat. §§ 57C-1-101 through 57C-10-07, became effective October 1, 1993.

Formation.   Articles of Organization must contain the following information: name; the latest date on which the LLC is to dissolve, if any; the name and each address of each person who executes the Articles; registered agent and office; address of LLC's principal office; and notice when all Members are not participants in management.

Minimum Number of Members.   One.

Default Rules. The following are examples of default rules provided by the North Carolina LLC Act. Unless otherwise provided in the Articles of Organization or Operating Agreement:

- Unanimous consent of the Membership is required for admission of new Members.
- All LLCs are Member-managed.
- A Member is not entitled to receive a noncash distribution.
- The unanimous vote of the Members is required for an assignee to become a Member.

State Classification. An LLC will be classified in the same manner as it is classified for federal income tax purposes.

State Entity Level Tax. None.

North Dakota

State Statute. The North Dakota Limited Liability Company Act, N.D. Cent. Code §§ 10-32-01 through 10-32-156, became effective April 12, 1993.

Formation. Articles of Organization must contain the following information: name; registered agent and office; name and address of each organizer; and the LLC's period of existence, if other than perpetual.

Minimum Number of Members. One.

Default Rules. The following are examples of default rules provided by the North Dakota LLC Act. Unless otherwise provided in the Articles of Organization or Operating Agreement:

- Members vote in proportion to their contributions to the capital of the LLC.
- The profits and losses of an LLC will be shared by the Members in proportion to their capital interest.

State Classification. An LLC will be classified in the same manner as it is classified for federal income tax purposes.

State Entity Level Tax. None.

Ohio

State Statute. The Ohio Limited Liability Company Act, Ohio Rev. Code Ann. §§ 1705.01 through 1705.58, became effective July 1, 1994.

Formation. Articles of Organization must contain the following information: name; duration; and any additional matters.

Minimum Number of Members. One.

Default Rules. The following are examples of default rules provided by the Ohio LLC Act. Unless otherwise provided in the Articles of Organization or Operating Agreement:

- The management of an LLC rests with its Members in proportion to their contributions to the capital of the company as adjusted from time to time to reflect any additional contributions or withdrawals by the Members.
- A person who is both a Manager and a Member of an LLC has the rights and powers of Manager and is subject to the liabilities and restrictions of a Manager.

State Classification. An LLC will be classified in the same manner as it is classified for federal income tax purposes.

State Entity Level Tax. None.

Oklahoma

State Statute.   The Oklahoma Limited Liability Company Act became effective September 1, 1992.

Formation.   Articles of Organization must contain the following information: name; duration; and principal office and registered agent and office.

Minimum Number of Members.   One.

Default Rules.   The following are examples of default rules provided by the Oklahoma LLC Act. Unless otherwise provided in the Articles of Organization or Operating Agreement:

- Silence with regard to the use of Managers results in at least one Manager being required.
- Managers will make decisions by majority vote.
- Interests of the Members are assignable in whole or part.
- An assignee is not liable as a Member unless or until he or she becomes a Member.

State Classification.   An LLC will be classified in the same manner as it is classified for federal income tax purposes.

State Entity Level Tax.   None.

Oregon

State Statute.   The Oregon Limited Liability Company Act became effective January 1, 1994.

Formation.   Articles of Organization must contain the following information: name; registered agent and office; notice address; whether there will be a Manager(s); name and address of each organizer; duration, if less than perpetual; and whether the LLC is to render professional services.

Minimum Number of Members.   One.

Default Rules.   The following are examples of default rules provided by the Oregon LLC Act. Unless otherwise provided in the Articles of Organization or Operating Agreement:

- The LLC is managed by the Members.
- Managers are elected and terminated by majority vote of the Members.
- On six months' notice, a member can withdraw.
- Members have no right to distributions in kind.
- The majority vote of the Membership is required for a new Member taking his or her interest from the LLC or an assignee becoming a Member.

State Classification.   An LLC will be classified in the same manner as it is classified for federal income tax purposes.

State Entity Level Tax.   None.

Pennsylvania

State Statute.   The Pennsylvania Limited Liability Company Act, 15 Pa. Cons. Stat. Ch. 89, became effective February 5, 1995.

Formation.   Articles of Organization must contain the following information: name and address of each organizer; office and agent for service of process; whether there will be a Manager(s); if a member's interest will be evidenced by a certificate of membership; if the LLC is to be a restricted professional company; and any additional matters.

Minimum Number of Members.   One.

Default Rules. The following are examples of default rules provided by the Pennsylvania LLC Act. Unless otherwise provided in the Articles of Organization or Operating Agreement:

- All the Members of the LLC will manage the company.
- A majority of the Managers or Members of an LLC shall be required to decide any matter.
- Voting is by Members on a per capita basis, and not in proportion to their profits interest or capital contributions.
- The LLC will have only one class of Members.
- A Manager shall serve for the shorter of:

    One year plus the time needed to elect and qualify a successor.

    The Manager's resignation, removal, or death.

State Classification. Pennsylvania taxes LLCs as corporations, even when they are recognized and taxed as partnerships at the federal level.

State Entity Level Tax. The LLC will be taxed as a corporation except for restricted professional companies.

Rhode Island

State Statute. The Rhode Island Limited Liability Company Act became effective September 21, 1992.

Formation. Articles of Organization must contain the following information: name; registered agent and office; and a statement of how it is intended to be taxed; and whether the LLC will be managed by Members or Managers.

Minimum Number of Members. Two.

Default Rules. The following are examples of default rules provided by the Rhode Island LLC Act. Unless otherwise provided in the Articles of Organization or Operating Agreement:

- Voting is by Members on a per capita basis.
- Interim distributions will be distributed on the basis of the value of the capital contributions made by each Member to the extent that such contributions have not been returned.
- The profits and losses of an LLC will be shared by the Members in proportion to their capital interests.

State Classification. An LLC will be classified in the same manner as it is classified for federal income tax purposes.

State Entity Level Tax. None.

South Carolina

State Statute. The South Carolina Limited Liability Company Act, SC Code Ann. §§ 33-43-101 to 33-43-1409, became effective June 16, 1994.

Formation. Articles of Organization must contain the following information: name; specific date of dissolution; registered agent and office; whether there will be a Manager(s); and name and signature of each organizer.

Minimum Number of Members. One.

Default Rules.   The following are examples of default rules provided by the South Carolina LLC Act. Unless otherwise provided in the Articles of Organization or Operating Agreement:

- Members manage the business affairs of the LLC.
- An LLC must maintain at its principal place of business:

    A writing setting out the amount of cash, if any, and the statement of the agreed value of other property or services, if any, contributed by each Member and the times at which or events on the happening of which any additional contributions are to be made by each Member.

    A writing stating events, if any, on the happening of which the LLC is to be dissolved and its affairs wound up.

    Other writings prepared pursuant to a requirement, if any, in any Operating Agreement.

- Only with the unanimous consent of the Members can an obligation of a Member to make a contribution be compromised.
- An assignment of an LLC interest does not entitle the assignee to participate in the management and affairs of the LLC or to become or exercise any rights of a Member or dissolve the LLC.
- Until the assignee of an LLC interest becomes a Member, the assignor continues to be a Member and to have the power to exercise any rights of a Member, subject to the other Members' right to remove the assignor pursuant to the statute.

State Classification.   An LLC will be classified in the same manner as it is classified for federal income tax purposes.
State Entity Level Tax.   None.

South Dakota
State Statute.   The South Dakota Limited Liability Company Act became effective July 1, 1993.
Formation.   Articles of Organization must contain the following information: name; duration; purpose; registered agent and office; description and amount of initial capital contributions; additional agreed upon contributions; and discussion of management.
Minimum Number of Members.   One.
Default Rules.   The following are examples of default rules provided by the South Dakota LLC Act. Unless otherwise provided in the Articles of Organization or Operating Agreement:

- Members manage the LLC in proportion of their capital contributions.

State Classification.   An LLC is not subject to state income tax regardless of the federal tax classification.
State Entity Level Tax.   None.

Tennessee
State Statute.   The Tennessee Limited Liability Company Act, Tenn. Code Ann. §§ 48-281-101 through 48-201-248, became effective June 21, 1994.
Formation.   Articles of Organization must contain the following information: name; office and agent for service of process; name and address of each organizer; address of principal executive office; statement as to whether the LLC will be board-managed or

member-managed; number of members at time of filing; dissolution matters if board-managed; reservation of power to expel a Member; and any additional matters.

Minimum Number of Members.   One.

Default Rules.   The following are examples of default rules provided by the Tennessee LLC Act. Unless otherwise provided in the Articles of Organization or Operating Agreement:

- Members do not have preemptive rights.
- An LLC does not have the right to expel a Member.
- The LLC will have only one class of Members.
- A majority vote of the Members, without regard to their capital or profit interest, is required for action of management in a Member-managed LLC.

State Classification.   An LLC will be classified in the same manner as it is classified for federal income tax purposes.

State Entity Level Tax.   The LLC must pay $50 per Member annually with a $3,000 cap.

Texas

State Statute.   The Texas Limited Liability Company Act, Tex. Rev. Civ. Stat. Ann. Art. 1528n, became effective August 26, 1991.

Formation.   Articles of Organization must contain the following information: name; duration; purpose; registered agent and office; name and address of each organizer; and provision discussing management.

Minimum Number of Members.   One.

Default Rules.   The following are examples of default rules provided by the Texas LLC Act. Unless otherwise provided in the Articles of Organization or Operating Agreement:

- The company is run by Managers who need not be residents of Texas.
- If the regulations are silent, written consent of all Members is required for admission of new Members.

State Classification.   An LLC will be taxed as a corporation.

State Entity Level Tax.   The LLC pays a tax of .25 percent of capital and 4.5 percent of earned surplus.

Utah

State Statute.   The Utah Limited Liability Company Act, Utah Code Ann. §§ 48-2c-101 through 48-2c-1902, became effective in 2001.

Formation.   Articles of Organization must contain the following information: name; purpose; registered office and agent; signature of initial registered agent; a statement appointing the director of the division as agent under certain circumstances; address of the LLC's designated office; name and address of each organizer who is not a member or manager; and if the company is to be Manager-managed or Member-managed; whether there will be a Manager(s).

Minimum Number of Members.   One.

Default Rules.   The following are examples of default rules provided by the Utah LLC Act. Unless otherwise provided in the Articles of Organization or Operating Agreement:

- The written consent of all Members is required to admit an additional Member.
- Management of the company generally rests with the Members in proportion to profits and capital contribution.

State Classification.   An LLC will be classified in the same manner as it is classified for federal income tax purposes.

State Entity Level Tax.   None.

Vermont

State Statute.   The Vermont Limited Liability Company Act became effective in 1995.

Formation.   Articles of Organization must contain the following information: name; address of initial designated office; registered agent and office; name and address of each organizer; duration, if the LLC is a term LLC; whether the LLC is to be Manager-managed, and, if so, the name and address of each initial Manager; and whether the Members of the LLC are to be liable for its debts and obligations.

Minimum Number of Members.   One.

Default Rules.   The following are examples of default rules provided by the Vermont LLC Act. Unless otherwise provided in the Articles of Organization or Operating Agreement:

- In a Member-managed LLC, each Member has equal rights in management.
- A transfer of an interest in the LLC does not entitle the transferee to become or to exercise any rights of a member.
- A transferee of a Member's interest in the LLC may become a Member if and to the extent that the transferor gives the transferee the right in accordance with authority described in the Operating Agreement or all other Members' consent.

State Classification.   An LLC will be classified in the same manner as it is classified for federal income tax purposes.

State Entity Level Tax.   None.

Virginia

State Statute.   The Virginia Limited Liability Company Act, Va. Code Ann. §§ 13.1-1000 through 13.1-1073, became effective July 1, 1991.

Formation.   Articles of Organization must contain the following information: name; registered agent and office; and address of principal office.

Minimum Number of Members.   One.

Default Rules.   The following are examples of default rules provided by the Virginia LLC Act. Unless otherwise provided in the Articles of Organization or Operating Agreement:

- Members manage the LLC.
- The Operating Agreements do not have to be written.
- A majority vote of the Members will fill a vacancy in the office of Manager.
- Managers can be removed by a majority vote of Members with or without causes.
- The liability of a Manager to the company cannot exceed the greater of $100,000 or the amount of cash compensation paid during the 12 months immediately preceding the Act or omission.

State Classification.   An LLC will be classified in the same manner as it is classified for federal income tax purposes.

State Entity Level Tax.   None.

Washington

State Statute.   The Washington Limited Liability Company Act became effective October 1, 1994.

Formation.   Articles of Organization must contain the following information: name; the latest date on which the LLC is to dissolve; registered agent and office; principal place of business; whether there will be a Manager(s); name and address of each person executing the Articles of Organization; and any additional matters.

Minimum Number of Members.   One.

Default Rules.   The following are examples of default rules provided by the Washington LLC Act. Unless otherwise provided in the Articles of Organization or Operating Agreement:

- Except as otherwise provided by the statute, the debts, obligations, and liabilities of an LLC, whether arising in contract, tort, or otherwise, shall be solely the debts, obligations, and liabilities of the LLC; and no Manager or Member of an LLC shall be obligated personally for any such debt, obligation, or liability of the LLC solely by reason of being a Member or acting as a Manager of the LLC.

- The affirmative vote, approval, or consent of more than ½ by number of the Managers shall be required to decide any matter connected with the business or affairs of the LLC in a Manager-managed LLC.

- A Member has the status of, and is entitled to all remedies available to, a creditor of an LLC with respect to the distribution at the time the Member becomes entitled to receive a distribution. A Limited Liability Company Agreement may provide for the establishment of a record date with respect to allocations and distributions by an LLC.

- An assignment entitles the assignee to share in profits and losses, to receive distributions and to receive allocation of income, gain, loss, deduction, or credit or similar items to which the assignor was entitled, to the extent assigned.

- A Member ceases to be a Member and to have the power to exercise any rights or powers of a Member on assignment of all of his or her LLC interest.

State Classification.   An LLC will be classified in the same manner as it is classified for federal income tax purposes.

State Entity Level Tax.   None.

West Virginia

State Statute.   The West Virginia Limited Liability Company Act, W. Va. Code §§ 318-1-101 through 31B-13-1306, became effective March 15, 1992.

Formation.   Articles of Organization must contain the following information: name; duration, if a term LLC; registered agent and office; address of LLC's principal place of business; whether the LLC is to be Manager-managed; and name and address of organizer(s).

Minimum Number of Members.   One.

Default Rules.   The following are examples of default rules provided by the West Virginia LLC Act. Unless otherwise provided in the Articles of Organization or Operating Agreement:

- Members manage the LLC.
- The Operating Agreements do not have to be in writing.
- A vacancy in management will be filled by a majority vote of the Members.
- Managers can be removed by a majority vote of Members with or without cause.

State Classification.   An LLC will be classified in the same manner as it is classified for federal income tax purposes.

State Entity Level Tax.   None.

Wisconsin

State Statute.   The Wisconsin Limited Liability Company Act became effective January 1, 1994.

Formation.   Articles of Organization must contain the following information: a statement that the LLC is formed under Chapter 183 of the Wisconsin Statutes; name; registered agent and office; whether there will be a Manager(s); and name and address of each organizer.

Minimum Number of Members.   One.

Default Rules.   The following are examples of default rules provided by the Wisconsin LLC Act. Unless otherwise provided in the Articles of Organization or Operating Agreement:

- Profit, losses, and distributions are allocated on the basis of value of the contributions made by each Member.

- The unanimous vote of the Members is required for assignees to become Members.

State Classification.   An LLC will be classified in the same manner as it is classified for federal income tax purposes.

State Entity Level Tax.   If the LLC is taxed as a partnership, the LLC is subject to a surcharge of up to $9,800.

Wyoming

State Statute.   The Wyoming Limited Liability Company Act, Wyo. Stat. §§ 17-15-101 through 17-15-145, became effective in 1977.

Formation.   Articles of Organization must contain the following information: name; duration; purpose; registered agent and office; amount of capital contributions of the Members; any additional contributions; right to admit new Members; right to continue; statement on the management of the company; and whether the LLC is to elect status as a "flexible" limited liability company.

Minimum Number of Members.   One.

Default Rules.   The following are examples of default rules provided by the Wyoming LLC Act:

- Unless otherwise provided in the Articles of Organization or Operating Agreement, the ability to contract or incur debt or liability for the Company is restricted to Members, if there are no Managers, or Managers, when Managers are authorized.

State Classification.   There is no Wyoming state income tax at either the personal or corporate level. Therefore, classification of an LLC for state income tax purposes is irrelevant.

State Entity Level Tax.   None.

APPENDIX B

Sequence of States' Adoption of Limited Liability Companies Laws

At the time this book was written, 48 states and the District of Columbia had passed LLC acts. It is likely that the remaining states will follow. For historical interest, the progression of adoption is as follows:

1977   Wyoming

1982   Florida

1990   Colorado, Kansas

1991   Nevada, Utah, Texas, Virginia

1992   Arizona, Delaware, Illinois, Iowa, Oklahoma, Minnesota, Maryland, Louisiana, Rhode Island, West Virginia

1993   Alabama, Arkansas, Connecticut, Georgia, Idaho, Indiana, Michigan, Missouri, Montana, Nebraska, New Hampshire, New Jersey, New Mexico, North Carolina, North Dakota, Oregon, South Dakota, Wisconsin

1994   Alaska, California, District of Columbia, Kentucky, Maine, Mississippi, New Jersey, New York, Ohio, Pennsylvania, South Carolina, Tennessee, Washington

1995   Massachusetts

APPENDIX C

Comparison of Business Entities

Table C.1 summarizes key characteristics of each of the different types of entity that you may consider for organizing your business or investment. The ability to view key items in a few pages can help you understand the main differences before you read a particular chapter of the book, or serve to summarize a portion of the book that you have just completed. When doing so, however, remember that the generalizations necessary to prepare this chart could obscure a nuance that is critical to your particular situation.

The entities summarized are generally those that provide the often vital element of limited liability.

CAUTION: The limited liability of a corporation, limited partnership, or LLC is not guaranteed. If you personally guarantee a bank debt (or any liability for that matter), the fact that a corporation or LLC is the primary obligor (the actual borrower responsible) will not relieve you of your liability. If you fail to respect the identity and formalities of the entity, limited liability benefits may be lost. For example, if you organize a corporation and have no minutes, no bylaws and never issue stock, a court may refuse to respect the corporation and find you personally liable. If you use a corporation, LLC, or other entity and commingle personal and business funds, a similar result may occur.

These entities include:

- *C Corporation.* This is an entity organized under your state's corporation law. Each shareholder should not be held liable for acts of the corporation. For tax purposes, however, the corporation is taxable as a separate entity from its owners. This can result in a two-tier tax—the corporation pays tax on its income and the shareholders then pay tax on the dividends distributed to them.

- *S Corporation.* This is an entity organized under your state's corporation law exactly like a C corporation. However, for federal tax purposes (some states and local governments recognize the S corporation tax status, others do not, and some in a modified format), the corporation itself is generally not taxed. Instead, the S corporation acts like a conduit for income and expenses to flow through to the individual owners.

- *Limited Partnership.* This is an entity organized under your state's limited partnership law. Every limited partnership must have at least two types of partners: general partner who is fully liable for all partnership debts and liabilities and limited partners who are not liable for partnership debts or liabilities except to the extent of their investment in the partnership. There are exceptions. In Table C.1, the general partner is assumed to be an S corporation (as previously described). The result is that all individual owners (i.e., the limited partners and the shareholder/owners of the S corporation general partner) can achieve limited liability.

- *Limited Liability Company.* This is an entity formed under your state's limited liability company statute. For tax purposes, an LLC can be taxed as a partnership (which is almost always the intent and which is generally the result) or a corporation (i.e., analogous to a C corporation).

The table, for comparison purposes also illustrates one entity where there is no limitation on the liability of the owners, a general partnership. This is then only appropriate to use for simple transactions where large claims or liabilities are unlikely.

CAUTION: Too often, people assume that if they buy insurance they needn't worry about acquiring the limited liability benefit of an entity. While insurance is essential, and securing adequate insurance coverage should be one of the first steps taken in planning any transaction, don't minimize the important protection an entity can provide. Insurance limits can be exceeded. Policies contain limitations, restrictions, and exclusions. The old maxim: "Better safe than sorry" provides the right approach.

For simplicity, Table C.1 omits many other types of entities, including professional corporations (a special type of C corporation or S corporation for certain licensed professional practices), limited liability partnerships (a variation of an LLC used by some professional practices), and trusts. Depending on your particular situation, one or more of these other approaches may be appropriate.

CAUTION: It's always best to seek the professional guidance of an accountant and business lawyer before selecting the entity for any particular business or investment.

Table C.1. Comparison of Business Entities

	C Corporation	S Corporation	General Partnership	Limited Partnership with a Corporate General Partner	Limited Liability Company
Statutes permitting formation	All states.	All states.	All states.	All states.	All states.
Limitations on minimum number of owners	None.	None.	Usually at least 2.	At least 2.	None, except Massachusetts, which requires at least 2.
Limitations on maximum number of owners	None.	Cannot have more than 75.	None.	None.	None.
Limitations on who can be an owner	None.	Individuals other than nonresident aliens, certain trusts, and estates.	None.	None.	None.
Allowable business purposes	Any, unless otherwise provided by statute.	Generally, same as C corporation.	Any for profit business unless otherwise provided by statute.	Same as general partnership.	Same as C corporation, but some states exclude certain activities.
Capital structure limitation	None.	Only one class of stock is permitted (classes that differ in respect to voting rights only are permitted).	None.	None.	None.
Formation of entity	Formal filing required.	Same as C corporation.	No.	Same as C corporation.	Same as C corporation.
Creation documents	Articles or Certificate of Incorporation.	Same as C corporation.	Partnership Agreement.	Certificate of Limited Partnership.	Articles of Organization or Certificate of Formation.
Personal liability of owners	None.	Same as C corporation.	All parties jointly and severally personally liable.	General partner liable. Limited partners not so.	None.
Default management structure	Board of directors.	Same as C corporation.	All partners participate.	General Partner.	Member managed in most states.

(Continued)

Table C.1. (continued)

	C Corporation	S Corporation	General Partnership	Limited Partnership with a Corporate General Partner	Limited Liability Company
Ownership participation in management	Shareholders elect directors.	Same as C corporation.	All partners may participate in the entity's management.	Only General partner. Limited partners risk liability by participating in management.	Depends on whether management is by Members or Managers.
Governing Agreement	Shareholders Agreement and Bylaws	Same as C corporation	Partnership Agreement	Same as general partnership	Operating Agreement
Voting rights of owners	Generally, pro rata to number of shares. May have voting and non-voting shares.	Generally, pro rata to number of shares. May have voting and non-voting shares.	Per capita or pro rata unless modified by partnership agreement.	As provided in Partnership Agreement.	Varies by each state, but generally pro rata unless modified by Operating Agreement.
Basic ownership unit	Share of stock.	Same as C corporation.	Partnership interest.	Same as general partnership.	Membership interest.
Rules for allocating profits and losses	Pro rata to number of shares (unless varied by other class(es) of stock).	Pro rata to number of shares.	Per capita unless modified by partnership agreement.	Pro rata to capital contributions less returned capital contributions.	Same as limited partnership unless modified by Operating Agreement.
Undistributed income of company	No current tax to owners.	Current tax to owners.	Current tax to owners.	Current tax to owners.	Current tax to owners.
Character of income and loss	Determined at entity level.	Same as C corporation.	Same as C corporation.	Same as C corporation.	Same as C corporation.
Deductibility of company's losses	No deduction to owners but entity may use current loss to offset unrelated income in certain instances.	Subject to certain limitations, losses pass through to owners on per share basis and are deductible against unrelated income.	Same as limited partnership.	Subject to certain limitations discussed below, losses pass through to owners according to their distributive shares and are deductible against unrelated income.	Same as limited partnership.
Flexibility of loss allocations	N/A	None.	Same as limited partnership.	Maximum flexibility since losses may be allocated by agreement to those members who will most benefit from tax deductions as long as allocations have "substantial economic effect."	Same as limited partnership.

Basis limiting deduction of losses	N/A	Owners' deductions are limited first by their bases in stock and then their bases in any direct loans to entity (basis does not include share of entity debt).	Same as limited partnership.	Owners' deductions are limited by their bases in their membership interests (basis includes their share of entity debt).	Same as limited partnership.
At-risk limitation on deductibility of losses	N/A	Loss deduction is limited by allocable share of at-risk amount, which includes amount contributed to entity, debt to extent the owner is personally liable, and qualified nonrecourse financing with respect to real estate.	Same as limited partnership, except that all general partners are generally at risk with respect to partnership recourse loans.	Same as S corporation except general partner is the only at-risk partner with respect to recourse partnership loans unless there are guarantees running from a limited partner to a general partner.	Same as S corporation.
Passive activity limitation on deductibility of losses	N/A	After the basis and at-risk limitations are applied, owner's loss deductible if active income if owner "materially participates." Income will be passive if owner does not "materially participate."	Same as S corporation.	Same as S corporation with question as to whether limited partner will be treated as S shareholder or as more restricted limited partner (more likely to be treated as S shareholder).	Same as S corporation.
Federal tax returns required to be filed	Form 1120	Form 1120S	Same as limited partnership.	Form 1065 with K-1 to members.	Same as limited partnership (unless set up to be taxed as a corporation (1120) or a single member LLC (member's 1040)).

(continued)

Table C.1. (continued)

	C Corporation	S Corporation	General Partnership	Limited Partnership with a Corporate General Partner	Limited Liability Company
Entity-level federal tax (assuming limited liability company and limited partnership are structured so that they will be taxed as a partnership for federal tax purposes)	Yes.	Usually not, but yes if passive income exceeds 25% of gross receipts and entity has earnings and profits. Moreover, usually not, but a built-in gains tax is imposed on sale or disposition of assets within 10 years of when corporation was C corporation and made an S election.	No.	No.	No.
Taxable year	Generally, calendar year or any fiscal year.	Generally, a calendar year.	Same as limited partnership.	Calendar year or fiscal year of the majority in interest partner or, if none, the principal partners or, if none, any other fiscal year for which the limited partnership establishes a business purpose; a fiscal year of September through November may be adopted even without a business purpose if the S corporation makes a Section 444 election and the required payments to compensate Service for cost of deferral.	Same as limited partnership.
Permissible accounting methods	Generally must use accrual unless entity is professional service corporation or small business with gross receipts of less than $5 million.	Same as C corporation.	Same as limited liability company.	Same as limited liability company.	May elect cash or accrual; tax shelters required to use accrual method.

Fringe benefits	Shareholder-employees receive tax qualified fringe benefits without restrictions of pass-through entities.	Greater than 2% owner-employees are generally ineligible for tax-free fringe benefits.	Same as limited liability company.	Same as limited liability company.	Owners are generally not considered employees so limitations apply.
Employment taxes	FICA tax is payable by both corporation and employee.	Same as C corporation.	General partner distributive share is subject to self-employment tax.	General partner distributive share is subject to self-employment tax; limited partner distributive share is not subject to the tax under Section 1402(a)(13).	Members generally subject to self-employment tax unless: (1) the Member is not a Manager in a Manager-ruled LLC, and (2) the entity could have been formed as a limited partnership.

GLOSSARY

Accrual Method. Rules provided in the tax laws for determining when you can claim a deduction and when you must report income. There are two major sets of rules. The simplest, which is used by individuals, is called the cash method of accounting. Under the cash method, you generally report income for tax purposes when you receive it and deduct expenses for the year when you pay those expenses. Under the accrual method of accounting, which many businesses, partnerships, and corporations use, income is reported and expenses are deducted in the year to which they relate instead of the year when they are paid.

Accumulated Earnings Tax. A penalty tax that is charged against a corporation if it retains excessive profits beyond the reasonable needs of its business, instead of distributing those profits to its owners. An LLC that is taxed as a partnership will not face this problem.

Adjusted Basis. Roughly speaking, your investment, for tax purposes, in certain property; the cost to buy or build a building (or any other asset), plus costs to improve it. If you have a casualty loss, it reduces your adjusted basis. Adjusted basis is used to calculate depreciation (multiply it by the appropriate depreciation or Accelerated Cost Recovery System percentage) and to determine the taxable gain or loss when you sell property (subtract adjusted basis from your net sales proceeds to determine your gain). If you are subject to the alternative minimum tax, your assets may have a different adjusted basis for the regular tax and the alternative minimum tax. Your adjusted tax basis in your LLC is based on your investment, reduced by income distributed, increased by certain loans taken out by the entity (where your LLC is taxed as a partnership), and so on. Your adjusted basis in your LLC interest will determine the amount of gain or loss on your sale of the interest.

Alternative Minimum Tax. A second parallel tax system that many wealthier taxpayers have to consider when calculating their tax.

The alternative minimum tax (or AMT) is calculated by starting with your taxable income determined according to the regular tax rules. Add certain tax preference items and adjustments required by the AMT. Only certain itemized deductions are allowed. Next, subtract an exemption amount. The result is multiplied by a flat tax rate. If the tax due exceeds the tax you owe under the regular tax system, then you must pay the larger alternative minimum tax.

Amount Realized.   The money and the fair market value of any property you receive when you sell property. It also includes the amount of any liabilities that the buyer takes responsibility for.

Annual Exclusion.   The amount of up to $11,000 that every person is permitted to give away per year to any other person without incurring any gift tax. There is no limit on the number of people you can make these gifts to in a year. To qualify for this exclusion, the gifts must be a gift of a present interest, meaning that the recipient can enjoy the gift immediately. This can present problems when you make gifts of LLC membership interests if there are no distributions, especially if there is no economic likelihood of distributions.

Articles of Organization.   The initial document filed with your state to form or organize your LLC; it may also be called "Certificate of Formation" or another name. It includes basic provisions concerning the life, nature, owners, and so on of the LLC and becomes a matter of public record.

Asset Protection.   The process of minimizing the risk of creditors or other claimants being able to reach your assets. This can include setting up a different entity, such as an LLC, for each property or business. Thus, if one particular property is subject to a suit (e.g., a tenant is hurt on one rental property), the claimant will be limited to the assets from that particular property or entity. This can prevent a domino effect against your other assets. An LLC, just like a limited partnership, offers important asset protection benefits.

At-Risk.   Rules limiting the amount of tax losses that can be deducted from a business or investment to the amount you have at risk in that investment. The at-risk amount includes the cash and fair market value of any property you have invested in the business. The at-risk amount (your deduction limit) also includes debts for which you are personally liable.

Basis.   Taxpayer's investment for tax purposes. Cost, less depreciation, plus improvements.

Beneficiary.   A person who receives the benefits of a trust or of transfers under your will. An LLC is intangible property. Thus, if you have real estate owned by an LLC that you own an interest in, the intangible or business disposition clauses of your will may govern instead of the real property disposition clauses. Be careful to have the will explicitly state where the LLC interest is to be given.

Bequest.   Property transferred under your will.

Blue Sky Laws.   State security laws that govern the right to sell interests in a security, among other matters. Anytime you form an LLC involving more than a handful of active and knowledgeable investors, always consult with a securities attorney to be certain you are not subject to any blue-sky, federal, or other security or reporting requirements.

Buy-Sell Agreements.   Contractual arrangements governing the transfer of ownership interests (LLC membership, corporate stock, or partnership interests) in closely held business. These often rely on insurance to provide the necessary funds.

Calendar Year.   The tax year that many entities are required to use (ending December 31).

Capital Gain.   The gain from selling a capital asset that is held for over one year. The gain is usually the amount realized (net sales price) less your investment (adjusted tax basis) in the property. Capital gains receive favorable tax treatment in that the maximum rate is set at 20 percent when the maximum tax rate on ordinary income is 38.6 percent. Your sale of your LLC may, depending on the circumstances, qualify as the sale of a capital asset that is taxed at favorable taxable gains rates.

Cash Basis.   A method of determining when income must be reported and when expenses can be deducted. Most individual taxpayers use this method. Certain partnerships (including LLCs taxed as partnerships), corporations, and other taxpayers may not be able to use it. Under the cash method, income is generally reported in the year that you receive the money, and expenses are usually deducted in the year that you pay the expense.

Cash Flow.   Cash generated by a business or investment. Since an LLC is a pass-through entity, each owner will have to report on his personal tax return an allocable share of LLC income, even if the LLC does not have adequate cash flow to make a distribution of that income.

C Corporation.   A regular corporation that pays taxes directly to the IRS. A C corporation can be contrasted with an S corporation, which generally does not pay taxes; instead, its shareholders (owners) pay tax on their share of the S corporation's income.

NOTE: The exact name of the following different types of certificates may differ from state to state.

Certificate of Alternate Name.   A certificate that may need to be filed if your LLC will operate under a different or additional name than the name under which it was formed. The laws vary significantly from state to state. A filing may be required in your state, county, both, or even elsewhere. Check with a local attorney.

Certificate of Amendments.   A certificate that you may find necessary, or prudent, to file amending the Certificate of Formation. It then also becomes part of the public record on your LLC. For example, if your state requires specifying the business purpose of the LLC, and this changes, it may be necessary to file a Certificate of Amendment.

Certificate of Cancellation.   A certificate that must be filed to terminate and liquidate your LLC. Caution: There will also be special tax filings with the IRS as well as state and local tax authorities.

Certificate of Formation.   The legal document that is required to be filed under state law to form or organize your LLC. Also called "Articles of Organization."

Certificate of Merger or Consolidation.   The certificate that must be filed where a partnership is to be converted into an LLC, or an LLC merged into another LLC (and/or another partnership). Caution: There are tax-filing requirements as well. You may also need permission of a landlord, lender, or anyone else with whom the LLC or other entity has contractual arrangements.

Check-the-Box Regulations.   The IRS rules permitting taxpayers to check a box on their tax form that indicates what tax status an LLC should have. Generally this option is used to assure partnership tax status, other than for one-member LLCs, which for income tax purposes are ignored as "disregarded" entities.

Closely Held Business.   A family business or a business owned by relatively few individuals. An LLC can be an excellent entity to own a particular business, or even key assets (e.g., equipment or a building to rent back to the business).

Contribution.   Property that you transfer to an LLC in exchange for your interest in it. This transfer is often referred to as a contribution of property to the LLC. Special tax rules will affect this. Generally, you will not have to recognize taxable gain on the contribution of property to the LLC for an interest.

Corporation. A legal entity separate from the individuals who own it (called shareholders). Corporations can be classified by the manner in which they are taxed, which include S corporations and C corporations.

Decedent. A person who dies. Assets of a decedent are disposed of by will or, if no will exists, by the intestacy laws of the decedent's state.

Default Rules. The state law that applies (by default) if you do not address a particular issue in your operating agreement. Most state LLC statutes are written in a manner that gives you as an LLC owner flexibility to select your own rules and arrangements.

Depreciation. The writing off of an asset's cost over its useful life or using methods prescribed by the tax laws. Depreciation is based on the idea that the elements, physical wear and tear from use, and so forth, wear down property over time. Depreciation (sometimes called "MACRS" deductions) of assets held by your LLC will be passed to your personal tax return and deducted there as part of the results you realize in that given tax year from your LLC.

Discount. A discount on the value of a gift of a minority (i.e., less than controlling) interest in an LLC that can sometimes be claimed. This enables the donor to give a greater percentage interest in the LLC as a gift in any year under the $11,000 annual gift tax exclusion (which may be inflation adjusted in future years) without, for example, using any of the donor's applicable exclusion.

Disregarded Entity. A one-member LLC that can be formed for legal liability protection, but can be ignored for income tax purposes.

Distribution. Cash or even property that you may receive as an owner of an LLC. However, your tax results are not limited to the amount you receive as a distribution where the LLC is taxed as a partnership. You will be taxed on your pro rata portion of LLC income or loss.

Donee. A person who receives a gift.

Donor. A person who makes a gift.

Election. Optional treatment of many different items provided for in the tax laws. Often the taxpayer must make an election (usually by filing a statement or checking a box on his tax return) as to which optional method will be used. An LLC, as a separate tax reporting entity, must make its own tax elections. Unless the operating agreement provides to the contrary, the manager of your LLC will likely have control over all these decisions.

Estate Tax.   On the death of a taxpayer, a tax that may be due on the transfer of wealth to family and others. Exclusions are provided for transfers to the taxpayer's spouse, charities, and so forth. The tax rate for the estate tax can reach as high as 50 percent (to be decreased in future years). A once-in-a-lifetime exclusion is permitted that enables you to pass property worth up to $1 million to others without having to pay an estate tax (increasing in future years).

Fair Market Value.   The price at which an item can be sold at the present time between two unrelated people in an arm's length transaction, neither under compulsion to buy or sell. Where a gift is made of an interest in an LLC, it must be valued at its fair market value. This may, however, be permitted to reflect a minority (lack of control) or lack of marketability discount.

Family Limited Partnership (FLP).   A limited partnership owned by members of the same family. An LLC is treated for income tax purposes in the identical manner.

Fiscal year.   The tax year, other than the calendar year, that a particular taxpayer uses. LLCs are subject to limitations on when they can use a tax year other than the calendar year.

General Partner.   A partner (owner) of a part of a partnership who is personally liable for all partnership debts and is permitted to participate in the management of the partnership. Every limited partnership must have one general partner. Often this general partner is a corporation to avoid any individual being personally liable.

General Partnership.   A partnership that has only general partners and no limited partners. This is the most common way for a few friends or investors to put their money together to buy a rental property or simple business. The risk is that in a general partnership all partners are personally liable, without limit, for all partnership debts.

Gift.   A term often used with reference to transfer taxes. If you transfer property without receiving something of equal value in return, the federal government will assess a transfer tax where the value of the gift exceeds the annual exclusion and you have exhausted your unified credit (e.g., you make a gift of your LLC interest to a trust for your child).

Gift Tax.   A tax that can be due when you give property or other assets away. You are allowed to give away a maximum of $11,000 per person (to any number of people) in any year without the tax applying (figure to be inflation adjusted). Above the $11,000 amount, you have a once-in-a-life-time exclusion that permits you to give away $1,000,000 (to be increased in future years for estate tax purposes, but not for gift tax purposes) of property without paying any gift tax.

Grantor. The person who establishes a trust and transfers assets to it.

Heirs. The persons who receive your assets following your death.

Interest. The term used to denote your ownership of a portion of an LLC; often referred to as your interest in the LLC, or your "membership interest."

Kiddie Tax. Unearned income (dividends, rents, interest, and so forth) of a child under age 1, which is taxed to the child at the parent's highest tax rate. This tax makes family tax planning much harder.

Lack of Marketability Discount. The value of an asset given away, say to a child, that is less than its initial or expected fair value. This may occur if, because of unusual circumstances, the asset is not readily salable.

Lease. A legal contract permitting one party to use property owned by another, usually for the payment of periodic rent. A common use of LLCs is to segregate valuable business assets (patent, trademark, real estate, equipment) in a separate entity, gift the interests in that entity to your heirs, and have them lease (or license) the right to use the property back to the business.

Limited Liability. Where an entity can be sued, but generally its owners cannot be held personally liable for debts, or losses of the entity. The classic limited liability entity is the corporation.

Limited Liability Company, or LLC. An entity formed under your state's LLC statute that has the legal characteristic of limited liability similar to that of a corporation, while it may qualify to be treated for tax purposes as a partnership.

Limited Liability Partnership, or LLP. Similar to an LLC but have less limitations on liability. Some states have enacted statutes (laws) permitting these entities so that licensed professionals (doctors, lawyers, accountants, etc.) can obtain some limitation on liability while still having the favorable tax status of a partnership. These entities are generally even newer than LLCs and caution must be exercised. Also, the nuances differ by state so be sure to consult a local attorney familiar with your state's rules.

Limited Partner. A partner (owner) in a limited partnership who cannot participate in the management of the partnership's business and who is not liable for partnership debts.

Limited Partnership.   A partnership with at least one general partner and any number of limited partners. See "Limited Partner."

Liquidation.   Termination and winding up of an entity, such as an LLC. A final tax return will have to be filed with the IRS, and with state and local tax authorities. A tax clearance certificate may be necessary from the state. Usually a Certificate of Termination (or something similar) must be filed.

Manager.   The individual charged with operating the LLC and making key decisions. The Certificate of Formation may specify who the manager is. The operating agreement should provide details as to the scope of the powers and rights of the manager, liability for acts, replacement, and so forth. Rights and responsibilities of managers also may be specified in the state law. The manager can be one individual, a group or committee of individuals, or even all members of the LLC.

Member.   An owner of part (or in some states, all) of an LLC. A member in an LLC is analogous to a shareholder in a corporation or a partner in a partnership. Some key characteristics and rights of a member may be set forth in the LLC's Certificate of Formation. An operating agreement should be drafted that provides details as to a member's rights, liability, and so on.

Nonrecourse Liability.   A liability for which no person is liable; only the property securing the debt can be used by the lender to satisfy the debt. For example, if your LLC buys real estate, it may be able to secure nonrecourse financing where no member is personally liable as a guarantor on the debt. If your LLC is taxed as a partnership, the partnership tax allocation rules could have important implications as to which members may claim a tax deduction for interest and other items related to this financing.

One Class of Stock.   A reference to the rule that an S corporation can generally only have one class of stock. Differences in the rights of shares that are permitted are very limited (e.g., some shares can be voting and others not). However, the return, distributions, and general economic rights of every share must be identical. Although there have been numerous proposals to liberalize these requirements, none have been enacted as of the date of this book being written. Absent liberalization of these rules, an LLC, which is taxed as a partnership, has substantial advantages over an S corporation in that the members are permitted great latitude in allocating income, profits, and deductions. The allocations must, however, meet the requirement of having Substantial Economic Effect.

Operating Agreement.   The written contract between all the owners (members) and generally also those in charge of operating the LLC (managers). An LLC operating agreement is analogous to a corporation's shareholders agreement and a partnership's partnership agreement. This agreement should address in detail the rights and obligations of members. It should contain buyout provisions in the event of the death of a member. If the LLC is an active business, the issue of disability should be addressed. Tax issues should be addressed: naming of a tax matters partner and defining his rights; allocation of tax benefits; and so on. It is almost always a mistake to try to save costs by omitting an operating agreement.

Ordinary and Necessary Business Expense.   A requirement for payments to be deductible expenses of your trade or business. Extravagant or personal expenses will not be deductible. These restrictions will apply to the LLC and thus affect your ability as a member of the LLC to claim deductions. Also, if asset protection is a concern, the payment of personal expenses through your LLC, in addition to tax problems, will increase the risk that creditors will be able to pierce the LLC's limited liability protection.

Ordinary Income.   Income or gain from selling property that is not a capital asset. Ordinary income is taxed at rates of up to 39.6 percent, which is less favorable than capital gains rates of a maximum 20 percent. There is an advantage for many taxpayers to realizing capital gains instead of ordinary income.

Partnership.   A syndicate, joint venture, group, or other arrangement, in which two or more investors join their money and skills to carry out a business as co-owners and to earn a profit. A partnership is generally treated as a flow-through (conduit) so that each partner reports his share of partnership income or loss on a personal tax return. The partnership files a Form 1065 as an information report with the IRS but does not pay any tax. An election is available to avoid being taxed as a partnership.

Partnership Interest.   The ownership of part of a partnership. Since most LLCs are taxed as partnerships, your ownership of the LLC (i.e., your member interest) will be treated for tax purposes as a partnership interest.

Passive Income.   The passive income and loss rules divide income into three types: (1) active (wages, income from an active business); (2) passive (income earned from rental property or as a limited partner investor); and (3) portfolio (dividends and interest on stocks and bonds). Passive losses (tax losses from rental property or from investments made as a limited partner) can only be applied to offset passive income. If you qualify as actively participating in a real estate rental, you may be able to deduct up to $25,000 of your passive tax losses against any income without regard to this limitation. Your interest in an LLC will be treated as generating passive or active income depending on the nature of the LLC's business and assets, as well as your involvement. Also, the provisions of the LLC operating agreement may also impact this determination.

Passive Loss.   Tax losses from rental real estate properties (e.g., as a result of depreciation write-offs) or from investments as a limited partner. Passive losses can generally only be used to offset passive income. If your LLC owns interests in rental real estate, the income or loss generated will be passive for your tax purposes unless you meet the requirement of being an active real estate professional.

Personal Property.   Furniture, equipment, and other movable property and assets. Buildings and land are not personal property; they are real property. Real property and tangible personal property are generally subject to probate in the state in which they are located on your death. If you are domiciled (permanently reside) in another state, you can avoid ancillary probate in the state where personal or real property is located by transferring those tangible assets into an LLC. Your ownership of an LLC will generally be viewed as an intangible property interest, not subject to ancillary probate.

Present Interest.   A gift that the beneficiary can enjoy immediately. To qualify for the annual $11,000 gift tax exclusion (figure to be inflation adjusted), a gift must be a gift of a present interest. A gift of an interest in an LLC to a child or other donee (and not into a trust) should generally qualify as a gift of a present interest. However, if you as the donor and parent have excessive controls over the LLC and the distribution of income, the IRS may argue that no gift was actually made. For example, if the LLC owns net leased real estate where there is no need for any services, but you take all of the LLC income as a salary (to avoid paying distributions to your children who received gifts of LLC interests), the IRS may argue that the gift of the LLC interests to your children was not a gift of a present interest.

Probate.   The process of marshaling assets of a deceased person, having the will recognized by the court (often called surrogate's court) and having the person designated in the will (personal administrator or executor) officially empowered to act (often by issuance of documents called letters testamentary). Ancillary probate is probate in a state other than the state in which you reside. Ancillary probate, and the attendant fees and time delays can be avoided, in many instances, through use of LLCs.

Pro Rata Share. A simple (from an economic perspective) LLC arrangement wherein each member shares a pro rata in the income, expenses, profits, and losses of the LLC. In a more complex arrangement, special allocations of income, expenses, profits, and losses may be used instead.

Qualified Subchapter S Trust (QSST).   A reference to specific requirements that must be met for a trust to own shares in an S corporation. An LLC is not subject to these complexities and therefore can be more flexible to use in an estate-planning context.

Recourse Liabilities.   Debts for which individuals, such as yourself as a member of the LLC that has taken the loan, are liable. Contrast with "Nonrecourse Liability."

Registered Agent.   A person specified in most types of entities, LLCs included, in the documents they file when formed (Certificate of Formation or Articles of Organization for an LLC). This is the person on whom notice should be given (served) in the event of a lawsuit or other matter. This designated person is often called a Registered Agent. If the person named moves to a new address, or is no longer appropriate (e.g., is no longer a member), be careful to file a Certificate of Amendment to change the designation.

S Corporation.   A corporation that makes an election to have income taxed to its shareholders thus avoiding a corporate level tax. An S corporation must meet numerous restrictions to qualify for this favorable tax treatment. An LLC is not subject to these restrictions and when structured to be taxed as a partnership (which most are) can have the same tax benefits of an S corporation with much greater ease and flexibility.

Sole Proprietorships.   A business run by you that is owned and operated without any legal entity (i.e., no corporation, partnership, or LLC). The advantage of using a sole proprietorship is simplicity and no cost. The tremendous disadvantage is that you will have unlimited liability for any problem. An LLC is not an option for a sole proprietor in most states since those states require at least two members to form an LLC. To form an LLC, you may need to make a spouse, child, partner, or business associate a nominal owner (member).

Subsidiary LLC.   An LLC owned by a master or parent LLC. This may be done to own real estate to avoid tainting other assets with the liability associated with a particular property.

Tangible Property.   Real estate, equipment, furniture, and other physical property. Where you own tangible property in a state other than the one in which you permanently reside (i.e., where you are domiciled), it will be subject to ancillary probate and potential additional taxes on your death. An LLC can avoid this.

Tax Basis.   The funds you invested to purchase property, plus the cost of capital improvements, less depreciation. That amount is your adjusted tax basis in that property. For an interest in an LLC, the calculation is more complex. Where the LLC is treated as a partnership for tax purposes, your adjusted tax basis could include the fair market value of property you contributed to the LLC, the amount you paid to purchase the LLC interest, your pro rata share of certain LLC debts, less amounts distributed to you, and so forth. Your adjusted tax basis is the amount used to determine any taxable gain or loss on your sale of the LLC or other asset.

Taxable Income.   Cash or certain economic benefits which you receive or have control over (constructive receipt) that are subject to tax (because no exclusion is allowed for them).

Trust.   Property held and managed by a person (trustee) for the benefit of another (beneficiary). The terms of the trust are generally governed by a contract that the grantor prepares when establishing the trust. LLC interests can be given to a trust for the benefit of your child or any other beneficiary.

Uniform Gifts (Transfers) to Minors Act (UGMA or UTMA).   A method to hold property for the benefit of another person, such as your child, which is similar to a trust, but is governed by state law. It is simpler and much cheaper to establish and administer, but is far less flexible and allows the child to get the assets upon reaching the age of majority.

Uniform Limited Liability Company Act (ULLCA).   A uniform act proposed for LLC laws. Many states have, or will eventually enact some version of this. Be careful not to assume that any particular state follows the ULLCA in all respects. There are often subtle, if not significant, differences between the statutes in different states even where those statutes are based on the same uniform act.

Unrealized Receivables.   A concept that, in certain cases, may result in the taxation of the sale of your interest in an LLC as ordinary income and not the more favorably taxed capital gains. Where the LLC has realized substantial income (and met other complex and rigid mechanical tests) from unrealized receivables, this may occur. The objective of this tax concept is to prevent you from using an LLC (or other entity) to convert ordinary income (taxed at rates of up to 39.6 percent) to capital gains (taxed at 20 percent). For example, if your LLC manufactured widgets to sell in the ordinary course of its business, ordinary income would be realized. But if just before making the sales, you were to sell all your LLC interests to someone else who would then sell the widgets, you would appear to have capital gains on the sale of your interests. This is because membership interests in an LLC are generally a capital asset producing capital gains. The widgets may be characterized as unrealized receivables, however, and you may have to report some or all of the gain on selling your LLC as ordinary income.

Value.   For purposes of making a gift of an LLC, the determination of the value of the interest given away. For tax purposes, the fair market value is the value to use. See "Fair Market Value."

INDEX